NO LONGER THE HERO

THE
PERSONAL
PILGRIMAGE
OF AN
ADULT CHILD

NANCY LeSOURD

A
JANET
THOMA
BOOK

D0180154

THOMAS NELSON PUBLISHERS
Nashville

Published in Nashville, Tennessee, by Thomas Nelson, Inc., and distributed in Canada by Lawson Falle, Ltd., Cambridge, Ontario.

Printed in the United States of America.

"Castle on a Cloud," by Claude-Michel Schönberg, Alain Boublil, Jean Marc Natel, and Herbert Kretzmer. From the musical *Les Misérables*, by Alain Boublil and Claude-Michel Schönberg. Copyright © Alain Boublil Music Ltd.
David Elkind, *The Hurried Child*, Copyright © 1988 by David Elkind. Reprinted with permission of Addison-Wesley Publishing Company.
Catherine Marshall, *Something More.* Copyright © 1974 by Catherine Marshall. Reprinted with permission of McGraw-Hill.
Excerpt from "Little Gidding" in *Four Quarters*, Copyright © 1943 by T. S. Eliot and renewed 1971 by Esme Valerie Eliot, reprinted by permission of Harcourt Brace Jovanovich.

Unless otherwise noted, Scripture quotations are from THE NEW KING JAMES VERSION of the Bible. Copyright © 1979, 1980, 1982, Thomas Nelson, Inc., Publishers.

Scripture quotations noted KJV are from the KING JAMES VERSION.

Scripture quotations noted NAS are from the NEW AMERICAN STANDARD BIBLE, copyright © 1960, 1962, 1963, 1968, 1971, 1972, 1973, 1975, 1977 by The Lockman Foundation and are used by permission.

Scripture quotations noted NIV are from The Holy Bible: NEW INTERNATIONAL VERSION, copyright © 1978 by the New York International Bible Society. Used by permission of Zondervan Bible Publishers.

Scripture quotations noted LB are from *The Living Bible* (Wheaton, Illinois: Tyndale House Publishers, 1971) and are used by permission.

Library of Congress Cataloging-in-Publication Data

LeSourd, Nancy.
    No longer the hero / Nancy LeSourd.
        p.   cm.
    "A Janet Thoma book."
    Includes bibliographical references.
    ISBN 0-8407-3346-1 (pb)
    1. LeSourd, Nancy.   2. Adult children of dysfunctional families—United States—Religious life.   3. Adult children of dysfunctional families—United States—Biography.   4. Psychologically abused children—United States—Biography.   5. Problem families—United States—Case studies.   6. Christian biography—United States.
I. Title
BV4596.A274L47   1991   2 3 4 5 6 7 8 9 10 - 97 96 95 94 93 92
248.8'6—dc20   91-29493
                                                                                          CIP

Nancy LeSourd['s]...emphasis on "choosing life" makes this book an inspiration. Other survivors and "Heroes" of dysfunctional families will find hope, inspiration, and a model for healing in this work.

Powerful, penetrating, and provocative—Nancy Oliver LeSourd has done a real favor to all in recovery who struggle with the belief that God is a caring, loving Father.

In this honest, harrowing, health-giving narrative there is wisdom and hope for many of life's saddest casualties. Thank you, Mrs. LeSourd, for going public with your story.

For all of us who have been trapped into the "Hero" role, ... Nancy shows us that God's love is greater than all our futile efforts to work to attain it. She has found the keys to set us free.

Not all will walk the difficult road that lay before Nancy LeSourd in and from her dysfunctional home, but every one of us can richly benefit from her honesty, candor, experience, struggles and ultimate victory. I...thank [Nancy] for using her beautiful gift of openness in her writing....

This book is not just for those who have experienced a dysfunctional family.... Nancy Oliver LeSourd has written a searching transparent book—a book about power and choice, and a book that assures us of God's love and hope for the future.

I discovered refreshing insight into the heart of the "Hero" and intelligent understanding of the heart of God. This book is a must read for anyone who struggles to believe that God really is a loving Father who intimately cares for His children.

Jan Silvious
Author of *Please Don't Say You Need Me*

Nancy LeSourd's touching account of facing her past and refusing to live in its grip will forever alter your perspective on the choices we make. As a writer and fellow overcomer, Nancy is a hero in my book.

Stormie Omartian
Author of *A Step in the Right Direction*

Many times God uses testimony as a powerful way of challenging His people. This is certainly what happens as Nancy Oliver LeSourd recounts God's work in her life. As you come to the end of her book you feel like applauding the Lord for the wonderful way he brings wholeness to his children.

David Mains
Director of "Chapel of the Air"

Unusual is the sharing of the...religious and theological struggle with the relationship with God. Pastoral counselors will find it useful not only to themselves but also to their clients struggling with the same issues.

Dr. Sue Webb Cardwell
Psychologist and professor emerita,
Christian Theological Seminary

[A] riveting personal story combined with educational descriptions of alcoholic family patterns.

Anne Grizzle, family therapist
Author of *Mothers Who Love Too Much*

Readers will be challenged, educated and inspired as they follow the author's transformation from living in denial and dysfunction to learning to walk in truth.

Sandra D. Wilson, Ph.D.
Author of *Counseling Adult Children of Alcoholics* and *Released from Shame*

To Bob Newman, counselor and friend,
who taught me the process of choosing life,

and

to my husband, Jeff, who invited me to
choose life, all through life, with him.

Contents

Acknowledgments

It is virtually impossible to thank all the people who have had a hand in this book. Special thanks to my father-in-law, Leonard LeSourd, who six years ago told me I had a gift in writing and asked me what I was going to do about it. My gratitude to Van Ardan and Mark Amerman and Robert Fraley, each of whom believed in me and urged me to tell my story.

A special debt of love is owed to all who prayed for me, encouraged me, and stood with me, not only during the writing of this manuscript, but also during the lifetime of experiences that formed the basis of the book. Of course, there would be no story to tell without the faithfulness of many of you assisting me to learn the truth about myself and about my Lord.

The members of my law firm have supported and encouraged me in this process. My special thanks to Wray Fitch and Chip Grange who have worked alongside me during much of my growth as a lawyer and as a person in the process of restoration.

My deep appreciation to Janet Thoma, my editor, for recognizing the importance of sharing a personal journey of recovery and for thoughtful and prayerful editing.

My special thanks to Margaret Shannon, whose tireless efforts in research provided me extra hours with my newborn son.

My utmost gratitude to my wonderful husband, Jeff, who believed in me and who committed countless hours to reading the manuscript, praying for me, caring for our son, and encouraging me in times of doubt and a wastebasket full of crumpled papers.

And, especially, to Luke, my son, who didn't learn to crawl until Chapter 10.

Preface

Each of our lives is a tapestry of memories. Some memories, like the day we first rode a bike unaccompanied by training wheels, are very good. These are warm memories we like to roll around in our minds until we have tasted again and again every tantalizing detail. There are other memories—disturbing, dark, disappointing. These memories are just as vivid but painful. These painful memories, such as the memory of hateful, poisonous accusations, the sound of doors banging after an argument, or promises unkept, have a power of their own. They flood the back roads of our minds, directing our paths so subtly, pointing us here or there, but always in the direction of death. For these memories steer us away from the efficacy of the cross and the power of life therein and catch us up instead in a quagmire of defeat.

Thankfully, God does not leave us to our own devices to rid ourselves of these memories. Because left to ourselves, we would deal with them in numerous, ineffectual ways—bury them, analyze them, overcompensate for them—all in an attempt to unravel the pattern these memories have woven. But thankfully, God initiates. He breaks into the pattern of sin and failure and confusion and pain and works wonders. This is my story of how God removed the sting of death from the wounds of my memories and wove a most wonderful and intricate tapestry from the threads of broken dreams and shattered hopes.

I chose to write this book in a personal, intimate format. I am a fellow survivor, the Hero in my family drama, who, like many of you, understands from experience what it is like to grow up in a dysfunctional home and to try to untangle the web of confusion this created in your adult life. Therefore, in writing this book, I use the familiar terms of

we and *us* as a recognition of the fact that we share a similar struggle. Our circumstances are different, but the patterns we developed as a result of those circumstances are
surprisingly similar. It is my hope that what I have learned
through eight heartrending years of counseling and study,
including almost every book I could find on healing the
pain caused by growing up in a dysfunctional home, can
encourage you to begin your journey—a journey that leads
to life and blessing—no matter how full of darkness, death,
and cursing the beginning of your life's path was.

Nancy LeSourd
P. O. Box 20311
Washington, D.C. 20041

PART ONE

The Battleground: The Dysfunctional Home

Chapter 1

The Challenge

*When I got tired of hurting, I started making choices. Big
choices. They meant risks and a change of lifestyle, but I knew
that if I didn't, I would live in the pain forever...During
this time my transformation started as I surrendered to choices
(behavior change) and faith (waiting for results).*[1]

Sharon Wegscheider-Cruse
The Miracle of Recovery

It was a sultry summer day in 1979 when the train
slowly pulled out of the Stony Brook, Long Island, station.
As it gathered speed, the backyards of each community began to blend together in flashes of color and contrasts. The
dilapidated cars swayed in rhythm, with the engine producing a cooperative cadence of motion and sound. Often
such a ride enabled me to relax, providing a respite from
the tyranny of thoughts. Not today. As the car rocked gently
back and forth, I closed my eyes and tried to calm the terror rising in my throat. I thought of all the reasons I should
turn back at the next stop. In forty-five minutes I would be
in Huntington. In one hour I would be at my first counseling session. Suddenly, the need that compelled me to set up
the appointment in the first place seemed insignificant.

I thought back to painful memories of the past. Recently

it seemed that these memories were surfacing with greater frequency and intensity. New memories had been flooding back and washing over me in waves. The intensity of emotions that accompanied these memories frightened me so. I would try to control these unbridled thoughts, yet all the energy it took to keep smashing them down left me depleted and numb. I felt as though I were in a tunnel, tumbling backward as all of life was rushing forward. At the suggestion of Anne Grizzle, a friend and trained counselor, I had set up this appointment, and now the train's squealing wheels alerted me to my stop and the reality of that decision.

A taxi took me to a two-story, red brick office building. I stared at the sign on the front of the building for a long time: Robert Newman, Suite 206. I didn't even know this man, and I was about to tell him my most secret thoughts—and pay him for the privilege of doing so? I was skeptical. Anne said she thought he was the right counselor for me, since his training in family development enabled him to understand the dysfunction that results from diseased family patterns. He was also a Christian whose professional expertise was tempered with a dependence on the Holy Spirit to guide in both the timing and issues involved in the healing of a wounded individual. Finally, Anne emphatically stated that he was well suited for me because he was a man. She had witnessed the results of how my deep-rooted fear of the controlling power of men had played itself out in my relationships with them. Interestingly, she believed that for me to have full healing, I needed to have a healthy relationship with a man, albeit a counseling one that would end at some point.

I climbed the stairs to the second floor and thankfully found a bathroom, which would give me a few more moments to collect myself. The mirror reflected deep, gray-blue eyes that seemed much older than their years. Even at twenty-five, I had several lines across my forehead. Looking at me now, I could see why. The tension I felt expressed itself in a furrowed brow and rigid muscles. My teeth were clenched, drawing my mouth into a tight line. I shook my arms and hands to release the tension. Brushing my long blonde hair back behind my neck, I forced myself to relax. My reflection mocked me.

Tenuously, I entered the small reception area of the counseling office. A long, narrow hall with a closed door at the end was off to one side. I sat down, and methodically paged through one magazine after another, not focusing on any of the articles. Why had I arrived so early? I tried to train my thoughts on the printed page. The temptation to escape was very strong. I had done quite well so far. I had finished college and a master's degree program, and moved on to a successful teaching experience. So what if there were a few difficulties in my family life before? I didn't live at home now; in fact, I lived a thousand miles away and had been on my own for seven years. Anyway, everyone had problems and that didn't mean they had to tell a stranger the most intimate details of their lives.

For every valid reason I came up with to leave, an equally compelling reason presented itself to stay. I had made a commitment. I could at least try one session and then put an end to Anne's encouragement that I seek professional help. Before I had time to resolve this internal debate, the door to the counseling room opened. I averted my eyes, pretending to be absorbed in my magazine so I wouldn't see the previous client. After all, I'm sure he would want anonymity. I knew I would.

"Nancy? I'm Bob Newman." I looked up and saw a man about thirty-five years old with dark brown hair. He wore a blue pullover sweater that enhanced the warm clear blue of his eyes. "Are you ready? Let's go back to my office."

As I walked through the open door, I quickly surveyed his office. Desk. Bookshelves. Two black vinyl chairs facing one another in one corner. A lamp, a box of Kleenex, and a Bible on a low table by one of the chairs. And a black vinyl sofa. Oh, no! I'm not about to lie down in any stereotypical fashion on a stereotypical couch in a stereotypical shrink's office. Guessing my thoughts, Bob smiled and suggested I take one of the chairs. He sat across from me in the other. "So, tell me about yourself."

"Well, I'm here because my friend, Anne, thought it might help to talk to you. I'm not sure what you want to know."

"Why don't you start by telling me something about your family," Bob replied.

Suddenly I poured it all out: "My father drank a lot and would strike out at whoever was near with cruel, hateful words. He made life miserable for my mother, who worked hard to bring in money and keep things operating smoothly, but it was too much for her. Just after I turned nineteen, she killed herself. That left us three kids with Dad; he told us we were all on our own now. At least I was in college, but my two younger brothers had to find places to live. I tried hard to help them, but nothing seemed to help. Now the whole family is a mess." I was shocked at how easy it was to share all this with Bob.

Equally surprising were the emotions that poured out in this narration about my mother's death. I had handled her death quite well, I thought. I had made all the funeral arrangements, taken care of the family, and comforted all those who came to express their sorrow at our loss. No time for emotions. Things had to be properly taken care of, arrangements made, people notified. As the eldest, I had to be strong. The family needed me. So why now, six years later, was I so overcome with the powerful sense of loss and grief?

Bob handed me a Kleenex and explained, "It is good you are able to talk about this. I see so much, and my tendency would be to jump right in, but God is in charge of your healing. We will need to be sensitive to His timing. It is very obvious to me that God has brought you to this point and that He has begun the process. Do you have any questions about therapy?" he asked.

"I suppose my primary one is, What happens in here?" I replied.

"You don't need to worry about what to say in each counseling session. God will bring to your mind what it is He wants to deal with during that particular forty-five minute session. There is no need to dwell on topics or force memories. We will work with whatever is happening in your circumstances to explore the reasons for your responses and reactions."

I left this first session encouraged. I knew that I needed help, and Bob seemed to be one who could help me. Yet the next Thursday, when I drove up to that same brick office building for my second counseling session, I was surprised to find myself even more terrified than before. It was 4:45 P.M.; I was right on time. Punctual, yes, but certainly not leaving myself any additional time to wait. In fact, Bob was waiting for me. As we walked down the hall to his office, I wondered, why did I get myself into this? My eyes darted to the front door. What danger did I expect from this unassuming, friendly man who just wanted me to talk? Why was I so tormented inside?

I took my same seat across from Bob and stared at a spot on the floor, not daring to look into those encouraging eyes. The clock pounded out its constant measurement of time, but I had nothing to say. The long silences were punctuated with Bob's simple encouragements, "Just say whatever comes to mind." But I just stared at the floor unable to meet his eyes. Twenty minutes passed. Bob patiently waited. I shifted my position but not my gaze. Again, he asked what I was thinking.

Without looking up, I finally said, "Nothing, only half thoughts."

The silence broken, Bob replied, "Nancy, it's good to find this out now. You've had a reaction to the idea of therapy."

I protested, "But last week I came in here and poured everything out."

"Yes, but last week you didn't know what therapy was. You've had a week to think about it, and you realize that this is going to mean getting at some very painful buried emotions. When I asked you what you were thinking and you said, 'half thoughts,' it was because as soon as one came to the surface you panicked and pushed it down again."

With my eyes still riveted on the floor, I considered what he said. Could I be afraid of what was buried inside of me?

Bob jarred me out of my thoughts with a question, "Nancy, is your father a powerful man?"

I scoffed at his question, angrily snapped my head up, finally meeting his eyes. My father—a powerful man? He is one of the weakest, most pathetic men I know. "No, of course not," I said.

"Did he have power over your mother?"

I sat up straight in the chair and answered bitterly, "Well, he certainly had the power to hurt her!"

"That's right," Bob said quietly. "In fact, if you believe your father is the cause of her death, then you've given him the power to control life and death, which is a very Godlike power. From what you described last week, Nancy, you've placed men in positions of power and control over you in all your relationships with them, whether family, dating, or work. And now, as your therapist, I am in that same position.

"In this therapy relationship, I am in control. If you give me knowledge about yourself, then you've given me the tool to control you. Knowledge is power, and in your case that power has been used to hurt." He paused for a moment, and then continued, "Nancy, who is the ultimate authority figure?"

I answered appropriately, "God."

"Yes. And as we deal with your pain and these buried emotions, you will experience God's response to this complete knowledge of you. You will learn that God accepts you just as you are. Do you believe that?"

I knew that as a Christian I should respond with a resounding yes, but my silent response to Bob's question implied a no. No, I didn't believe God accepted me just as I was. God the Father was no different from my earthly father. In fact, at times He acted just like my father. My father would promise to do something for me and then forget, over and over. The promises in the Bible were like that—sometimes they worked; sometimes they didn't. My father loved to toy with me, baiting me into trusting him and then turning on me. God seemed to want me to trust Him, only so He could pull the rug out from under me. God, like my father, was not to be trusted, but I desperately wanted to say yes to Bob's question.

The tears poured down my face. I yearned to know what it was like to be totally known by a man or even God and not be rejected. I wanted that more than anything else in my life, but how could I believe that acceptance would be the result of sharing who I really was—all my ugly thoughts and wounds. As I struggled to answer, the tears escalated into sobs. I hung my head, unable to respond, broken at the glimpse of something which was at the same time wonderful and unattainable.

The tenderness in Bob's voice reached out to me as he said, "Well, you will learn that God loves and accepts you. God wants to heal you. Now is His timing, and you'll find that as you can open up to the real feelings inside of you—your anger, bitterness, and fear—that He loves you still. God wants to heal you, but He can't do it as long as you're strong. He is breaking down your defenses. Now you have to make a decision whether or not to trust this process. Are you willing to do that?"

When I left counseling that day, I asked that question over and over again to myself. For years I had simply regrouped whenever powerful feelings came to the surface.

As Larry Crabb identified in *Inside Out*: "When we reflect deeply on how life really is, both inside our soul and outside in our world, a quiet terror threatens to overwhelm us. We worry that we simply won't be able to make it if we face all that is there. In those moments, retreat into denial does not seem cowardly, it seems necessary and smart. Just keep going, get your act together, stop feeling sorry for yourself, renew your commitment to trust God, get more serious about obedience."[2]

Yet I was weary. The great amount of energy required to keep memories suppressed for many years had taken its toll on me, leaving me too tired to fight the memories down anymore. I was at a crossroads. The sense of hopelessness I felt at the repetitive patterns in my life had become so intense and intolerable that the potential pain of examining these locked-away memories, on balance, was becoming bearable.

Was probing the past really necessary anyway? Didn't Paul admonish us that we are to forget those things that are behind? As a Christian, was I giving too much power to past experiences when I should just be living in God's grace in the present?

Yet I had tried to forget the past and live in grace. And I had tried Scripture memory. And prayer. And more Bible study. And more faith. In fact, concerned Christian friends who puzzled at my continuing emotional struggles to be at peace and to feel loved by God would suggest that I just needed to pray more. Then I would rush to the bookstore and buy scores of books on prayer and devour them to try to unlock the secret to God's heart. Others would suggest it was a matter of more faith. Off I would go to the bookstore and read every book on fath. The more I struggled to know Him, however, the more confused I became. Could it be that something in my past was preventing me from knowing that reality?

Could I make this choice to examine my family background? Would I be willing to discover the patterns I had learned from my earliest years that were creating my present struggles? I had to decide. It was my choice alone—one that could forever change my life. I pulled over on the side of the road and bowed my head. In a brief moment of commitment, I said, "Yes, Lord, whatever it takes, I am willing to begin this journey."

This book tells the story of that journey. It begins by sharing my childhood, with its war of words and anger and explains how I developed specific and effective survival techniques to cope with the battleground of a dysfunctional home. The second part describes my young adult years and the troubling patterns that emerged in family, work, and romantic relationships as I continued to rely on these survival techniques. The third part explains what happened in counseling when I began to examine these patterns and to risk changing them. The fourth part shares the greatest test of all that I had learned in counseling: the ability to trust in a relationship.

It would not be an easy journey—encompassing eight years of counseling, much study of recovery literature, and many painful changes—but it would lead to freedom and to life. This is my story, shared to make it easier for someone else in pain to accept the challenge to explore self-defeating patterns that have led to death and start on a journey of faith to choose life instead.

Chapter 2

The Battlefield: The Dysfunctional Home

When parents have unmet or unresolved needs, they generally are unable to meet their children's needs. This promotes at least two problems. One is that their distortions, hurts, and needs will likely be passed from one generation to another. Secondly, and maybe more importantly, their children will lack the fundamental resources of perception, affirmation, and strength necessary for coping with the many and varied problems in life.[1]

> Jim Craddock, Pat Springle, Robert S. McGee
> *Your Parents and You*

When I grew up in the 1950s, the typical television script for the happy American family heralded Mom in her crisp shirtwaist dress, pouring orange juice out of a glass pitcher at the breakfast table, while Dad, dressed in a grey flannel suit and starched white shirt, engaged in cheerful morning repartee with his family before leaving for the office. Smiling boys and girls ate their cereal, kissed Mom and Dad good-bye, and hopped on the bus for school as their faithful dog, Spot, wagged his tail in approval.

But life at our home on Yorkshire Road in Atlanta, Georgia, was quite different. The laughter of children playing was silenced when Daddy walked in the door. I, being the eldest, had the important role of chief scout. Stationed by the living room window, I took the evening watch. Would this be a night of yelling and screaming or would we have a reprieve?

The steel gray Plymouth rolled into the driveway. A large man, bald except for graying hair on the sides of his head and several long strands on his forehead combed back, emerged from the car. Sometimes his hair would stand out in tufts on the sides. Combined with his full, gray-speckled beard and his dark eyebrows drawn together across the bridge of his nose in a scowl, it gave him an appearance of evil. Priding himself on being a maverick, he wore knit golf shirts with a string tie—an odd combination and certainly a contrast to the other blue pinstripe-suited lawyers in his profession.

As soon as Dad got out of the car, I scanned his face. I had learned to read my father's emotions: when his eyebrows were drawn together in a deep frown, which was most of the time, trouble was ahead.

Yet my father hadn't always been like this. My parents had met in law school and married shortly after they graduated. My mother had told me that for the first few years, things were fairly normal. Dad was moody at times, but not hurtful. Then sometime soon after I was born, apparently something happened to cause a shift in his personality. He became bitter, vindictive. I often wondered what caused this. Did he lose an important case? Was he humiliated in some way? If Mom knew, she never felt she could tell me.

On this night, I ran to alert the troops. My younger brothers first: "Pete, Sam, Dad's home and he's mad." Then Mom. I'd rush into the kitchen, knowing I had only moments to spare before he would walk in the door. "Mom, Dad's home and his eyebrows are together." It was a simple code but it worked.

My brothers and I quickly scattered and immersed ourselves in quiet activities in our rooms. It was important to lay low. Don't draw too much attention to yourself.

My father slumped in the swivel rocker in the living room and began to light his pipe. It was a ritual. First he cleaned the pipe stem. I was struck by the funny noises he made as he cleared the stem by blowing air through it. Then came the crinkling of the orange and black striped bag of Sir Walter Raleigh® tobacco as he scooped up the tobacco for his next smoke. The match struck, hissed, then faded as the slurping noises he made as he sucked on his pipe took precedence. He leaned back in his chair and closed his eyes.

Sometimes I watched from the crack in my bedroom door and wondered what his day had been like. As a title attorney, he often had to travel to different cities to check the deeds of property in record rooms. I knew that made him tired. At times when he came home, we would work on a crossword puzzle together. My father, skilled in his use of the English language, would work for hours on the puzzle. He would let me help by looking up words in the dictionary and suggesting possibilities. I felt so proud when he praised my selection of a word that fit the blocks. On nights when he came in with his eyebrows together, however, I would stay in my room and pray, *Dear God, please, don't let Daddy get mad tonight.*

But my prayers always seemed to bounce off a glass ceiling. Dinner was always the catalyst. We gathered around a round table, the type strategically used by companies to offset a pugilistic, confrontational approach. Not so at the Oliver home. The dominant presence at dinner was my father, a combatant lying in wait for his prey. The three of us kids kept our heads lowered, concentrating on the meal. No eye contact. We'd learned early that to meet his gaze was to assert a challenge and no one wanted that. We'd wait. Which of us would bear the brunt of his abuse?

Tonight it was my youngest brother. "So, Pete. I see you made another D. How stupid! Why can't you be more like your sister," challenged my father. Pete looked up in terror. I hated it when he compared Pete to me. He was only in second grade but had shown no interest in school or reading and had had a hard time of it. Sam, a fourth grader, and I, a sixth grader, on the other hand, took to school well, since by getting good grades we could find some affirmation from our father.

Dad pushed his chair back from the table, and leaned back in it, resting his elbows on the arms of the chair, the fingers of one hand mirroring those of the other. Suddenly, he pointed at Pete and shouted, "You arc an embarrassment to your mother and me." He continued, "What are you good for? Nothing. You can't read. You can't work math. All you do is stay in your room."

Pete shrank back in terror. I could see him begin to shake, and I knew he was trying to hold back his tears.

That was it. I'd have to step in. Anything to get Dad off Pete's back. "Daddy, my ballet recital is next week. Are you going to come?"

"And see your fat legs pounding across the stage! I wouldn't miss it for the world." He turned his full attention to me now. I heard Pete breathe a sigh of relief and lower his head. Sam kept his eyes glued to his dinner plate as well. "Come on, boys, tell her. Isn't she a sight? Elephant legs. That's what you boys should call her. Come on, Sam, tell her. Elephant legs."

I hated the change in my body as much as my father apparently did. I had gone from a spindly fourth grader to a rotund sixth grader. I didn't understand what had happened. In the fourth grade, I was thin and agile. I could race with the best of them, and I loved to ride my bike and to twirl around on the ballet dance floor. But now I was almost as big around as I was tall. The other girls in my class were developing nicely, but I was still flat-chested, fleshy, and awkward. I was uncertain in ballet now that I had moved up to toe shoes. It was much more difficult to maneuver across a dance floor on the tips of my toes and with my body shaped the way it was, and I had begun to hate dressing in leotards and tights. Elephant legs. Those words marked me forever. I was ugly. He knew it too.

"I suppose I have to pay for another one of those queer ballet outfits. What is it this time?" he asked.

I hated to tell him. Four of us were doing a dance number to "Waltz of the Flowers." "A pansy," I replied.

"A pansy! It figures. I have to spend twenty dollars to see my little girl plod across the floor for five minutes as a pansy! You kids cost me a fortune—it's always some fool thing for your enrichment. When are you ever going to pay me back?"

We had faced off. The battle was between the two of us now. With her face drawn tightly, Mom sat by quietly and Pete and Sam kept their heads lowered close to their plates, shoveling in food to look busy. I needed to maintain control. I was determined he was not going to win, but it was a difficult challenge. My father had a way of twisting everything you said. It was always a battle of words. Hurtful words.

"But, Daddy, I make all A's and help you proofread legal documents." I always liked this time because he wasn't yelling at me. It was almost like normal.

"Yeah, but, girl, you'll never be able to pay me back. All the money I've invested in you. Look at this." He reached behind him and pulled out some large, light green ledger sheets on which he recorded what he had spent on each of us. "See, here: $323.44 the last quarter. Just for you, Elephant Legs. What do I get out of it? Any appreciation? No, it's just, Daddy, can I have this, Daddy, can I have that?"

Try as I could, I could not keep the hot tears from flowing down my cheeks. My head pounded and my heart raced. As he continued his tirade, I felt weaker and weaker. He knew how to harp on your most sensitive areas until he had beaten you down, making you feel worthless and powerless.

How to stop it? Don't listen. Just shut him out of your mind. I issued these commands to myself as his tirade got louder and louder. Don't explode at him. Then there would really be hell to pay. Stay in control. My chest rose higher with each breath. I knew I was breathing too fast again, but it seemed like the only way I could keep my anger from exploding. Close your mouth, Nancy, that will slow down your breathing. I could hear the sound of my own breath rush in and out of my nose. My chest continued to rise faster and faster. I felt light-headed, and I knew I was going to do it again. That's the last thought I remember.

When I awoke, Mom was sitting next to me on my bed. She was a small woman, only 4 feet, 11 inches. Her short, black hair, fashioned by bobby-pinned pincurls each night, framed her delicate features. Unadorned by any makeup, her face seemed like an empty canvas, with only a splash of color from her green eyes. She placed a cool washcloth on my forehead and stroked back my hair. "Nancy, Nancy, when are you going to learn? You just have to learn to take it. Just take it."

This was her method of dealing with my father. Often he drank late at night. Sometimes he drank himself into a stupor. Other times he was sober enough to hound her with his irrational tirades and unfounded accusations until early into the morning. She used to try to dialogue with him, but my father, a lawyer and a master of words, had turned his greatest gift into a tool of hatred. So Mom learned to be quiet, to "just take it," and to not try to defend herself.

This must have been hard for her, since in her legal career she was accomplished and confident. For five years, she had been the only woman trial attorney in Atlanta and had gained the respect of the judges she appeared before and the opposing counsel she was up against. When I was born, she switched to tax work, which enabled her to keep a more regular schedule. She continued trial work pro bono, however, usually with juveniles. At times she took me, as a young girl, with her to the juvenile detention centers so I could learn about her work. This Jane Oliver was far removed from the pain in our home. When the door shut behind her in our house, however, she changed. She responded to my father's attacks with what she deemed the most strategic tactic—a passive quiet—to not exacerbate an already painful situation.

Often, it wouldn't work. At two or three in the morning, Mom would awaken us and drive us to the Holiday Inn on the interstate a few miles from our home. She had to get some sleep since she worked full time to provide for many of the family needs. The next morning we would have breakfast at the Krystal before being dropped off for school on Mom's way to work. For the longest time I thought that this is what most families did.

One day at recess, however, I learned that my home was different. My best friend and I raced to the swing set for our favorite game. We pumped our legs harder and harder to see who could get the highest. The chains would swing and jerk, then arc dangerously close to the top pole of the swing set. Then we effortlessly sailed through the air, letting our legs dangle until the swings came to a rest. We wrapped our arms around the chains, and I leaned back trying to make my hair touch the ground. It was then that I let out our family secret. I told her how two to three times a week, Mom would take us kids to a motel in the middle of the night, and then we would have waffles for breakfast at the Krystal on the way to school. Clair's eyes got wide as she stared at me in disbelief. "Why does your mom do that, Nancy? You go in the middle of the night? A couple of times a week?" The amazed look on her face said, "Your family must really be odd." The memory of that look kept me from telling anyone about my family again for a very long time.

WAS YOUR HOME A BATTLEFIELD?

If your childhood home was filled with verbal, emotional, or physical abuse, it was not a normal home. Verbal and physical assaults become the weapons directed by the dysfunctional parent to destroy the health and well-being of the spouse and the children. Those of us who have grown up in these types of homes understand the dynamics. It is war. We have experienced the outright battles, and the carnage that is left.

Other types of dysfunctional homes are just as devastating, but their battles are not as obvious. These homes are engaged in a cold war, but the loneliness and pain are just as close a companion to this child as the child from alcoholic or abusive homes. Many times adults from these types of homes feel they have no reason for their present struggles; their stories pale beside their friends from violent homes. Sure, they think, it's alright to see your family of origin as a reason for your present struggles if your parents beat you or drank, but what if they just ignored you or cared for you too much?

Andrea, an only child, came from such a family. Her father was often absent from home due to military obligations. When Andrea was born, her mother put her career on hold for seventeen years and focused entirely on her new daughter. Andrea became her mother's exclusive world, and she soon began to sense she was responsible for her parents' happiness. At Christmastime, for instance, she was acutely aware of these two people staring intently at her, waiting for her reaction to the many presents for her piled high under the tree. She felt she had to generate as much noise and excitement as several children, so she worked hard to scatter paper and ribbons with verve and exclaim with glee.

Her mother, an accomplished teacher who had become well respected in her field, was a perfectionist. If someone ran water in the aluminum sink, she would be right behind them to mop it out so that it sparkled. When Andrea was given chores, her mother was right there, redoing what Andrea had just finished.

When Andrea began to develop her own friendships, her mother was frequently ill. She would often say, "You used to be so nice when you were little. We used to spend so much time together." Andrea soon realized her mother resisted her having her own life. Then her father died when she was in high school, and Andrea's first thought was, "Oh, my God, this woman's happiness depends entirely on me."

When Andrea graduated from college, she held a series of broadcasting jobs, which led to a plum position with a national network. Yet she never felt satisfied. She could never enjoy her awards and accolades, and she beat herself up for "average" performance. When she became a Christian, it was just one more arena in which she had to be perfect. This exacting God certainly couldn't accept her as she was, but if she was just good enough, then maybe . . .

Jim came from another type of dysfunctional family, one whose secret was hidden from the family. His parents had never told him about his grandfather, Tom, who had been an alcoholic. His father determined never to drink and Jim's mother agreed. There was to be no alcohol in their home. Although Jim never saw his parents drink and was never abused verbally or physically, Jim grew up in a family that was rigid and cold. He shared many of the characteristics of his friends who came from such homes. He seemed to sabotage his own success in business and felt fearful much of the time for seemingly no reason. He often broke off a relationship as soon as it became apparent that the woman really cared for him. As a Christian, he doubted that God loved him or had his best interests at heart. When Jim had his own family, he subconsciously recreated the home he had grown up in. This dysfunctional home was handed down from generation to generation, but Jim saw no reason to look at his family of origin as a source of his present struggles since no alcohol or outward, dramatic signs of abuse were present.

Sensitive, accomplished individuals, like Andrea and Jim, perceive someone like myself as deserving to express their pain, while they feel they have no excuse. Yet, as Leo Tolstoy so aptly explained in *Anna Karenina*, "All happy families are like one another; each unhappy family is unhappy in its own way."[2] Your pain from the cool rejection of your parent is as deep, piercing, and destructive to you as my pain from the violent behavior of mine.

THE DYSFUNCTIONAL FAMILY SYSTEM

Families develop systems to cope with the stress associated with the dysfunctional parent—all other individuals are defined in relation to the dysfunctional parent. When the dysfunctional parent is the standard by which the other family members measure their responses and actions, the scales are already tipped toward unhealthy and unsatisfying relationships. Rather than the family becoming the place in which it is safe to explore one's own gifts, abilities, and character as an independent person, the family sacrifices the individual to preserve the family unit.

The dysfunctional family has certain characteristics that create negative relational patterns in those of us who grew up in them. I spent eight years of counseling and over twelve years studying the dynamics of dysfunctional homes, identifying the characteristics of the dysfunctional family system and the patterns this system had created. It's often a long process, but unless we can identify, acknowledge, and change these patterns, we are destined to repeat this family system in our own families.

Code of Silence

The secrecy in dysfunctional family systems is inviolable. No one in this family is permitted to talk about the family—either within the family or to outsiders. The family must appear normal. Family members band together to preserve that image. The code of silence provides the dysfunctional family a rallying point; it works to preserve the integrity of the family system.

In my family, my mother steeled herself to "take it" when my father railed on, and urged us to respond the same way. Rather than question the abnormal behavior of my father, she, and ultimately her children, made a tacit agreement to adjust to it, thereby supporting the abnormal behavior.

I rarely had friends over to play because I never knew how my father would act. To make this seem normal, I came up with what I thought were acceptable reasons why I was always available to play at my friend's house but never able to have her over. Those reasons never focused on my father.

When my father's outrages were too great, we were scooped up to go to a motel. This skulking around in the middle of the night reinforced the code of silence. No one was to know that this was what we did. Silence, secrecy, shame—an unending cycle, but an effective one for keeping the family secrets and pretending life was normal.

Crisis-Orientation

A healthy family will have crises. Yet in a healthy family, these periods are time-limited and the skills exhibited by the individual members to cope with these crises are healthy. Family members attempt to find a solution together and rely on one another for strength to get through this intense period of need. Most importantly, after the crisis has passed, the family returns to normal living.

In a dysfunctional family, the family lives from crisis to crisis, and when there is not an overt crisis, the family lives in expectation of one. The tension in this type of family is palpable. When the code of silence has been invoked, however, the individual family members cannot talk to one another about it, and there is a great sense of isolation and loneliness. Since we have also been taught to preserve the family secret at all costs, we cannot share our concerns with outsiders. We often isolate ourselves because we are afraid of what our friends will see or hear if they visit our homes.

These crises are sustained and frequent, and this becomes normal life for us. When we reach adulthood, we feel uneasy when things are going smoothly. Often, we attempt to sabotage our own success in relationships or at work to create a crisis and bring back that comfortable feeling of chaos. We thrive on change and dislocation because it creates new arenas for crisis management. We often procrastinate in tasks or projects because the encroaching time deadlines raise the project to a crisis level. We may become great crisis managers, rising to the occasion and impressing all with our ability to cope. But life is not meant to be lived in a sustained crisis mode. Much of life is meant to be lived on the plains of our emotions, but for us, the mountainous highs and deep, treacherous lows feel comfortable and provide the greatest security.

Unpredictability

In a healthy family, the children learn to expect certain responses from their parents for specific behaviors. Promises made are promises kept. In a dysfunctional home, unpredictability and confusion reign. Certain behaviors get one type of response from the parent at one time and another at a different time. Outbursts occur for seemingly no reason. Promises are broken. The children attempt to figure out what they are doing to cause this. This is the beginning of one of the lifelong curses of growing up in this type of home: blaming oneself for the unreasonable behavior of others.

Since the children do not talk to anyone about the reality of their circumstances, they begin to guess at what normal behavior is. They are never really sure if they're acting appropriately, and later, they will spend a great deal of their adult life attempting to guess what behaviors and emotions are proper in different settings.

Repression of Feelings

Emotions are extremely powerful in dysfunctional homes because they are usually explosive. Many feelings of rage, hurt, fear, terror, loneliness, disappointment well up in us, but the expression of such emotions is not permitted. Again, the code of silence operates to keep us from discussing this with others, so we never learn that many of our feelings are appropriate or how to express them properly. We submerge these powerful feelings because we don't know how else to cope with them. I was deeply angry at my father for his verbal attacks, but my mother taught me to stuff that feeling. She thought it was the best thing for me, since to express my anger, as she once had to him, only brought more vindictive abuse.

Inability to Trust

In a healthy home, a child develops trust from the very beginning of life. The baby cries; the mother responds by tending to the need for food or a change of diapers. This happens over and over. The infant begins to trust that a communication from him will be heard, understood, and responded to by his parent. As the child develops, the consistency with which the parents relate to him breeds trust. The child knows what to expect and he feels secure. Even in matters of discipline, the consistency and reasonableness of the parents permit the child to explore his own environment within safe boundaries.

In a dysfunctional home, the boundaries are often violated. The child is called upon to be an adult, often a parent to his parent. Rather than my mother interceding for my brothers, I became the protector. This inversion of roles creates confusion of boundaries. The child is no longer developing toward an autonomous individual; instead, the child is increasingly confused as to where he ends and his parent begins. When I was only nine or ten, my mother used to ask me for advice about whether she should leave my father. I was called upon to dispense great wisdom on the institution of marriage at an age when I should have been playing with Barbie® dolls.

Roles in the Family System

Roles begin to evolve in a dysfunctional family system as the members of the family find their places and adjust to the dysfunctional parent. Sharon Wegscheider-Cruse devotes six chapters in *Another Chance* to examine the five primary roles that occur in an alcoholic family: the Enabler, the Hero, the Scapegoat, the Lost Child, and the Mascot. Today, we would call the Enabler, Codependent. These roles are present in most dysfunctional families. When I first learned of this family paradigm, I easily identified the roles each of my family members adopted.

The Enabler

The Enabler is most always the spouse of the dysfunctional parent. However, all individuals in the family "enable" the dysfunctional parent to continue in his abuse because the family system operates to keep them from questioning the appropriateness of that behavior. Individuals in a dysfunctional family subjugate their own development to the performance of their role in sustaining the family system.

When the dysfunctional parent acts in ways that are irresponsible, embarrassing, or destructive, it is often the spouse who steps in to compensate and to soften the effects of his actions. This enables the dysfunctional parent to continue acting irrationally, for he is not having to face the consequences of his actions.

The Enabler often begins his role by taking over the duties and responsibilities of the dysfunctional individual. This accomplishes two goals: it helps preserve the family unit, and it presents a together front to the world. When the dysfunctional parent is an alcoholic, the spouse may call in sick for him when he is hung over. This protects that person's job and the income source to the family. Perhaps the dysfunctional parent is a workaholic; then the spouse takes on more and more of the child-rearing responsibilities in the absence of that parent.

My mother was the Enabler in our home. This role fell to her by default. It was unusual in the 1950s for the woman to be the primary breadwinner, but Mom realized that if we were to have consistent support, she would need to provide that. She had been raised in a very rigid home where her mother had never once told her she loved her. Nothing my mother did was good enough for her mother, yet she was the dutiful daughter, who after her father died when she was in college, tended to her mother's needs. Since my father abdicated his parenting responsibilities, my mother —caring very much that this family be whole—picked them up, playing both mother and father to us. She amazed many, juggling her work, her parenting responsibilities, her caretaking of her mother, and her varied civic responsibilities. But I rarely saw her laugh.

What is the individual payoff? The Enabler develops a sense of importance, even self-righteousness, that becomes his raison d'être. Since the dysfunctional parent typically

causes the spouse to feel inferior, the additional responsibilities bolster the Enabler's self-esteem and importance to
the family.[3] Obviously, the longer the dysfunction goes on,
the more the Enabler feels inferior and the more he needs
this role to elevate himself. He can become addicted to that
role, which is why it is so hard for a spouse who is codependent to make significant changes in this role, even
once he recognizes his codependency.

Wegscheider-Cruse notes that there is a price for continuing in this role. As the dysfunction deepens, the dysfunctional parent deals with his pain by projecting his guilt
and self-hatred onto the spouse. He becomes supercritical
of all aspects of the spouse.[4] My father despised my mother's career and her ability to support the family. His frus-
tration with the obstacles to his own career advancement
were taken out on her as he would condemn her efforts,
hitting at her vulnerable areas. He would tell her that she
was an uncaring mother for being out in the work force,
when she saw her need to work as essential to providing for
her children. This, coupled with her already low self-
esteem, pulled her down even further. Although deeply
angry—at himself, at his spouse, at God—the Enabler often turns that anger inward on himself. This can result in
disease or, as in my mother's case, even death.

The Hero

Most often the firstborn, the Hero realizes that something is wrong in the family system. Heroes cope by com-
pensating for these problems by being good, often very,
very good. We succeed in school, often getting kudos and
approval from otherwise abusive or disinterested parents.
We work very hard to reestablish a balance in the family,
but our efforts never pay off.

The Hero also projects the image of a successful family.
After all, if little Johnny or Susie can be so good, so responsible, so accomplished, something must be right within

this family. This is particularly accentuated when the Hero begins attending school:

> When our Hero starts going to school, he finds a whole new world of ways to "be good." He can be good at his schoolwork and bring home A's. He can be good at music or sports and make the family proud. As a bonus he discovers that kids who are good at things are popular with teachers and other kids, too. At some level he says to himself, "I'll show the world this family is okay. A family has to be okay to have a kid who can do things better than other people, doesn't it?" And when he does well, he feels okay, too.[5]

There is a price to be paid for this role, however. The Hero's efforts at overachievement are focused on restoring balance to the family. Since the dysfunctional parent is not changing, the Hero redoubles his or her efforts to chase the rainbow. We typically avoid any involvement with areas in which we are not successful, which would be enjoyable for healthy individuals even if they were only average in them. For example, academic subjects were easy for me, but my athletic abilities were minimal. I learned early to avoid all games unless they were board or card games requiring mind skills. The fear of failure and the extraordinary drive to achieve kept me in the arenas where success was possible.

Because we are usually the firstborn, we learn our style of relating to the dysfunctional parent from the Enabler. We can become "little Enablers."[6] This is particularly damaging in adult life as we seek to establish a relationship with a life partner. Our style of relating easily attracts those who are either chemically dependent or dysfunctional themselves. Thus we perpetuate the generational cycle unless we can break these patterns.

The dysfunctional family system creates a particular pattern of destruction for the Hero which is rewarded by society. After all, who would think a super-responsible, hard-working achiever isn't okay? So the Hero continues these patterns as a result of positive feedback. At some point, however, the confusion and pain become so unbearable that even these societal payoffs may not offset it.

This book focuses primarily on the Hero—what life is like as a Hero in a dysfunctional family, what happens when that Hero grows up and leaves the family system, and how to break the dysfunctional patterns and behaviors. Since I was the Hero in my family, I will share what growing up in this role has done to my life. Many of you are Heroes. Others of you are married to Heroes or have a sibling who was a Hero. This book is meant to help you understand yourself or others who have had the burdensome and lonely role of being perfect, achieving all, and chasing success only to find it no longer provides enough payback.

The Mascot

The Mascot is often the youngest child. As the "baby" of the family, the family secret is kept from him. Of course, he senses the craziness, but when he inquires about it, the Mascot is only given vague reassurances.[7] This creates increasing tension, because he knows there is something very wrong with this family. He learns to release the tension through his antics or jokes. He becomes the family clown, again diverting attention from the real problems and providing some release of tension for the family:

> The Mascot who creates fun wherever he goes has some things in common with the Hero. Both manage to get positive attention for themselves and at the same time bring good feelings to the family. When the other members laugh at him, it relieves their tensions too. Everyone seems to forget, at least for a moment, how grim it all is.[8]

The Mascot also pays a price for this role. Few people really know him since his outward persona is that of the clown. He is lonely even while others surround him with attention. It also stunts his social development, because his main interactive skill has been to joke.[9] He often remains immature in his communication skills.

Wegscheider-Cruse has found that Mascots are the most affected by stress. Since Mascots have learned to deal with problems by clowning around, joking, and shifting attention to their acts, they often escape into further delusion. Mascots may have serious psychiatric problems and may be misdiagnosed as paranoid schizophrenic. This occurs because they are torn between their flippant, carefree exterior and their terrifying fears within. Learning to dull their pain with drugs or alcohol, they may also become chemically dependent or suicidal.

My brother, Sam, was our Mascot. Although he was second-born, he was very close in age to me. He was also tall and many people mistook us for twins. We liked that comparison. We did a lot together, had similar friends, and even roomed together with bunk beds for much of our younger years. This closeness in age and attitude may explain why Sam adopted the Hero role for the first part of his childhood.

Yet individuals in the dysfunctional family system may switch roles when one role becomes too uncomfortable or is no longer working to provide the defensive protection it once did.[10] Somewhere around age eleven, Sam also became our family Mascot. Quick-witted, he provided many laughs. He'd clown around at dinner and keep the attention on himself to divert it from our father. With a strong facility for words, he gained approval for the entire family by his weekly humorous letters submitted to the Mail Bag, a column in the *Atlanta Constitution* newspaper.

The Scapegoat

Whereas the Hero attempted to distract the family from its problems with his success, the Scapegoat enters the family system, observes the ineffectiveness of that approach, and tries an alternative method. Instead of being very, very good, he is often very, very bad. The Scapegoat draws attention away from the dysfunctional parent to himself and his escapades. He may get into trouble to get any attention, even negative, from parents who are otherwise occupied with their own roles.

When our mother died, Sam switched roles again and turned more to the drugs that were a part of his teen years to numb the pain. He graduated from high school a year early and went on to the University of Georgia at the age of seventeen. He was only there for a semester when it became clear it was too difficult for him to manage. His drug use had caused him to do poorly in school for the first time.

Back home, he lived with my father, and the two of them got into physical as well as verbal battles. They would drink together and then throw the furniture around the room. He became very manipulative. My mother had left a small amount of money in a bank trust fund that was to be used only for education. Sam learned to con the bank trustees by signing up for classes at Georgia State, submitting the tuition bills, and then withdrawing on the last day in which you could get a 90% refund. Several years later, when the bank trustees finally caught on and stopped this source of income, Sam began to live off the streets of Atlanta and in state mental hospitals. Named after my father, he had become just like him, addicted to drugs, mentally ill, and suicidal.

So what is the payoff for the family and the individual? The family can turn to the Scapegoat as the one who is the troublemaker. Instead of confronting the dysfunctional parent, the family can say that all their problems are caused by the Scapegoat and focus on changing him instead.

The Lost Child

This child enters a family already in the midst of chaos.

He is a loner, spending much time on his own, staying out of the way of the others and laying low. The Lost Child makes few demands. He often is found playing alone in his room. This isolation protects him from some of the negative effects that attention (good or bad) brings to the Hero and Scapegoat.[11]

However, this same isolation exacts a price. The Lost Child has had such little interaction in the family that he has few skills for coping with the outside world. It is difficult for him to make friends, and he further withdraws. Loneliness becomes the primary characteristic:

> While he is young, the safety of his solitude may be worth the cost, but as his personal world expands beyond the home, what once was a sanctuary becomes increasingly a prison. All around him he sees people involved in human relationships, yet he cannot seem to get past the bars of his own solitary habits and social inexperience to participate. Aloneness turns into a deep, aching loneliness, with its companion feelings of sadness, confusion and fear.[12]

The Lost Child often has doubts about his own sexual identity and sometimes can be confused about sexual preferences.[13]

My youngest brother, Pete, was our family's Lost Child. His bedroom was his sanctuary, and he often spent hours upon hours there. He had trouble scholastically and withdrew from peers with whom he could not compete. Within the family structure, he was the one most often targeted by our father. His inadequacies in school and within the family structure itself were clear opportunities for verbal abuse. He was never going to receive approval and he knew it. So why try?

Pete was fourteen when our mother died. He lived for a time with relatives and then spent his last few years in high school in a boarding house. Despite his poorly developed academic skills, Pete was a hard worker. He did not want to be dependent on our father and worked several jobs to pay his rent. I admired his grit and determination. It was during this time that he had his first homosexual experience and began experimenting with drugs.

Our family's Lost Child is truly lost to us now. As an adult, he moved away, leaving no forwarding address. Despite efforts to locate him, no one knows where he is living.

The Battle Plan: To Survive

There is a castle on a cloud,
I like to go there in my sleep.
Aren't any floors for me to sweep.
Not in my castle on a cloud.

There is a room that's full of toys.
There are a hundred boys and girls.
Nobody shouts or talks too loud.
Not in my castle on a cloud.

There is a lady all in white.
Holds me and sings a lullaby.
She's nice to see and she's soft to touch.
She says, "Cosette, I love you very much."

I know a place where no one's lost.
I know a place where no one cries.
Crying at all is not allowed.
Not in my castle on a cloud.[1]

"Castle on a Cloud"
from the play *Les Misérables*

Wilfrid Noyce was an avid mountaineer whose dangerous mountain-climbing exploits led him to be interested in the characteristics that enable people to survive in situations of exceptional hardship and danger. In *They Survived*, written just before he fell to his death in 1962 while climbing Mount Garmo in the Pamirs of the Soviet Union, he focused on people who had survived extraordinary physical conditions, those who faced treacherous hikes, excursions, explorations, earthquakes, and internments in concentration camps. In his conclusion he explored the question of why some people survive ordeals that destroy others.

Noyce surmises that survival depends on the ability of a person to be conditioned by gradual stages to the intense conditions they must face. He notes that, "The climber who goes up by gradual stages can operate comfortably at 26,000 feet, a height at which the unacclimatized, dropped from an aeroplane, would die. Similarly the Channel-swimmer is able to immerse himself for longer and longer periods, the skin of the Antarctica explorer's fingers hardens until he can handle metals at −40°."[2] Noyce hypothesizes that this ability to adapt both mind and body to changing conditions, along with the courage it demands, is the main quality common to all survivors. "Whether you are trapped in a coal-mine or beset by disease, lost at sea on a raft or avalanched down an ice-slope . . . you will survive according to your ability to adapt to conditions as they arise. According as you adapt, you become the new unit, climber-and-mountain or sailor-and-sea, with greater possibilities of endurance than climber or sailor alone."[3]

This is what happens to survivors from dysfunctional homes. We learn to adapt to our environment, to change with it in whatever ways are necessary to protect our lives. In so doing, we learn to be passive, to accept our environment's requirements, and to respond to that environment in a way that ensures our survival and the survival of the family. We become one with the mountain.

Over the last twelve years, as a part of my own journey, I have studied most everything that has been written on dysfunctional families, alcoholic family systems, and recovery. As I considered the role Heroes play in the family drama and examined my life and the lives of other Heroes I have known, I identified six primary survival techniques Heroes develop to cope with their families of origin. In this chapter and the next, we will examine these survival techniques and demonstrate how they are used in the family system. Each of these survival techniques, though effective to deflect the pain of childhood for a time, exacts its price from the individual.

POST-TRAUMATIC STRESS DISORDER

Recently, experts have begun to expand the condition of Post-Traumatic Stress Disorder (PTSD), originally confined to war veterans, to victims of crime, witnesses of suicide or other traumatic deaths, and children in abusive homes. Dr. Andrew Slaby, in his recent book, *Aftershock*, also notes that trauma may be event-specific, such as a war, a death, or an accident, or it may be more subtle, such as growing up in an alcoholic or otherwise abusive environment.[4] Dr. Slaby underscores six characteristics that make a trauma a trauma: (1) expected versus unexpected news, (2) element of sudden shock, (3) element of personal history in which you fear repetition of the painful events, (4) unfairness, (5) powerlessness, and (6) blame and guilt. Not all are required, but they each signal a crisis and the possibility of aftershock or Post-Traumatic Stress Disorder later on.[5]

The last four characteristics are often present in children from dysfunctional families. Dr. Slaby explains that when a traumatic, stressful life event does not ease, one's reaction can become more and more debilitating.[6] The cumulative result of this response to sustained trauma can result in PTSD.

What Happens to Individuals Suffering from PTSD?

Post-Traumatic Stress Disorder occurs when one has experienced stress or a traumatic event of such intensity and nature that it is outside the range of usual human experience and would be markedly distressing to almost anyone. Imagine what can happen to children who experience the collision with violent, explosive personalities on a daily basis. Living in the sustained stress environment of a dysfunctional home, particularly an emotionally or physically abusive one, can bring about PTSD in many of these children, which may not manifest itself until their adult years.

PTSD is often characterized by the traumatic event being persistently reexperienced in at least one of the following ways: (1) recurrent and intrusive distressing recollections of the event, (2) recurrent distressing dreams of the event, (3) sudden acting or feeling as if the traumatic event were recurring, (4) intense psychological distress at exposure to events that symbolize or resemble an aspect of the traumatic event. I believe that I experienced PTSD in college after my mother's death. For a year I would see her lying on the floor surrounded by blood in my weekly nightmares. When I saw the movie *Chinatown* a few years later, which has a scene where a woman is shot in the head, I became physically ill, rushing out of the movie theater with my heart pounding, letting the cool evening air calm my terror. To this day, I am unable to see graphic movies in which a person is physically hurt in any way. The image of my mother is linked up with these seemingly unconnected Hollywood stories.

Persons with PTSD will often avoid any thoughts or feelings associated with the trauma, any activities or situations that arouse recollections of the trauma, or any important aspect of the trauma.[7] Although we did not sell our house until three years after my mother's death, I never could go down to the basement where the first suicide attempt occurred or into her bedroom where she died. I mentally shut off that part of our house.

Often one of the problems for us in trying to get in touch with our childhood is remembering our childhood. The pain of those years is so deep that repression mechanisms work hard to keep the feelings associated with the events of those years submerged. When similar events occur, often in other venues such as work, we overreact to those events, attaching the emotions of the past to the present situation.

Dr. Timmen L. Cermak, author and speaker on many issues surrounding adult children of alcoholics, states that the effects of PTSD can be especially severe if the stress is caused by a series of traumatic events and is of human origin.[8] He further asserts that the effects of PTSD are even more severe if the individual under stress has rigid coping strategies or if their support system includes those who deny the source of the stress.[9]

One of the most devastating aspects of this disorder is a condition called psychic numbing, a sense of estrangement from other people and a sense that there is no place or group to which one can belong. Dr. Cermak has found that the lack of spontaneity and extreme emotional control of people exhibiting PTSD are often displayed by adult children of alcoholics.[10] Emotions can become frozen, making intimacy with others or with God impossible.

> Their survival depends upon their ability to suspend feelings in favor of taking steps to ensure their safety. Unfortunately, the resulting "split" between one's self and one's experience does not heal easily. Until an active process of healing takes place, the individual continues to experience a *constriction of feelings*, a decreased ability to recognize which feelings are present, and a persistent sense of being cut off from one's surroundings.[11]

What we developed to help us survive may later paralyze us. We become stuck in relationships or job situations, anxious and worried about repeated failures, fearful we will be found out, and disillusioned with the elusive quest for happiness. Although desirous of acceptance and freedom to feel and express our true selves, we are so assured of our rejection that we isolate our true self from ourselves and others.

In childhood, that was absolutely necessary. We were in a life-and-death situation, and we responded to the perceived threat to our very being with these techniques. We survived as a result. But when we repeat these childhood patterns of survival as adults, we are surprised to find ourselves in more and more constricting and confusing situations. What protected us in the past is the very thing that is destroying us now. When we can recognize these survival techniques and the patterns as they are played out in our adult lives and summon the courage to change them, then the traumatic event (or often, many repeated traumatic events) will lose its terrible power over our lives. Let's look at six of them now: fantasy, denial of feelings, super-responsibility, overachievement, flight, and burden-bearing.

SIX SURVIVAL TECHNIQUES

Fantasy

In a dysfunctional home, the child is left to his own devices to make sense of what is happening. Since children are naturally creative and imaginative, they build a fantasy family with happy endings and secure "ever afters" as a solution for the inadequacies of their own families.

I created my fantasy world in my closet. There I found a safe haven from the arguing and tirades. A piece of wood, 8 inches by 8 inches, covered a hole in the drywall, which had been cut to fix the plumbing in the bathroom next to my bedroom. Rather than re-drywall, the plumbers had simply put a block of wood over the hole. Anytime I wanted I could go into my closet, shut the door, remove the wood cover, and have enough light from the basement windows to play for hours without being afraid. No one knew where I was, and often I was not missed.

All my stuffed animals and dolls were neatly arranged in a circle on the floor of one end of the closet. There were to be no outsiders in my fantasy family. In this family, there was a mother and a father who loved one another and especially loved their children. There was no fighting or screaming. Everyone was extraordinarily polite to one another, careful not to hurt through inconsiderate actions. Since I was very young and had little contact with other families to know how they should act to show love, there was a formality in their interactions. Yet the daddy doll always came home from work happy. He loved to pick up his little girl doll and swing her around the room. He would then put her on his knee and tell her how pretty she was and how much he loved her. The mommy doll did not work. Instead, she stayed home with the little girl doll and played with her all day long. This picture, as far removed as it was from the reality of the Oliver family, made me believe things could be better one day, somehow.

This may sound irrational, but I grew up in the era of classic television programs such as "Leave It to Beaver," "Ozzie and Harriet," "Father Knows Best," and "The Donna Reed Show." These composite families were my standard of reality. Then there were the wonderful movies such as *The Sound of Music, Mary Poppins,* and *Pollyana.* In all these movies, a hardened character, incapable of loving, was softened, warmed, and transformed by the love of a woman or the children. Somehow, the movies always ended with the disjointed family put right again. Now I was sure that if I could just be that kind of child—warm, precocious, and loving—then my father, too, could be transformed.

And if not, there was always the possibility of a miraculous savior. After all, children's literature and movies focused often on the mystical fairy godmother who could grant a child's heart's desire. Why, if Dorothy could only get to the Wizard of Oz, she would get back to Kansas. Cinderella's wicked stepmother and stepsisters would be put in their place if she could just become that princess desired by the handsome prince. Lo and behold it was Cinderella's fairy godmother who just happened on the scene with the glass slipper solution. The message was clear: just believe, and it, too, shall come true for you.

I yearned for these miraculous, magical endings for my family. But, just like the books and movies, I needed an outside agent—a wizard, a Mary Poppins, a fairy godmother—someone who had the power, desire, and ability to effect the happy ending.

I was raised in a Christian environment where my mother read Bible stories to us, held family devotions, and took us to Sunday school and church. There I discovered a likely candidate for my fairy godmother—God. I still have a piece of construction paper on which, at the age of seven, I had drawn a big red heart on one side and printed the words, "I love you, Mommy" and a large yellow cross on the other with the words, "Please God, help my Daddy."

Much of childhood is play and fantasy, as it should be, but when children begin to fantasize to escape pain, it becomes a psychological defense that can wreak havoc when carried over into adult relationships. It made it difficult for me to identify truth and reality. When painful events occurred in relationships, I often responded with wishful thinking, belief in some magical cure or change, and inordinate patience in waiting for these hoped-for changes to occur. After all, I had spent a lifetime as a child believing that life in the castle was right around the corner.

Fantasy also affected my view of God. Since God, more than the fairy godmother, has all power to change circumstances, He became my greatest hope to end the embittered conflict at home. When we develop a fairy-godmother type of relationship with God, then it often continues into adult life, preventing us from spiritual intimacy with Him. Also, an inability to separate reality from fantasy makes it especially difficult for us to know God as Father when we confuse His character with that of our earthly fathers or mothers.

Denial of Feelings

Growing up in a dysfunctional home, we do not learn to identify and respond appropriately to the vast array of feelings we experience. An early lesson in our homes is that it is inappropriate to feel anger, shock, shame, disgust, or disappointment at or with our alcoholic or dysfunctional parent. As Heroes, we had to display to the world that all is right with the family. We learned to deny the pain experienced in the family setting, especially to those in our outer worlds of school, friends, and work.

My father was noted for his public displays of outrageous behavior. It made a simple trip to a restaurant a torturous affair. The waitress would turn to him to take his order and he would begin. "I ain't nothing but a south Georgia jackass. I ain't got no couth. So whataya recommend?" I suppose it was meant to be cute, but it was only embarrassing. My mother and brothers and I lowered our eyes to the menus as if that would somehow hide us from the connection with this man. Then when it was our turn to order, we would be especially civil, somber, and polite. Perhaps if we acted exceptionally well-mannered and educated, then no one would suspect there was something wrong with the family. Our roles in the family drama were clear. Project to the outside world that this is an acceptable family. Deny that there is anyone marching out of step. Maybe they'll believe us.

When I was in the eighth grade, I suffered another periodic outbreak of eczema. It was located behind my knees and on the inside of my elbows. The doctor had prescribed some very dark green cortisone cream, which left me looking severely bruised. I escaped attention with long sleeves and long dresses until P.E. class with its shorts and T-shirts. My gym teacher asked me to come by her office after class. In a deeply compassionate tone, she encouraged me to be forthcoming about the obvious child abuse that had occurred. I was horrified. How could she even suspect such a thing? I had to absolve our family. Immediately I began to assure her that this was nothing more than medicine and that I had a very happy home. I prattled on about family outings, birthday parties, vacations, spilling out any happy memory I could summon. Now why did I go overboard? Why not just explain about the green cream and have a good laugh about it? I was terrified she was getting close to our family secret. I had to make certain that she never suspected that our family was anything but a loving, caring, safe place to be.

The same thing had happened several years before. Pete had ventured to share with an especially caring second grade teacher about the verbal abuse he received from our father. That teacher sought me out, since I was the oldest, to validate this information. I assured her everything was fine, that it was just a typical spat, and all was now well. She was convinced, and I had served to reinforce the code of silence for my brother and to give him the message again, "Don't talk about this to anyone!" Of course, we didn't ever talk about it with each other either. Even though Sam and I shared bunk beds and heard the same arguing and yelling in the nights, even though we both heard our mom crying late into the evening, and we went to the motel together at 2:00 in the morning, we never talked to each other about what we heard.

It was easy for us to keep up a public denial of a private pain. My mother was always serving in some capacity or another in civic and school functions—PTA president, Neighborhood Association president, Girl Scout leader. She was admired and appreciated. She had two children who did very well in school. We all attended church together. All of this added weight to our assurances to anyone who would venture to ask if all was okay.

One of the most devastating techniques of denial that we learned was to stuff our feelings. We were terrified of our father's nightly dinnertime tirades, but it was important not to show it. If you did demonstrate weakness, it made you the likely target for that night's barrage. Even though the three of us kids were close in age, we never talked to one another about our family until we were grown. So each night, at the dinner table, we kept our heads low, shoveling food into our mouths to look busy. We stuffed our fear down with every bite. Later I learned to placate my fears, uneasiness, or pain with food. My brothers turned to drugs and alcohol. But we'd each learned to deny our feelings and keep them from surfacing by anesthetizing these powerful monsters.

Denial also occurred verbally. "It doesn't matter; it's okay" was my frequent response to my father's forgetting promises he had made. I got to be very good at this lie.

When I was a junior in college, I was tapped for Mortar Board, an organization recognizing service, leadership, and scholarship in college students. At Agnes Scott College, it was considered a very high honor and the tapping service was quite a production. Weeks in advance the school notified all the parents of the award and told them to keep it a secret from their daughters. That evening, all the juniors gathered at the quadrangle, anxiously wondering who would be tapped. The Mortar Board seniors, in caps and gowns, marched single file, singing the Mortar Board song and holding candles. As they marched around the inner circle of the juniors, one at a time, a senior would tap a junior on the shoulder and that junior would fall in behind them. The parents who had flown in from many parts of the country were hidden away and observing the ceremony from inside a building on the quadrangle. The seniors then led the juniors into this building where there were great exclamations of joy and excitement as parents met their daughters. My father was there and stiffly congratulated me. He then said that he would come to the 10:00 A.M. induction service to be held in the school's auditorium the next day and quickly left. I understood because my father had never been big on touching father-daughter moments.

The next morning I was seated with the other newly tapped juniors on the platform of the auditorium. As I waited for the service to begin, I scanned the auditorium, row by row, searching for my father. He wasn't there. The service began. I could hardly pay attention to the speaker as I searched the auditorium over and over. The speaker was nearly finished. My father was not coming. I felt the sinking loneliness of years of broken promises welling up in this moment. I fought back the tears, trying to enjoy this important moment in my college career. "That's okay," I said to myself. "It doesn't matter. He was here last night."

But it did matter. It mattered deeply and yet I was denying it to myself and later to my father. When we talked later that week, I asked him why he didn't come. He couldn't even remember that he had said he would come. I didn't understand about the alcohol at the time—how it causes people to have short-term memory loss. All I knew was that I was not important enough to my father to have him remember this one event in my college career. All I knew was that I ached—deep, uncontrollable waves of pain seared my heart. But I said to myself, "It's okay. It doesn't matter."

Denial enables us to live with the pain of our families. We learn to rationalize, minimizing the reality of the situation and denying the force of the pain. It provides a measure of sanity in an otherwise crazy situation. Since there is no one outside the home we can talk with to validate what we are feeling, it becomes easier to deny those feelings than to live with these unexplained and intensely powerful emotions.

But denial exacts its price in adulthood. We are unable to interpret situations correctly and to respond to them appropriately. In relationships, we will rationalize the most abusive, inappropriate behaviors of others, rather than confront the reality of their actions.

In our spiritual life, we lose again. Although God cares intimately about us and desires that every care be cast on Him, we minimize the pain, rationalize the hurt, and tell Him, "It's okay. It doesn't matter." In so doing, we cannot develop a deep and intimate personal relationship with God because we are unable to express the truth about our feelings to Him. I also found that I needed to provide God an excuse for seemingly not hearing my plaintive cries for help for my family. Just as it seemed to be my responsibility to make the family look good to the outside world, when I came into a relationship with God, I undertook the responsibility of making Him look good to others. Minimizing my pain and the need for help kept Him from looking bad, just in case He didn't come through.

Super-Responsibility

I was every mother's dream. Other mothers liked me to play with their kids because I was so good. I would help out in their homes like a dutiful daughter. Of course, what they didn't know was that other kids' homes were my refuge. I could go there and feel normal for a while. If I spent the night out, I had an evening's reprieve from the arguing at home. If I helped in the kitchen or learned to sew or bake from another kid's mom, I could live my fantasy family for a moment. My mom was too busy making a living to have time to make cookies. So I learned to be very good, a pleasure to be around, so that my friends and their moms would have me over again.

At home, not only was I the lookout, the one who scouted out, evaluated, and reported daily on my father's moods, but I took it upon myself to come up with some diversions to keep things on a light note. I would even enlist the help of my brothers. Sometimes these schemes were quite elaborate. One night we hung a sheet from a metal jungle gym in the backyard, spread blankets out on the ground, popped popcorn and gathered bubble gum and Coca-Colas®, and retrieved family movies from the neighbors for a night at the drive-in (well, sit-in). Surely he wouldn't get abusive in front of the neighbors. Or I would volunteer to proofread legal documents for him. Keep him busy. Keep him away from Mom. Let her have some peace. It often worked.

It was important to be responsible at school as well. The teachers loved me. Homework was always done on time and completely. Behavior problems? Not from me. I sat erect, spoke when called upon, and never cut up. I became devastated if I made a B because not only was my self-esteem wrapped up in my grades but so was the family's. I was their prize, their trophy, and I needed to shine.

Chores became another area in which I could take charge. By the fourth grade I began helping my Mom with some of the bookkeeping jobs she took on, on the side. I knew her burden was heavy and I wanted to lighten it. We didn't have much disposable income, because my mom was the major breadwinner, so I learned to sew. I didn't want to add to Mom's burden, so I began working at a very early age, trying to provide money for my needs and to take pressure off her.

When I became a Christian in the ninth grade, I found a new arena for performing my duties. Even at that young age, I began regular prayer and fasting for the deliverance of my family. I had much to accomplish. I had to convince God Almighty to deign to care for us. No, even more impossible, it was my responsibility to convince God to change my father. Then all would be okay. Prayer was not dialogue with a loving, effectual God; it was just another tool of this super-responsible child.

Super-responsibility is a survival technique that evokes much societal approval both in childhood and later years. Therefore we don't even recognize these patterns as self-destructive. In fact, in the workplace and career, our unresolved compulsion to correct the family's ills often translates into compulsive overwork, which brings us great rewards—praise, money, and status. However, as we will see in the next chapter, achievements secured out of these deep internal needs do not satisfy for long since they did not accomplish the motivating goal underlying each achievement—to change our families. We will consider the last three survival techniques there.

Chapter 4

More Weapons from the Arsenal

I saw that I was just another Robinson Crusoe cast away on an uninhabited island, with no society but some more or less tame animals, and if I wanted to make life bearable, I must do as he did—invent, contrive, create, reorganize things; set brain and hand to work, and keep them busy.[1]

> Mark Twain
> *A Connecticut Yankee in King Arthur's Court*

The Hero, burdened by his sense of super-responsibility—that the stability of the family is dependent on his being good—finds the many and varied opportunities that school presents a perfect platform for performance. As a result, overachievement is a parallel survival technique often developed by Heroes to cope with the family system.

Overachievement

Academic and athletic opportunities for achievement abound in the school setting. Doing well in school feeds a deep hunger in the Hero. He begins with such a profound deficit of security and love, however, that achievement often spawns overachievement. It takes more and more success to feel okay, because no matter how well one does, it does not bring about the desired change: a healthy family.

I was good at achievement but I was excellent at over-achievement. Take the sale of Girl Scout cookies, for example. I couldn't just sell the most boxes in my troop or in my school. No, I had to sell the most boxes in the entire city of Atlanta. Girl Scout badges received the same earnest effort. The small embroidered circles swooped down one side of my sash and up the other until there was no more room. Then there was the public library's summer reading program for elementary school students. If you read ten books, you got a certificate. I read over a hundred. At church, we earned a gold star for every hymn we memorized. Once we had accumulated enough gold stars, we got a plastic figurine of a composer. Dozens of those little plastic heads marched in a row on top of our piano.

One day, the principal came into my third grade class and called the names of several students and told us to clean out our desks. I was terrified. What had we done wrong? They ushered us into a combination third/fourth grade class. The idea was to combine the top third grade students with the bottom third of the fourth grade students to enhance the learning of both groups. Suddenly I was being asked to do math problems one year ahead of where I was. Each math paper came back with an F on it. My hands would shake as I took the paper from my teacher. I felt my chest heave as I began to panic and swallowed air in gulps. How could I take this paper home?

I begged the smartest student in our class to let me come over every afternoon and learn how to do long division. I told my parents I was going over to Diane's to play. I drilled myself over and over again until I had conquered this. My parents never had to know how hard I worked. I had to make it look effortless. I didn't want them worrying about me. Perhaps if I just regrouped, redoubled my efforts, and applied myself, I could make that A in math. That philosophy, learned at the age of eight, began to color everything I did, and I made it through high school sporting a 4.0 average with valedictorian and National Merit Scholar honors.

It was a funny thing about making all A's in high school. As each succeeding A piled up on the other, the pressure to achieve increased. It was no longer enough that I was good, or even very good; I now needed to be excellent, perfect, superlative. If anything is worth doing, it's worth doing well. Isn't that what we are told? But for the Hero, the desire to achieve is founded on the need to assure yourself that you matter, that you and your family have worth.

In the turbulent sixties, there were causes to be championed, and who better to lead the fight for justice and reform than our Hero. My high school was often singled out for special media attention since Dr. Martin Luther King's children attended there and it had been the first high school in Atlanta to be integrated. The media seemed to assume that if there was to be any racial violence, it would happen at Grady High School.

Interestingly enough, because Grady High was the first school to be integrated six years before, there was relatively little disharmony between blacks and whites. In fact, there were many solid, warm friendships between blacks and whites. But as a downtown high school, Grady had been singled out as a potential trouble spot because of its high ratio of blacks to whites. It was a time of court-ordered desegregation and mandatory teacher transfers to bring school black/white ratios to the 70/30 percent split reflecting the Atlanta population. There were evening curfews on high school students in the city of Atlanta as anger and violence flared up. Mike Flores, a Hispanic transfer high school student, began writing about racism at Grady High and encouraging a sit-in in *The Great Speckled Bird*, the Atlanta underground newspaper.

One day in my senior year, when I arrived at school, police cars were stationed around the building. Policemen stood armed with tear-gas guns. Many of the students just stood around outside and watched. As I got nearer the building I heard the shouts, "Hell no, we won't go." "Black and white we must unite—Same enemy, same fight." Inside the building were students sitting down with their backs against both walls. They pounded their knees and then the floor in time with their chants. The noise was deafening.

I got word the principal wanted to see me. As co-president of the student body, I was to try to quell this uproar by offering a compromise to Mike Flores. Move the entire sit-in to the cafeteria where they could "discuss" the issues. As a sweetener the principal had agreed to permit the media to be there. I walked down the hall, picking my way through the bodies on the floor, and approached Mike. As he saw me coming, he stood up, and swung his arm around and around to orchestrate the volume of the chanters even louder. He had a determined look in his eye.

I tried to speak to him over the roar of the students. I told him there would be television cameras in the cafeteria, and he could have full opportunity to say whatever he wanted there, not only to the students but to the entire city of Atlanta via the media. Screaming louder and louder, "Black, white, we want a fight," Mike pulled his arm back quickly and released it, socking me in the jaw. I took that as a no.

Later that day, the Atlanta superintendent of schools proposed a televised debate that he would moderate between Mike Flores and me. A major Atlanta television station had volunteered to sponsor the debate on racial desegregation. Now this was really exciting. Here was a wider arena in which to shine. The whole city would know that Nancy Oliver was okay and that her family must be so too. As student body president, I had initiated an interschool council, composed of the student body presidents of the twenty-six Atlanta public high schools to act as a liaison between the students and the Atlanta School Board, which had to implement the court-ordered desegregation. I had given much thought to ways that this could occur peacefully in our city.

The half-hour debate pitted Mike Flores, a sixteen-year-old self-avowed Communist, against a seventeen-year-old conservative student leader. The issues of race relations in the schools and how to best implement federal policy were discussed. Without a crowd to generate shouting support, Mike disintegrated as I peppered him with fact after fact and he responded with loud, polemic slogans.

My parents were in a sound booth, watching. I knew I had done it now. Surely, this would touch a chord in my lawyer father. Now he wouldn't need to drink and get crazy. But life doesn't work like that—relief is only temporary. The irony, however, is that each time the Hero discovers that stellar performances do not achieve the desired goal, he just redoubles his efforts, thinking maybe the next achievement will be the one that tips the scales.

The Student Council advisor, writing to my parents to let them know I was to receive the *Atlanta Journal* Cup for Best All-Around Senior stated, "Nancy is one of the finest and most pleasant young ladies that I have ever had the pleasure of knowing. You did an excellent job of rearing Nancy, and I know that you are extremely proud of her. You showed her the right way, and she will always bring much pleasure to you." I had done it. I was so very good, so accomplished that my parents had gotten the credit. So we were okay after all.

But overachievement, for all the societal good it may produce, can develop into a self-destructive pattern when our Hero grows up. Most often it is in the arena of the workplace where these destructive tendencies are displayed. The workplace rewards Heroes. Heroes make excellent employees in many respects. They are very responsible, hard-working, successful employees. But the goal for each of us is to thrive as God's special creation, unique in motivations and talents to be energized and channeled in an outward expression. When our desire to succeed and achieve is driven by an internal need to feel and be okay, then we are only realizing a portion of the joy God intended when He made us creative, inventive individuals. We become needs-driven. That is why many Heroes suffer periodic burnouts at work. Each new mountain climbed reveals yet another on the horizon to be conquered. And as long as there are mountains, our Hero is driven to conquer them.

Something internally compels the Hero forward to continue to prove to the world that he is okay long after he has left his family. Success is not sweet; it is fleeting. Drinking deep satisfaction from his work and achievements is difficult because he is never good enough. Why? Because no matter how much he tries, no matter how hard he works, his family never changes.

Flight

Behaviorally, it has long been recognized that individuals under stress exhibit either aggressive or withdrawal behavior, the "fight or flight" phenomenon. The child in a dysfunctional home perceives the danger and has a choice of escaping from that danger or facing it. Because of children's perceived and realistic assessment of their inferior status for fighting, and because of the family system's code against confrontation of the real issues, flight is most often the chosen response to stress.

As we have already seen, flight can occur through a mental escape. Paul Tournier, in *The Healing of Persons*, notes that flight can occur through escaping into the past or the future. Escaping into the future by constantly making plans, according to Tournier, is a way of escaping from the imperfections of the present.[2] Tournier also speaks of "noble flights," which enable us to escape through work and noble achievements. In each instance, flight provides the psychological escape from pain.

Once school began to offer extracurricular activities, I had acceptable ways to escape family pain. I could spend long hours either in the activity or preparing for the activity. After all, Girl Scouts was only two hours a week, but I needed hour upon hour to complete the requirements for each badge. I could escape to my room or a friend's house to "work" on these projects. I could escape with books, spending long hours sitting outside in the grass reading. No one minded. These were all good things to be involved in, but the impetus for my involvement was to clear out of a lonely, fearful, angry house.

When I turned sixteen I bought my first car, a 1961 VW bug, for $150. My car became my "grown-up" closet. When the yelling got too unbearable, I would grab my keys and go driving. It didn't matter where or how far. A full tank of gas cost $3 in those days, and I could spend hours upon hours driving around. I can remember the exhilarating feeling I got as I escaped out of that house. I turned the key, engaged the clutch, and bolted. I had done this when I was younger with my bike. But I could only get five to ten miles away on my bike. Now with all this horsepower, I could cover a lot of territory. The further away I got from my house, the better I felt. The cold air on my face as I drove would soothe my terror, and I could begin to breathe normally again. Sometimes I would pray out loud, begging God to change my family, and try to make sense out of what was happening.

Learning to flee potentially harmful, even dangerous, conflict is a wise and important survival skill. When a child from a dysfunctional home consistently responds to this type of conflict with physical flight from the ongoing battle, he conditions himself to respond to conflict later in life in the same way. Heroes do this easily, and it is often the workplace that becomes that "closet," that place of safety

and security, in which they can close the door on the conflict and tension and immerse themselves in work.

Heroes can do this in relationships as well. Conflict is
not an invitation to deeper communication and growth. It
strikes terror in our hearts and evokes years of flight response mechanisms. Often when I was in a relationship
and a fight or disagreement arose between us, an inexplicable uneasiness fell over me and a sense of foreboding
deepened. Something more than a conflict was brewing.
All my conditioned flight instincts were awakened. Whereas
he wanted to talk out the issues, I had uncontrollable urges
to jump in the car. I just needed time to think, time to cool
off, I'd assure him, but what I wanted to do was escape the
pain of the conflict.

I want to be careful here, but I feel it is important to
mention another area into which we can flee from our deep
emotional pain—Christianity. My own personal commitment to turn my life over to the Lord came in the ninth
grade at the age of fourteen. However, I had "walked the
aisle" some six or seven times before. I just never felt like it
took. But what I later realized was that I saw turning my life
over to Jesus as a magic-potion type of solution. When
nothing changed in my family, I walked the aisle again,
committing myself again, this time more fervently, more
intently repentant, and more enthusiastically determined.
Each such effort was a reaffirmation of my inability to accept the assurance of eternal salvation and that nothing,
yes, nothing would now come between me and my Lord
(Rom. 8:35–39).

I was so entrenched in trying to earn the healing of my
family through being good and trying to please them. Now
I was in a whole new family—God is the father and all
these church people are my brothers and sisters. Now I
needed to please God. This created a fearful and fruitless
relationship as I tried to please a perfect God with my imperfect offerings of time, talent, prayers, and obedience.

God wanted me to know him as Father, as the unconditional lover of my soul. I was much, much too busy trying to win Him over and get Him to try to save my family to really get to know Him.

I am not trying to say that anyone from a dysfunctional home who becomes a Christian is not really a Christian. However, I would venture to guess that most Christians from dysfunctional homes have a deep need to know God cares— really cares—about their personal circumstances. There is likely a lack of intimacy, perhaps even a fear, as this Christian relates to God. If we flee into religion, into church service, or even into obedience with the objective of winning over this apparently capricious, uncaring God, then it becomes a self-destructive pattern that needs reformation.

Unless we resolve these conditioned flight mechanisms— whether mental or into various social, religious, or career activities—we will remain captive to conflict, rationalizing our escape behaviors with our need to finish a project at work, do good at church, or just cool off for a while.

Burden-Bearing

The eldest have always been thought to take responsibility for the younger children and assist in their parenting. In a dysfunctional home, however, the Hero often must include his parents in his duties. He sometimes takes care of the alcoholic parent physically. Or he may strive to meet the needs of the dysfunctional parent by working very hard to please them in tangible ways. He often counsels the enabling parent directly and at least indirectly assists him in his enabling. The Hero, through his accomplishments and heightened sense of responsibility, becomes both parents' source of strength. He becomes a little adult very early and undertakes the tremendous burden of making everything right.

My father threatened suicide on a weekly basis. One

might say he was all talk and no action. But a nine-year-old child did not understand his threat as a manipulative tool. She responded by doing all she could to get Daddy to want to live.

After dinner, my father usually retired to a basement office where he would sit in a Lazy Boy® recliner, watch television, and drink. That gave us all some release from the tension until late in the evening. He would typically emerge from the basement after the 11:00 news, ready to engage an adversary. His facility with the English language and his pugnacious nature may have given him an edge as a lawyer, but it created a very adept verbal abuser when coupled with alcohol and prescription drugs. He would go on a search-and-destroy mission. Fortunately for us kids, we were already in bed. Unfortunately for our mom, even if she was in bed, she shared his bed. He would crawl into bed beside her and begin to tell her how worthless she was and reiterate every conceivable mistake she had or could ever make. Since my mother was a lawyer too, trained to respond to arguments with logic and reasoning, it must have been difficult for her to just lie there and "take it."

Since our house was small, I could hear him drone on way into the early hours of the morning. My mind was always racing, playing out scenarios: What if he were to hit her, what should I do? What if he comes into my room? Should I pretend to be asleep? If only I had kept my cool at dinner and not let him get so agitated, maybe he wouldn't be yelling at Mom now.

One evening I heard him announce his imminent suicide once again. But this time he did so waving a gun in the air. He went down to his office in the basement and closed the door. I waited and held my breath. Silence. I crept down to the basement in my pajamas and listened at the door. Silence. I tried the doorknob and it wouldn't turn. He had locked the door. "Daddy, Daddy, I love you. Please don't hurt yourself." I cried through the door. Silence. I was terrified. What was he doing in there? Why wouldn't he answer me? "I'll be good. I promise. I won't let you down." I entreated. Silence.

I panicked. What if he had shot himself and I just hadn't heard it? What if he needed me? I had to find out. The basement window! I raced upstairs and out the front door. I tore across the front lawn and down our neighbor's driveway to the side of our house. A small 3-foot-by-1½ foot window looked down into that basement office. I pressed my face against the window. He was still alive. He was sitting in the Lazy Boy® recliner with the gun on his lap, smoking his pipe. I lay on the ground all night keeping watch. I thought for some reason that as long as I was there as a vigilant observer he wouldn't kill himself. When the morning arrived and he was still alive, it validated my interpretation and gave me an inordinate sense of power and control. Unfortunately, that only added another burden; now I was responsible for my parents' very lives as well as their happiness.

I felt a great sense of responsibility for my mother as well. I knew she was deeply troubled by her marriage. I knew this because we would take walks in the early evening and she would inquire, "Nancy, should I divorce your father? I'm considering it." What ten- or eleven-year-old child is going to have enough wisdom, objectivity, and compassion to answer that question? The last thing I wanted was a divorce. To split up the family would be the ultimate verification that I had failed in my responsibility to save the family.

One morning I heard my mom shout out, "Nancy, Nancy, come quick. Help me! Help me!" My father was standing over her in the kitchen with a raised hammer in his hand. I rushed up to him, grabbed the hammer out of his hand, and hurled it out an open window onto the neighbor's driveway. I then proceeded to give him a lecture.

This inversion of parental roles is extremely dangerous for the adult child from a dysfunctional home. Children need boundaries. They need to know where they end and their parents begin. For example, when a child comes from a home in which the parent places an inordinate amount of pressure on the child to perform in ways that please them and looks to the child to meet deep unmet needs in themselves, then the child's identity becomes submerged in the parent's. He knows he is their reason for being and feels enormous pressure to live up to their expectations of him. He may try to be that parent's confidante, best friend, closest advisor. He must rise to the level of that parent and put away childish responses, even though he is yet a child.

When children come from homes in which the parent is incapable of functioning, as in the alcoholic home, they actually pick up physical tasks that are ordinarily the responsibility of parents. He may have to undress the alcoholic parent and put Mom or Dad to bed after he or she has passed out on the floor. He may take care of siblings. He may take charge of the household, setting everything in its proper order and schedule.

Whether the child parents the dysfunctional parent by caring for him and the household, or parents the codependent parent by providing counsel, advice, and peer friendship, there is a truncating of the child's psychological development. Dr. Annie Herman, early childhood expert, noted that

> The child *needs* to be dependent on the adult, has a right to this feeling. If the adult is just like the child after all, then the child can't really depend on him. And yet that stage of childhood when children believe in parental omnipotence helps develop a basic, life-giving trust, a trust that carries with it half of life's enjoyment long after childhood has ended.[3]

Dr. David Elkind, author of *The Hurried Child,* noted that

hurried children are stressed children. Children who are hurried into mature decision making and responsibility may end up with a distorted sense of their power and capacities and may appear to be more mature and secure than they really are.[4] Elkind explains that sometimes children are hurried into mature interpersonal relations because the parent is under stress and needs a confidante. That relationship of confidante, however, is distorted, since at the age of eight or ten years, no child has the experience and intellectual and emotional security to truly advise the parent.[5] These requirements placed on children by parents leave them in a chronic stress situation.

In recent years there has been increasing interest in children who appear to respond positively to sustained stress situations. Researchers have found five qualities in individuals who seem to survive stressful home situations. First they have *social competence*. They seem at ease with peers and adults and are able to make others at ease with them. They also have *impression management*, where they are able to present themselves as appealing individuals. They often appear eager to learn and win adults over to them easily as mentors. They have *self-confidence*, primarily in their ability to master stress situations. They are independent and think for themselves. They often find a place for themselves in which they can create an environment where they can exercise this *independence*. Finally, they are *achievement-oriented*. They are often exceptionally original and creative. Elkind suggests that, born to a different family, they might even have been prodigies.[6] Born to a stressful home, however, they utilize these achievement orientations to survive.

Much of this research was done prior to the examination of what happens to children who grow up in alcoholic or otherwise dysfunctional homes. Yet these five characteristics are an apt description of our Hero. Our Hero has so learned to manage his environment that he appears to exude social competence and self-confidence. Others looking at him without knowledge of his family background would likely extol the fine stock from which he must come. One wonders what the Hero could have accomplished if his abilities had been supported and nurtured for the expression of these gifts, rather than his having to call upon these gifts to survive the sustained stress situation.

Each of these survival techniques—fantasy, denial of feelings, super-responsibility, overachievement, flight, and burden-bearing—provides the Hero what he needs to cope with his family of origin. These survival techniques work both to protect the integrity of the Hero as an individual and to preserve the Hero's role within the family system. These techniques also become the first line of defense when painful events occur.

Because they are so deeply ingrained, these survival techniques are easily called into action when the Hero has to respond to a painful or stressful event. Rather than evoke a desire to examine one's life and foster change, the painful event typically propels the Hero into action. The Hero, conditioned to turn to these survival techniques, and so often resilient no matter how desperate the circumstances, simply takes a deep breath, faces the situation, and does what must be done. After all, he is the Hero, the one equipped with these special survival skills to rescue others.

Chapter 5

Retrenchment

It was death—Davy's death—that was the severe mercy....
That death, so full of suffering for us both, suffering that
still overwhelmed my life, was yet a severe mercy. A mercy as
severe as death, a severity as merciful as love.[1]

Sheldon Vanauken
A Severe Mercy

A warm gentle breeze was blowing in the spring of my
freshman year on the evening of March 13, 1972. I pulled
into the driveway behind my mother's car. My friend,
Karen, and I were stopping off here to tell my parents
good-bye before we drove down to Florida for spring break.
I took the stairs two at a time, excited about our adventure.
As we entered the living room, I saw my father and my two
brothers in a state of panic. "We can't find your mother
anywhere," my father explained. He was standing in the
middle of the room, immobile, and ashen-faced. Sam was
busy dialing one number after another, calling her friends.
Pete sat distraught on the sofa with tears streaming down
his face. "She wasn't here when I got home from school
and that was five hours ago!" he cried. My mother's pocketbook and car keys were on the dining room table, but she
was nowhere to be found.

I quickly stepped in and took charge. "Have you called the hospitals? Have you notified the police? What about Carroll? Have you called her? Could she be visiting a neighbor? Maybe she's just on a walk. It's a beautiful evening. Okay. I'll run Karen back to school and be right back. Call the police in the meantime. And don't panic. I'm sure she just lost track of time." I got Karen back to Agnes Scott in record time and turned the car around for home. I prayed aloud, "Dear God, help Mama. Please protect her wherever she is." Thoughts of kidnapping or rape entered my mind. "Lord, if she is in any danger, surround her with your love. Don't let her die, Lord. Oh God, please don't let her die."

I admired my mother. Like myself, she had been student body president of her high school. She then went on to Agnes Scott College where she served as president of her freshman class, majored in political science, became president of student government, and then went on to be the only woman in her law school class at Emory University. I had decided to attend Agnes Scott College with my sights on a legal career. I rationalized my choice to turn down Duke and Vanderbilt, since Scott provided the most financial aid. Behind that decision, however, were two thoughts. First, I couldn't go away very far from home; they needed me. Agnes Scott was twelve miles from my home. Second, I couldn't ask my mother to pay more money at another school. So in September 1971, I launched my college career, picking up the freshman class presidency, deciding on a political science major, and planning for a legal career. I wanted to be just like my mother.

At about the same time I was calling out to God, my mother, lying in a pool of blood next to the washer and dryer in the basement utility room, realized she wasn't going to die. "You're not going to let me die, are you, God?" she asked. "Okay, then I want to live." She could hear activity upstairs in the house and knew that if she could call for help, someone might hear her. Pete had searched the basement, Dad's office, and the family rec room, but had not thought to look in the small utility room at the back of the basement. She tried to reach for the handle to the door of the utility room. Her hand fell limp at her side. She had cut her arms so deeply that she had severed tendons and her useless arms would not respond to her desire to live. She knew she had lost a lot of blood. Now her will to live was flowing back into her in deeper measure. "They're not going to find me," she thought. "I've got to let them know I am here." She dragged herself by her elbows to the door and tried to push it open with her body weight. Fatigued she fell against the door, but the latch held firm. "God, I do want to live, help me," she whispered. Suddenly, inexplicably, the latched door opened and she slumped unconscious to the ground outside the utility room.

"What was that?" Pete exclaimed. "I heard a noise downstairs." He raced down the steps and saw our mother bleeding profusely with an eight-inch carving knife by her side. When I returned to my house, there was a note on the door. "Pete and Sam with the Jordans. Your mother tried to kill herself. At Grady hospital.—Pop."

The surgeons worked on her for hours, attempting to repair nerves, tendons, and ligaments badly severed. She had zero blood pressure when the ambulance arrived at the emergency entrance. The doctors told my father it was doubtful she was going to make it. She had lost too much blood. My father waited, and I prayed. "God, you've got to let her live. We can't make it without her. We need her, Lord, please don't let her die. Please God. Oh, please God, don't let her die." Miraculously, she survived.

The next day, I slipped quietly into her darkened hospital room. Her eyes were closed and her arms were so bandaged that she looked like she had on elbow-length boxing gloves. I leaned over her and brushed her wavy brown hair back off her forehead, over and over in the same way she used to brush my hair back off my face after I had passed out at the dinner table. She opened her eyes and lowered them quickly in shame. "It's okay, Mama. I love you. It's going to be okay," I assured her.

With a passion I had never seen in her before, she entreated, "Nancy, don't ever lose your faith in God. Satan can make you do things you never thought you were capable of doing." Then she lapsed back into a drugged sleep. I stood, staring, trying to comprehend what she had just told me. We were the only two in the family who shared a faith in God, but frankly, this talk about Satan was a bit weird. We had gone to the Methodist church where one heard as much about John and Charles Wesley as about Jesus. Satan was rarely mentioned. What did she mean?

For the next two months she was hospitalized at a psychiatric hospital, spending time in individual and group therapy and undergoing many hours of physical therapy to try to regain the use of at least one of her arms. I juggled my final weeks of school, caring for the family, and visiting my mother at the hospital on a daily basis. I changed my plans for summer work, deciding to spend the summer at home taking care of the house and shuttling my mother back and forth to doctors' appointments.

Six weeks after Mom entered the psychiatric hospital, I received an urgent message in biology lab. I was to come to the dean's office immediately. Dean Gary explained that my brother, Pete, had had an accident. He was in his eighth grade woodshop class when he caught his hand in a band saw, severing his finger. He had been taken to Grady hospital. Once again I jumped into my car and raced to the hospital. Dr. Klinkscales, a well-known Atlanta plastic surgeon, was working to repair the damage to Pete's finger. When I visited Pete later in the recovery room, I was struck by the irony. There he was in the same hospital, with the same surgeon, with the same elbow-length boxing glove bandages as my mother. Was he trying to duplicate her experience, accidentally, of course?

My summer was a whirlwind of activity. Since my mother had limited use of her arms, I helped dress her and take care of her basic needs. I shuttled her to and from physical therapy appointments, treasuring these moments alone to talk. And we still continued our walks around the block after dinner. We spoke of life...and death.

I remember one unusual lunch toward the end of the summer. We split a roast beef sandwich, which I cut up for her. By this point, there had been some healing in the nerves of her right arm to enable her limited use. I was encouraged. I just knew she would recover fully. After all, I was praying so diligently for her every day, fasting once a week, and certain that the God who heard my prayer last March would answer all these other prayers too.

"Nancy, I want to tell you some very important things. I want you to listen carefully. You'll need to know these things should I ever die."

"Mama, that's ridiculous. I won't need to know that kind of information for years now," I replied sharply.

"Think about March. What if I had died? Remember, my father died while I was in college and I realize you don't know anything about where important papers are. I'm depending on you, Nancy. You're the oldest. There is important information you'll need to know to take care of the boys." She then proceeded to explain about bank safety-deposit boxes, wills, insurance policies.

I blocked it all out. *I don't want to be responsible*, I screamed inside my head. You cannot die. Not now. Not ever. I need you Mama, don't you understand that? But I just nodded my head when she asked, "Now can you remember all that?"

My father's tirades that summer were thematic. With hospital and doctors' bills skyrocketing for both Pete and my mother, he had plenty to gripe about. When drunk, his tirades were merciless. "Why didn't you just finish the job?" he screamed at my mother. "It would have been cheaper to bury you than to fix you up."

I decided to stay out of school that fall, but my mother insisted that I go back to Agnes Scott. She wanted to know that I was okay, she said, and the only way she could be sure that her attempted suicide did not ruin my life was for me to go back to school. More out of a desire to assure her everything was okay, I returned to Scott in mid-September for my sophomore year.

On Saturday morning, September 29, 1972, I awoke to our first really crisp cold fall day. I love Atlanta falls. They last forever and the trees luxuriously rotate their colors so slowly that you can enjoy the subtle color changes for weeks. I threw open my dorm window and drank in the cool air. I let the wind that rustled the golden leaves rush over my face. It was a glorious day.

I was going to a Georgia Tech football game that afternoon, but the weather had turned so cold that I had no jacket to wear unless I went home. I hopped into my VW bug and made the quick twenty-minute trip home. I sat at the breakfast table with my mother and shared a cup of coffee. We laughed about the antics of the juniors who had set up the entire dining hall out on the quad during the wee hours of the morning. Then I grabbed my jacket, kissed her good-bye, and told her I loved her. She stood at the front door waving as I pulled out of the driveway to go back to school. By the time I arrived at my dorm room, she was dead.

My roommate told me to call home. My father said, "Nancy, she's done it again." I knew she needed me. After all, I was the only person she spoke to for weeks after her first suicide attempt. So I jumped back into my car and raced for home. When I arrived, I saw a police car in the driveway. I bounded the steps two at a time. The policeman was standing in the living room with my father. "Where is she?" I demanded.

My father said, "Back in our room. But, honey, you don't want to go back there."

I spun around and retorted, "I have to go. She needs me." I had no idea she wasn't alive, and my father didn't stop me.

I saw my mother, lying on the floor. She had shot herself in the mouth with a small pistol. Undaunted, I knelt beside her and prayed aloud, "God, You can do something. You could raise this woman from the dead if You wanted." I held her close, her body still warm, and sobbed, realizing this was one prayer that would go unanswered.

When I walked back into the living room, the coroner had arrived, and there was much to be done. I had to call the funeral home, the minister, relatives, friends. I churned into action, emotionless.

The next several days were spent caring for everyone. As we stood in a parlor in the funeral home, receiving mourners paying their respects, I found myself in the position of comforting them, making it easier for them to say kind things. After all, it was awkward. A suicide. I spent most of my conversation assuring them that everything was okay.

On the day of the funeral, I stood in front of my closet for a long time. I didn't own anything black. My high school science teacher had said that black is the absence of color. Think of that: when all of color is no longer, that is black.

We drove to the funeral home. When we arrived, no one else was there. I knew that soon there would be people coming to pay their last respects to my mother. I walked into the funeral parlor. There at one end of the room was a walnut casket, polished and gleaming from a few rays of early morning light filtering in through the lace curtains. The room itself was dark. I didn't understand that. It was a brilliant fall day. Why draw the curtains, closing out the day and closing in the darkness? I walked over to the windows and shoved the curtains aside.

I walked over to the casket and stared a long time at the body of my mother. The billowy satin cushions around her seemed incongruous with the life of violence she had known. I smiled at the glowing rouge on her waxy cheeks and the creamy red lips. Mom had never worn makeup. And now in her death, they made her up to look alive. The absence of color, however, that was reality.

The minister said something about God's permissive will being done. I remembered very little. The family was seated in a small alcove off to the side. I sat next to my father on one side and my brothers on the other. When the funeral was over, we were left with each other. What would we do now? How would the three children, terrified of their father, deal with the loss of the one who had sacrificed her own life for all those years to act as a buffer between him and us?

We had a number of relatives in Atlanta on my mother's side, but once she died, we never heard from them again. They were glad to be rid of their connection to Carl Oliver, but it left us children feeling even more abandoned. My father had one brother, and he and his wife volunteered to take Pete in for a while. A child psychologist had explained to them that Pete had a symbiotic relationship with our mother and was so close to her that he had even tried to duplicate her experience a few months back with the saw accident. Left to live in that house with my father, the psychologist explained, Pete would likely have another "accident," which could kill him. Sam, sixteen years old, was very bright. At that point it was in vogue to skip your senior year in high school and attend college a year early. Although much of his identity was tied up in being editor of the high school newspaper, which had won Southeastern regional first-place awards under his direction, he left Atlanta and went to Athens, Georgia, to attend the University of Georgia. There his drug use from high school was exacerbated into full-blown addiction.

I returned to school. I worked double shifts to make enough money to stay in school and dropped out of all activities, except church. I wasn't going to be like my mother. I would change my destiny. No more political offices, no more sights set on student government or law school. I would be different. It was then I began to plan for a career in teaching.

My father sat in an empty house and drank.

Throughout my college years, I maintained one hope: that one day I would marry and my family would not be at all like this. Over and over I had prayed as a young girl, "Dear God, please don't let me have a marriage like my parents'." That earnest prayer continued. I just knew God could bring me a good man, a man exactly opposite my father, who would love me.

But that was just the problem. The more my family fell apart and my efforts to restore them either through prayer or my rescuing attempts failed, the more important became my little girl fantasy family. That fantasy family loomed larger as I cloaked its future reality with a supernatural power to make up for my past.

A real comfort to me during those college years was the works of Catherine Marshall. Through her writings, I learned much about prayer, waiting on the Lord in seemingly impossible circumstances, and the Holy Spirit. How thrilled I was to be her weekend companion the October of my senior year in 1974. She was coming to Agnes Scott College for a Board of Trustees meeting and to sign copies of her latest book, *Something More*. As president of the Christian organization on campus, I was the obvious choice of the Agnes Scott College president, Dr. Perry, to escort her to meals and accompany her on campus.

Toward the end of our time together that weekend, we walked down the brick path toward the president's home where she was to join the other trustees for tea. It was a gorgeous fall afternoon. The sun glinted off the windows of

Winship Hall as we stopped to admire the dell. We drank in the crisp air and exclaimed over the brilliant reds of the maples and golden leaves of the ash trees, which framed the dorm. As she stood admiring the trees, I stood admiring her. She had been more than cordial to me that weekend; she had been warm and engaging. We had talked of life, of faith, of the students at Agnes Scott and what they thought about Christianity. She had listened intently to my answers as she questioned me about my plans after graduation.

Catherine Marshall was somewhat of a celebrity figure at my college. After all, she met Peter Marshall while she attended Agnes Scott College in the 1930s, and the filming of her blockbuster book, *A Man Called Peter,* had taken place on our campus. Her book *Adventures in Prayer* had chronicled her lesson in faith as God made it possible for a young minister's daughter from Keyser, West Virginia, to pursue her dream of higher education. Her intensity of faith in a caring God was evident not only in her writings but now in her sharing with me.

As the time neared for her to be at the president's home and for us to say good-bye for that weekend, I began to get very nervous. I desperately wanted to ask her about my most secret fear and deepest longing. She had known my mother during their tenure on the Agnes Scott College Board of Trustees together. She was aware of the nature of my mother's death and something of my father's reputation. The minutes were slipping away. If I was to ask her about this, I had to do it now.

"Mrs. Marshall, given my family background," I asked, "would a strong Christian family be willing to accept me into their family as their daughter-in-law?"

She looked evenly at me and then glanced away, thinking for several moments. She started to answer, then paused again. Finally, she turned and said, "Nancy, it would be very hard. A family would be right to be concerned about the extensive amount of mental illness in your family lines." She continued to explain but I heard nothing more that she said. I was devastated to hear this pronouncement that my deep desire for a normal family was unlikely to be fulfilled. My heart sank and I lowered my eyes. I didn't deserve such a family. My generational patterns and lines declared otherwise.

This was my first glimpse of the painful path ahead. These foundational years from childhood through college had underscored the sensibility of relying on these survival techniques to cope with the pain and chaos of my family. What made sense in childhood, however, would bring disaster in adulthood as I attempted to operate in the major spheres of life—family, work, and romantic relationships—in a healthy manner. Part Two describes the negative results in a Hero's life of continuing to operate out of childhood survival skills.

The Battle Scars: Wounded Warriors

Chapter 6

Home Is Where the Heart Is

This is the evil in the serpent's promise to Eve, "You will be like gods." God made human beings as creatures, not as creators. If you believe you are a god, you ignore your limitations, creatureliness and mortality. Human beings do not have the power, wisdom, or goodness, the independence or permanence of God, no matter how frantically they try. Such confusion of self with God ends in destruction.[1]

Karl A. Olsson
Meet Me on the Patio

Mom had been the glue that held the family together. It was she who made the holiday and birthday efforts. With Mom gone, the logical person to step into her role, or so I thought, was me. I made massive preparations for this Christmas, only three months after Mom's death. Yet, in the midst of overdoing, I was in incredible denial. We had all just lost a very important, very central person to our existence. We should feel lousy this Christmas. But I was going to make sure we were one happy family.

I was also determined to help my father. I knew he was grieving the loss of his wife. Even though she was the butt of much of his abuse, I knew that her death had created a void in his life. They had been married for twenty-four years. I appointed myself my father's guardian—his little angel to bring him the help and salvation he needed. I thought that perhaps now, with Mom gone, he would be open to letting God in his life. Maybe now, he would be asking questions that might lead him to God and health and wholeness, and of course to his proper place in my made-for-television Christmas.

Four days before Christmas, I drove to Conyers, Georgia, with my best friend, Leigh, to a Trappist monastery, an ideal place for me to go when I wanted to escape. There, under a particularly favorite oak tree, I could write in my journal, pray, and daydream. I wondered why we decided to come to the monastery on this particularly abysmal day. It was pouring torrential rain as my little VW bug sputtered its way up the long drive.

When we went to the bookstore, I knew God had wanted me to come. There was a little book on grief. On impulse I bought it. On the way back to Atlanta, Leigh read it out loud to me. It was perfect for Dad. It discussed the stages of grief, how to deal with them, and how to keep grief from deteriorating into a depression. Curiously, I did not give the book to my father directly. I left it on the breakfast table where he might just pick it up. And, of course, I prayed. It was like leaving a letter for Santa Claus. I was hopeful that my indirect attempts would pay off. My fairy-tale Christmas might just come true.

On Christmas Eve we put up the Christmas tree. Dad helped string the lights. We popped popcorn and began stringing our traditional popcorn and cranberry garlands. We wrapped presents and made Christmas cookies. We even sang carols. The highlight, however, was when my father called me into his bedroom and said he wanted to show me something that had really helped him. He held out the grief book. I recorded my ecstasy in my journal:

"Thank you, God, for letting me be your little angel for the day!" I just knew that God and I could pull this family together.

Then came Christmas morn. Dad called a family meeting to discuss the financial condition of the family. He brought up his journal sheets to show us what we were costing him. He then began his tirade about money. He especially turned toward Pete and the costs of the operation on his hand. I whisked Pete out of the house, ostensibly to deliver a Christmas present. We had a few hours reprieve before we had to be over at our grandmother's house for Christmas dinner. Did we talk about what had happened? No. We just went to a movie.

That night at Christmas dinner, Dad began again. His tirades were directed at everyone, even his own mother. No one could quiet him down. He got louder and more vicious. Sam split to be with friends, and Pete and I excused ourselves to deliver another present. When we left, we went to our uncle's house. He said he had been expecting us to show up. He tried to explain to us how difficult it was for Dad to receive love. With all the "to do" I was making over Christmas, trying to make our home love-filled and warm, Dad was feeling more and more pressure, he told us. The nastiness and meanness pushes us away, he explained, and gives him some space from the love he can't accept.

My uncle encouraged me to break away, emotionally, at least, from Dad. I argued that this seemed to be against all my principles. I had to help now. There was no one else; I was the oldest. I could do what Mom had done. "Honey," he tried to explain, "your father will either make it or not. What I'm worried about is how many people he'll drag down with him."

I could not accept this. I was a Christian. Wasn't I obligated to love my father? Wasn't I supposed to forgive seventy times seven? If I abandoned him now, who would help? Who would lead him to the Lord? How else could he find wholeness? I measured my uncle's counsel but found it lacking.

After I graduated from college, I moved a thousand miles away to Boston for graduate school. After three years in Boston, I moved to Stony Brook, New York, but distance didn't stop me from trying to help my family. It made things logistically more difficult, but did not temper the fervor with which I tackled my task. And besides, I had God, for whom distance is not an issue, to help me.

EMOTIONAL ATTACHMENT

Our Hero is away from home physically, grown up and on his own in a career, but the home in which he grew up is carried in his heart, empowering his concerns and actions. Often unaware of the power of his family to direct his life, he responds the same as if he were still residing at home. He becomes a little messiah, compelled to control the outcome of the lives of family members. The Hero is often certain that no one else can accomplish it the way he can.

Especially when the family troubles continue into adulthood, the Hero is racked with more guilt. Since he could not redeem the family in his youth, he redoubles those efforts as an adult. It becomes more and more important to him to see the family restored and whole.

When family issues aren't dealt with, the Hero brings the same patterns of relating that he learned in his family of origin into all his adult relationships: those with his family, his friends, his spouse or dating relationships, and work. He tries the same techniques learned in his home but does not understand why they do not work now. The survival skills, adopted in childhood to endure the homelife, become counterproductive now. Yet it is often all he knows. Old patterns of control and manipulation must be recognized and given up for healthy ways of interrelating. The Hero must face squarely the patterns of control and power as they have evolved in his relationships before new patterns can be created.

Control

Many times in recovery literature or therapy, you will hear that you must stop trying to control others and, instead, take responsibility for your own life. Recognizing the ways you control or attempt to control is the first step to taking responsibility for yourself.

When our Hero grows up, he should relate to his family as a mature adult. The only problem is that the little child who tried so hard to hold that fragile situation together with his super-responsibility and burden-bearing knows no other interpersonal skills with which to respond to his family as an adult. He is still taking full responsibility for holding the family together. In essence, it is the young child in adult garb seeking to control the outcome of the family. Because of his deep unmet needs for a wholesome family, he strives to rescue the wayward family members now, rope them back in and make them behave as he has always hoped and dreamed.

How does the Hero control? He may attempt to manipulate events and circumstances to effect a change in the family member. He may, in love, of course, involve others who in his perception have a better chance at getting them to change. This may include securing the advice of professionals (counselors, drug treatment specialists, pastors) in the hopes that these folks can reach the wayward member and bring wholeness to him.

After my mother's death, for instance, I renewed my efforts to save my family, but our dysfunctional childhood now became evident in the choices my brothers made. When my brother, Pete, turned sixteen, he wanted to live on his own. We searched for a boarding house in our old neighborhood, and he began to live an even more isolated existence than before. He kept wanting to talk about why

Mom committed suicide, but I didn't hear his cry to break through all this denial and confusion and understand the pain he grew up with. I explained Mom's suicide away. She worked hard. She was tired. It's all for the best now; she doesn't have any more pain. But Pete didn't want the pain explained away; he wanted the wounds lanced and examined. Yet I had stepped into the role of the little Enabler. I wasn't able to discuss the sickness and meanness of our father. Rather I had to save him, save the image of a happy family I so longed to experience.

Sam returned to Atlanta to live with our father. He found college too overwhelming and wanted to wait out another semester. Since he had graduated early from high school, he had little to do. His drug use increased, and he and my father had violent arguments. Both tall men, they would hurl furniture at each other in drunken rages. The police were often called in to stop the violence. Within one year both were hospitalized in mental hospitals for several months at a time.

It was a good thing that I had curtailed my college activities, for I had much caretaking to do during these years. I shuttled back and forth between work and mental hospitals and later jail and halfway houses as Sam deteriorated even further. I wanted so to restore the family. Perhaps if I just prayed enough, Sam could be the same old person again, the one who made us laugh, the brother who shared bunk beds with me.

Parkside Hospital, one of the mental hospitals to which Sam was admitted, was a forty-five minute drive from my college. On the way to my first visit, I prayed, asking God to restore my brother's sanity. "God, I know You love my brother. Do something, please, to help him. I know You can if You would just want to." I fasted and prayed for him several times a week—especially on the days when I would visit.

I parked the car and stared at the hospital for several minutes. They had tried to make it appealing. It was a low, three-story white building with many trees surrounding it. The sun shone brightly off the stone walkway as I approached the building. I took several deep breaths and walked inside. After signing in, I secured my visitor's badge on my shirt collar and went down the corridor. At the end of the long hall was a thick, steel-reinforced door with bars across the small, eye-level window. I rang the buzzer and an attendant came and inspected my pocketbook. He then escorted me to my brother's room.

It was awkward. I didn't know what to say. How do I act normal when I am here behind several layers of security?

"How are you doing, Sam?" I asked.

"They've got me on some drugs and tell me I'll need to take them for the rest of my life. Hey, do you still have that guitar? I sure would like it in here." Sam told me they had diagnosed him as paranoid schizophrenic and had put him on lithium.

"Yes, I have it. I'll bring it the next time I come. Sam, I've been praying for you."

"Ain't no need for that, sister. I'm doing fine on my own. Now why don't you get out of here before they lock you up too, for talking to the Big Man. Hey, don't forget the guitar, okay?"

I left the hospital, praying again for my brother's healing. During those years I entreated God to change my father, to heal my brother, and to bring us all together again. Sometimes my prayers would drift to thoughts of a happy family reunion. I would picture my father begging our forgiveness, the three of us kids maturely dispensing grace and all being forever-after happy. I just knew God could do this—if He wanted to. I tried to do anything—and everything—I could to make this happen.

An Attempt to Control the Environment

If our Hero is in a position to do so, he will control aspects of his environment. For example, just as a child may have attempted to seek and destroy the bottles of alcohol, now as an adult, he may attempt to structure the environment of the dysfunctional parent so that he will not respond in a particular pattern. Suppose the dysfunctional parent is a verbal abuser. The Hero may monitor the conversations to prevent outbursts from occurring. Well aware after years of abuse how the tirades begin, he may learn to structure the conversation to divert topics and thus quell potential outbursts. He becomes a master at manipulating conversation to keep things on an even keel and keep the explosive issues from arising.

Watch the Hero in any family conflict. He will be the one who, like a super-cop, jumps in to referee and soothe. Peace at all costs is his motto, and he perceives that he is the only one clever enough and proficient enough to institute it. If things begin to get tense between family members at a special gathering or holiday, he will be the one to deflect attention and attempt to change the direction of the conversation to less explosive subjects.

Even as an adult, the family drama continues and our Hero becomes the director. His heightened sense of responsibility for the outcome of the family causes him to foster situations that are scripted to effect his goals. He becomes immensely frustrated when the players do not act appropriately. Yet, he redoubles efforts to control their destinies, partially because he has assumed God-like power over their lives. Our Hero has been called forth to redeem the family, if not through his own achievements, then certainly through his skillful efforts at effecting change in the lives of others.

I tried to control my brother Sam's environment, for instance, in an effort to overcome his dependence on drugs. I began researching the drug addiction programs in the Southeast for a Christ-centered program. When I discovered Teen Challenge, I talked with the staff for many hours. I was just sure they could help my brother. Now if only I could convince him to give it a try. Although we had always been very close, I knew he hated me right now. He especially hated my "religion." If I were to suggest any drug treatment program, he would hit the ceiling and start threatening me. So, I did what anyone would do, or so I thought. If he wouldn't listen to me, maybe he would listen to ex-addicts and others who tried to convince him to submit to a treatment program. But he knew I was behind it, and it steeled him even more against the idea. "You're just trying to control my life. Get the hell out of it, sister. I don't need your help or that of your Jesus freaks. Leave me alone and quit messing up my life."

In 1980, Sam was arrested and served a jail term. Now I knew I could help. If only the courts and his parole officer could be persuaded, he could be released into a drug treatment program. In fact, many of Teen Challenge's program participants were ex-offenders, court-ordered to the program. If I could get him into this program, his life would be turned around, he would meet Jesus, get clean, and be the old Sam I once knew. This program had to be the answer, and I began to try to set this answer in motion.

One night I received a phone call. It was Sam calling from prison. "What the hell do you think you are doing? You have no right to interfere. Leave my parole officer out of this. If I hear of you trying to interfere with my life anymore, I am going to kill you. Do you hear me? I can get a gun and I will. I'll come up to New York and blow you away. Do you hear me? Leave me alone." Then he hung up.

I sat there dumbfounded, holding the receiver. I burst into tears. "Lord, I just want to help. I just want him to be okay again. Why is this happening? Why can't my brother get help? Where am I going wrong?"

I didn't understand at the time that the more I tried to control my father and my brothers, the more enmeshed I became in their lives. I no longer knew where I ended and they began. It became important to my sense of well-being to know that I could help them change.

If you are trying to determine if you are overly enmeshed with a family member, ask yourself, "What is my motive? Is it to help my parent or sister or brother or to rescue me from shame?" Much of what I was doing sounded right, but my motive was wrong. If only I could make my brother better, then I would be okay too. This family had to be restored. It was very important to me and I didn't understand why at the time. It had to happen. And I had to make it happen. God and me together.

My youngest brother, Pete, did not escape my machinations. Pete, our Lost Child, had struggled with his sexual identity for years. When he confessed his homosexual experiences to me and his desire to change, I whirled into action once again. Now it was up to me to find the best counselor possible for Pete so he could explore these issues. I was convinced that family issues were at the root of his confusion. If only he could talk these out with a skilled counselor, I just knew he could be helped.

But when I found the perfect counselor, Pete didn't want to go. He was content with his lifestyle, he assured me. But he had to go. Didn't he see? This could help him. I would pay for it. Wouldn't he just try it?

Pete was resolute. No, he did not want to go to counseling. I was so frustrated. It seemed the more I tried to help my family, the more they pushed away from me and the more rooted they became in their problems. Didn't they see I loved them and only wanted their best? I was the one who would save them—their little messiah.

The Little Messiah

The Hero recognizes his central role to the integrity of this family. His sense of power heightens and his need to control the outcome of his family members' lives becomes more ingrained in his personality. He has become the little messiah—the long-awaited one who will save and heal the broken family. But what happens when our Hero is a Christian and comes face-to-face with the real Messiah?

At the root of any relationship with Jesus Christ is the issue of power. You would not need a savior, a messiah, if you could achieve acceptance by God on your own. You would not need the Holy Spirit to empower you if you were able to live in constant obedience to the Lord. You would certainly not need a God who had the solution to man's problem of sin if God were not omnipotent and you a mere mortal. Yet when an individual like our Hero has grown up in a dysfunctional home with an extraordinary vision of his power and ability to control people, then an intimate relationship with God becomes unobtainable until he addresses the issue of power.

The spiritually sensitive Hero, perhaps the Christian Hero, believes in a God who must care about his family's health more than he does (if He is to be God), but who must be instructed by the Hero. God becomes an errand boy of the Hero's admirable goals—to redeem and restore a broken home. The Hero is still calling the shots.

Since none of my family would respond to my efforts and offers of assistance, I had nowhere to turn but to God. If they wouldn't take my help, maybe they would take His. So I prayed and I fasted and I sought others to do the same. I just knew if we all concentrated our prayers at those doors of heaven, God would have to answer. He would have to perform a miracle. Wasn't what I was asking for worthy of His response? Wouldn't it bring glory to His name? Of course. So I prayed all the more fervently and aggressively. This, too, was my responsibility, my battle plan for helping my brothers and my father. God could do it, if I could just convince Him to act on our behalf.

Now I had a new arena for activity. The little messiah could not save her father and brothers directly, so all efforts were focused at indirect salvation. I employed the same efforts toward God I had toward others who might be able to help: I pled my case, I sought possible avenues of help and suggested them to the Lord, I got others involved to pray, and I believed. Oh, how I believed! It was so important to never doubt that God would come through. He was my last avenue of hope for saving my family. He couldn't let me down.

It gets very confusing because often what the Hero is requesting is just and right. The Hero may be praying for health, wholeness, salvation in its fullest sense for each member of the family. All these things are good and worthy of being brought to a loving God who cares for each individual. But when the Hero does so as part of his agenda for saving the family, the tables turn. God becomes the tool by which the Hero will accomplish his will. He becomes just another professional that the Hero consults in order to effect his plan. Even obedience and Christian service can be brownie points, used to cajole this unwilling God into effecting your heart's desires.

Until the issue of power is resolved, the Hero is thwarted in his desire for wholesome relationships with his family. He is also prevented from true intimacy with God. Often he may determine God doesn't exist or isn't who He says He is. Those with beginning spiritual interest or as young Christians will determine that He is unloving and uncaring and most of all, lacks power. It becomes too difficult to get to know Him; He seems so different from what our Hero would like Him to be.

To tell the Hero to let go of his control is to strip him of his primary motivation for being. Without replacing the drive to control or healing its root cause, letting go of his control can become just another tool for controlling. He may come to the belief that if he lets go, then his family will get well. He then empowers the letting go with the ability to effect the change he so desires. If that does not create change, then he often is enraged at the impotency of the very thing counselors or others are telling him he must do. The Hero's need for control over these important people is so deep that to admit that he is powerless over these persons is incredibly difficult. He has become a minigod in their lives. To give up this position of great authority and power requires him to reevaluate who he is at the very core of his being.

Empowerment

Because the primary motivation for the Hero is to control, he becomes empowered at seeing others change due to his efforts. When they move toward change, he is affirmed. When they backslide, he is repudiated. Who he is depends on what they do, how well they perform according to his estimation of what is wholeness. The members of his family are on a constant performance basis in their relationship with him. Their future, their well-being, have become so wrapped up in his self-esteem that he needs them to change to validate the meaning of his own life.

We all operate from motivations. We are infused with power to act in certain ways on the basis of these motivations. The Hero gave the family its reason for being. He displayed to the outside world that all is right with the family. Just look at me. You can see how good my family must be. This creates in the Hero an inordinate sense of power. The family looks to him to prove its worth to the world.

When the Hero becomes an adult, this role is still active. There has been no curtain closing on the family drama. Instead, we are in Act 2 and the Hero is still bringing the applause to the family. He continues to prove to the world that something good can come out of his family.

He still wants to be the star. He still needs his family to continue to affirm his role. He learned his style of relating from the Enabler and now as an adult, he rushes in to rescue the perishing. Only he is capable. Because of the silence that still pervades the family secrets, he is the only one with enough information, enough savvy to effect a result. He is empowered by his ability to effect change in these family members. He is empowered by a false sense of the heroic as he arrives just in the nick of time to save them all from themselves. He is empowered by his sense of mission and calling. His whole life has been geared just for this: to take charge and to enable these family members to become whole. It fell to him as a child to bear the burdens of this family; why not even more so now?

Unfortunately, I never escaped this role, even after I moved to Boston to attend graduate school. Then my father continued his rantings and ravings by long-distance telephone. They were more limited when he called me, due to the expense. When I called him, the one-sided conversations would usually last about an hour until I had dissolved in tears. Once that had been effected, he would then terminate the call—his victory achieved.

His phone calls were thematic. His hatred and venom toward my mother spilled out. "She blew my life apart. She stripped me of all my finances and left me with nothing. I worked my whole life to build this family, and with one gunshot she blew it apart. I had a good family, good kids that loved me, and now none of you care. She did it. She turned you against me."

"But, Dad," I would interject, "our family had problems long before Mom died. We were never a happy family."

As if he didn't hear me, he would continue, "Jane was an impossible woman to please. She wanted me to work all the time to provide for you kids. I had to work so hard and now she's blown it all away."

I began to steam inside. He work hard! My mom was the one who had to work hard. She was the main provider in our home because my father's efforts were so tentative. Then I knew what was coming next: the will. I began to brace myself.

"And another thing. The final knife in my back was that damn will. Your mother did that to spite me and only you can correct it. You know, honey, that I care for you kids. I'll take good care of you. I'll make sure you have everything you need. Just sign over to me the money and tell that bank I'd be a good trustee of those funds. You know I love you kids. I'll do what's best for you."

This was a constant theme, since I was the only child who had reached the age of maturity and could make legal decisions about the trust. Six months before she died, my mother changed her will, which originally bequeathed her estate to my father and named him as executor, and now instead, named the Fulton National Bank as executor and trustee of her marital property. It wasn't much money, but what was there was only to be used to provide for the three children as the bank deemed appropriate. It is an unusual estate plan, but one that made sense to my mother as she looked at my father's ability to manage the funds for our benefit.

Now as his ability to make money dwindled, he saw the trust as a source of funds. I refused to comply with his request that I sign over any rights.

If I defended my mother's memory, his vituperative thoughts became even more antagonistic and directed at me. "You're just like her, ya know," he'd start. "You're mercenary and only care about yourself. You don't give a damn about me. You and your religion. If you really wanted to treat me like Jesus treated others, you'd give up your rights to that money. He turned the other cheek. Why can't you? I know why—cause you're just like her. You're mean and spiteful and greedy. You're going to make someone a great wife one day. Ha! I doubt anyone will have you. Not when I finish telling him what you're like."

His tirades would go on and on. I could feel my spirit weaken. I tried not to listen. I tried not to let what he said affect me, but I became weaker and weaker. I felt so defeated.

Often I would try to close out what he was saying by praying silently. "Oh God, please help Daddy. Please help him calm down. Please, God, help me not to respond in anger. Help me to know what to say to him. I ask again for his salvation and healing. Help me to know how to help him." Yet I felt so defeated. How often had I prayed this prayer and others like it, and yet there seemed to be no help for my father. He only seemed to get worse.

He didn't like my being so far away and would often threaten to kill himself unless I returned to Atlanta. As soon as the threat of suicide was mentioned, I went into action. The responsibility to save his life yet one more time was mine. I would talk to him for hours, often long into the night to convince him to live. In one instance, I was so convinced that he was going to take drastic action that I told him I would be on the next plane out of Boston, called him from the airport so he could know I was on my way, and rushed from airport to plane to airport to taxi to his apartment. When I got there, he was fine. I see now that he was thrilled with his ability to control my life.

The battle scar of power brought about by years of burden-bearing and super-responsibility wounds our Hero now in adulthood as he attempts to relate to his family and to God. His deep desire to see his family whole is good, but his methods to effect that desire create a block in his own development which must be broken. At its root is the issue of power and control. These issues must be resolved before healthy relationships with our families can begin.

Chapter 7

The Working Wounded

*The idea of flight may lie at the origin of the finest career.
...But such a vocation will always carry a certain bitterness in it, because its origin lies less in a positive call than
in an escape, an attempt to forget a failure.[1]*

Paul Tournier
The Healing of Persons

When our Hero enters the workforce, he carries with
him the wounds of his childhood. The survival techniques
that served to protect him as a child continue to operate as
he selects a career, engages in meaningful work, and relates
to others in that environment. As a result, he is troubled.
He is never satisfied—either with his personal performance
or his choice of work.

Something just isn't quite right, but it may be difficult
for him to define. After all, our Hero's overachievement in
school translates well in the workplace. Often he is a very
responsible, dependable, and accomplished worker. Society
applauds competition and achievement, and the Hero's
success is rewarded by promotions, salary, and prestige.
Any success he achieves, however, is often bittersweet. He
feels driven to perform but unable to enjoy the benefits of

his hard work. Compliments are downplayed; criticisms replayed.

Job satisfaction is elusive. He feels constricted in various job situations, often changing positions or jobs frequently. There is an uneasiness with coworkers. He is often driven by perfectionism. He is one of the working wounded with whom we associate daily. He may even be one of us.

Work was intended by God to be deeply satisfying. God was able to stand back from His endeavors, evaluate them, and find pleasure in them. Adam and Eve, before the Fall, were given a work assignment: the commission to tend the Garden. "The Lord God took the man and put him in the garden of Eden to tend and keep it" (Gen. 2:15). It was only after the fall that work and sweat became related (3:17–19).

Why, then, is work so often a difficult place for us to experience satisfaction? This is a perennial question for many, but even more so for the adults from dysfunctional homes. We seem to keep repeating negative patterns over and over. We move on to different jobs, different cities, different careers, and yet the same problems plague us in the workplace. What are we doing wrong? Where is that ability to stand back from our work and pronounce it good? Where is our ability to rest from our work?

OVERWORK: THE HERO'S ACCEPTABLE ADDICTION

When our Hero was a child, he learned especially during the school years that achievement provided two important requirements for his survival. First, it deflected attention away from the family problem and onto his accomplishments. For a while, at least, the family appeared happy and proud. Often, if the dysfunctional parent placed a high value on education or success, this was the only time he received any affirmation or validation from that parent.

Second, achievement provided a way to protect the family secret. Perhaps no one will suspect that there is anything wrong with his family if he just achieves enough success in his school or social setting to cause others to assume he comes from a loving, nurturing environment. After all, if he can accomplish this or that feat, then the stock he comes from can't be all bad, can it?

These motivations, unrecognized and unchanged, compel the Hero just as forcefully when he enters the workforce. He overachieves there as well, often becoming driven. Particularly, in the late twenties and thirties, as psychological defense mechanisms such as repression begin to lose their ability to keep childhood pain down, he may work to dull the pain of what he is really feeling. He is troubled, but denies the pain by throwing himself into his work.

It's round and round the carousel, grabbing for brass ring after brass ring. One achievement mastered, it's on to the next. No time to sit back and enjoy the accomplishment. No time to dream and let creative intellect pursue perhaps uncharted territory. The Hero needs defined goals, outlining his path to success. Rung after rung he climbs the ladder, each step a forerunner to the next, the never-ending staircase to success.

Catch your breath, perhaps. Evaluate the next step, perhaps. But ever onward, ever upwards goes our Hero. For what? What is he looking for? What does he need so desperately from his work?

My first teaching job was at a small Catholic high school in the Boston area. The demands by the administration for teacher involvement in extracurricular activities were very minimal. I could have been home each day by 3:00 P.M. Instead, in the two years I was there, I created a joint American history/American literature teaching program, became Social Studies department chairman and revamped the entire curriculum, started a scholarship award program for the study of Congress, and coached the cheerleaders. I was also in my final coursework and completion of my thesis for my master's degree. If that were not enough, I had a burden for these kids to have a personal relationship with Jesus Christ, so I began a Young Life club at the school, creating a need for fifteen to twenty more hours a week in planning club activities, meeting with leaders, and contact work with kids.

My next teaching job required overinvolvement from the beginning; it was at a boarding school. The demands on a boarding school teacher are high by nature: teaching, coaching, and living in a dorm provide a round-the-clock work environment.

Then it was on to Georgetown law school. I chose a highly competitive, highly expensive school, necessitating long hours of study and many hours of outside work to pay bills. Again, overwork was no stranger. The old adage about law school is true, "The first year they scare you to death; the second year they work you to death; and the third year they bore you to death." The first two years were jam-packed. Thirty to forty hours of work at a law firm were crammed into non-class hours. Law review and litigation clinic hours ate up more time. Then, of course, my outside interest in religious freedom cases and involvement with the Christian Legal Society needed their measure of time.

By the third year, a time to relax perhaps and be "bored to death," I was heavily in debt. I pumped up my work hours as a law clerk, often spending the night at the firm to complete a project. I was at Georgetown Law Center by 5 or 6 A.M. and at the library or work until midnight most nights. I thought nothing of this. After all, it's law school—the paper chase years.

The law firm experience is set up to capitalize on this pattern of long hours and hard work in law school. As an associate in a law firm, you must work long hours for a number of years to demonstrate a commitment to the firm if you want a chance for partnership. With the increased financial pressures on firms in the eighties to offer larger salaries to young associates, this translates into 2,000-plus billable hours per year, which makes it difficult to maintain a personal life as well.

Why did I do this? Why did I select a career that blatantly puts such a premium on hard work and long hours? Why did I take a reasonable teaching job and fill it with unreasonable hours and multiple projects?

Dr. Bryan E. Robinson has called work the "drug of choice" for many adult children from chemically dependent and dysfunctional homes.[2] He claims that excessive work anesthetizes the childhood pain and yet can create many of the same patterns of a drug- or alcohol-addicted person. Many times I have thrown myself into my work to seek stability when my personal relationships felt out of control. I could become self-absorbed in work that society or my church pronounced worthwhile—all the time running as fast as possible from my inner pain. Being away from work can make you feel uneasy. What do you do with yourself? Saturdays, if not spent at work, were certainly not spent at play. Projects! Weekends were times to see how many things I could cross off of my "to do" list.

Many times Heroes, especially those from alcoholic homes, pride themselves on not succumbing to alcohol or drugs like their parents or siblings. More insidious, however, is becoming dependent on work to create your sense of self-worth and to mask the pain. Like an addictive agent, however, this kind of working may create more problems for the worker than it solves:

> The irony of the disease is that work addicts suffer more problems on the job than their colleagues. Work addicts are generally not team players and often have difficulty cooperatively problem-solving, negotiating, and compromising. Because they are over-invested in their work,

they tend to suffer extreme stress and burnout, and subsequently their efficiency declines.[3]

The twenties and thirties are years often spent building up one's career, trying out different career paths, and working hard. Why should that be any different for the Hero? The two central issues for the Hero in evaluating whether he is overworking are his motivations and balance. The Hero finds himself running from one project to the next, even one job to the next. Is his hard work primarily motivated by enjoyment of what he does? Is he called to that work? Or is he driven? The Hero should also look at the question of balance. Hard work is not to be condemned. Hard work, to the exclusion of the time spent alone, with God, or with others, should be examined, however. If the Hero spends inordinate amounts of time in the workplace because it becomes a place to hide from oneself and others, then it is not healthy. Busyness becomes a catch word for avoiding relationships. "Wish I could join you, but I have to finish this project." "Sorry, son, I know I said I would come to your baseball game, but this emergency came up." "Honey, we'll celebrate our anniversary next month; it's just a bad time at work right now." Adult children were such loners as children, never feeling like we fit in no matter how successful we appeared, it is easy to duplicate this pattern in adult life. It feels so right, so comfortable.

Douglas LaBier, author of *Modern Madness* and a psychotherapist whose practice is made up of patients whom he calls "troubled winners," notes that oftentimes a spiritual vacuum is created as individuals make compromises for success in their careers: "I found that the drive for success—and its criteria of money, power and prestige—exists alongside a parallel, but less visible, drive for increased fulfillment and meaning from work."[4] He hints that meaningful work, such as an investment banker who can use his skills to help develop low-cost housing, is the panacea to this spiritual vacuum. However, Pascal noted that each of us has a God-shaped vacuum in our hearts, and we have been scurrying around trying to fill that aching void.

For the Hero who has developed a self-identity circumscribed by his achievements, it can be very easy to allow success, work, and achievements to become an idol. Meaningful work, even that which advances the causes of Christ such as ministry, is only an attempt to fill this aching void. Our Hero, who so desperately needs to know he matters—to his father or mother, to his heavenly Father, to himself—drives himself to achieve. Until he has found his call first in the love of God for him and then in expressing his unique gifts and talents in the professional realm, he will be frustrated. Done backwards—seeking affirmation of self and validation of worth by God through his work—his accomplishments become less and less fulfilling. He begins to recognize how inadequate success is to provide him the love and wholeness he has yearned for his whole life.

What are some of the characteristics of the working wounded? How can you know if unresolved childhood issues are a part of your current struggles in your job?

Burnout

Many adults from dysfunctional homes suffer from periodic burnout. Their inability to express their frustrations and their high level of intensive work combine to produce depression and burnout. Much has been written on corporate burnout as experts review the eighties' focus on work to the exclusion of other relationships. Recently, *USA Today* cited the high employer costs of burnout. Employers were surprised to learn that one of the main reasons for rising health care costs is mental health expenditures. The National Institute of Mental Health estimates 5.8 percent of Americans suffer from depression and burnout, costing more than $27 billion in lost productivity, $17 billion just from lost workdays.[5] Douglas LaBier found in his research that 45 percent of career professionals suffer from work-related emotional problems, such as stress, burnout, malaise, and value conflicts.[6]

Dr. Herbert J. Freudenberger, in his book *Burn-out: The High Cost of High Achievement*, defined burnout as wearing oneself out by excessively striving to reach some unrealistic expectation imposed by oneself or by the values of society.[7] As a child, our Hero learned to emphasize his capacity for achievement and activity to receive the attention or love he needed. He also learned that his accomplishments deflected family pain, at least temporarily. When he enters the workforce, he carries these patterns of relating to the task at hand into his work. Hardly ever questioning the wisdom of piling yet another responsibility on his already full plate, the Hero manages to draw from within the ability to sustain yet another commitment. As typical with the Hero, he will usually do all things quite well.

Heroes have an enormous capacity to handle many things at once, often amazing friends and coworkers with their abilities. However, this energetic approach to all of life may be a facade. When the burden of sustaining this facade becomes too unbearable, the Hero can face a burnout. Burnouts most often occur in the workplace, but they can occur in the home as well. The Hero typically will take on more and more responsibility for the home and family as well. He will care for home and hearth, managing the home corporation and its attendant organizational and financial responsibilities, as well as the very important interpersonal needs. Rush Susie to swim practice and then drop Jimmy off at his soccer game. Swing by the grocery store. Don't forget Aunt Ellen's birthday card. Tonight is family night; have you planned that game yet? Stop by the gas station, the dry cleaners, the photo shop. Got to get

these pictures in the album by Saturday when Gran
gets here.

Another time to observe this overcommitment
Christmas. Typically a season of many activities, our
goes into high gear. Why? More than likely, holidays w
tense time in his childhood home. When he has his
family, these holiday periods are imbued with larger-t
life expectations. Everything must be perfect. Coo
must be homemade. The home must be decorated sp
didly, inside and out. Christmas cards written. Activ
planned. Parties attended and given. The presents mus
perfectly selected for each family member and tied u
ribbons and bows. He races around throwing all of tl
responsibilities into his already overscheduled mix of
ties. By the first of the year, he is depressed. He is bur
out.

Dr. Freudenberger notes that not every personality t
experiences burnout. Typically burnout occurs in "dynar
charismatic, goal-oriented men and women or determi
idealists who want their marriages to be the best, tl
work records to be outstanding, their children to shi
their community to be better."[8] When we look to our wor
whether in or out of the home—to sustain our vision of
ideal family and to make up for a lost childhood, we sut
Not only do we suffer burnout, but we suffer repeated c
appointment. No job, no amount of effort placed in our
reer success, no solicitation from our current family
going to make up for the past. The past must be healed
the present to be freely lived.

A burnout in work, like a failed relationship, howev
may be just what the Hero needs to shake up his patter
enough to ask significant questions. It is only in asking t
questions of why self-destructive patterns continue to ex
that one can get beyond the seeming failure of his copi
mechanisms to the root childhood issues. Seven questio
we need to be asking are: Am I always trying to be safe? I

I tend to be rigid? Do I tend to try to flee rather than fight? Do I tend to avoid conflict? Do I prefer working alone? Do I tend to avoid criticism and reject praise? Am I able to take a break?

1. Am I Always Trying to Be Safe?

I have been drawn to friends who take risks when it comes to work. One friend thought nothing of taking her medical skills from the hospitals in Boston to the Cambodian refugee camps in Thailand. Another started his own law firm in Manhattan. Another friend left a thriving legal practice to manage a struggling publishing company. When I left teaching to go to law school, you might think that I, too, was taking a risk. Underlying this change, however, was my great need for safety.

One thing I knew I did well was academics. I rolled right out of college into graduate school because I knew I could succeed there. Later, when I was trying to determine what track to take after teaching high school for five years, I looked at three avenues—school, school, or school. I examined a graduate program in counseling at a seminary, a doctorate in education, and law school.

Why didn't I look at a variety of new job options? Why did I return to school instead? I knew I could succeed at school, and if I was to embark on a new endeavor, I would learn the skills for that through my safe haven. No need to maximize any chance for failure.

One of the hazards of growing up as the Hero is that success comes with such a high level of expectation for what it can do for family harmony that you dare not engage in suspect activities—those with a possibility of failure. Rather than try new avenues of work, the Hero may cling tenaciously to those jobs in which he can do well, even if it is limiting his current growth. He may stay in a job that has predictable, safe requirements long past the time that job has provided him any challenge and stimula-

tion. Dr. Patrick Gannon, clinical psychologist, observed that many survivors are in jobs that fit their fears and not their talents.[9] Safety, even predictability, is what the Hero seeks.

2. Do I Tend to Be Rigid?

However, this predictability can lead to rigidity in an adult from a dysfunctional home and create a problem in the workplace. The needs of most businesses require individuals to be open to change, willing to learn new skills, and adapt to new programs. A person seeking predictability and safety can exhibit an extraordinary amount of resistance to change. A new computer program is introduced. Four of the employees are interested in learning the new software; two sit stone-faced, arms crossed as the supervisor explains the new program. They are not reacting to the computer program; they haven't even tried it yet. Instead, they are reacting to change.

The business has hit a down period. To avoid having to downsize, the company streamlines some procedures that will make the work more efficient. The end result should be to protect everyone's job. However, a number of the employees are subtly sabotaging these procedures. They know that they could lose their position if the company has to downsize, but they just can't seem to accept these new methods.

Rigidity also works against creativity. Effective problem-solving requires an openness to discussion, an expansion of possibilities, and objective evaluation. When one of our working wounded gets involved in problem-solving, he may view any evaluation of his avenue of expertise or sphere of authority as a threat to his self-worth. He may limit the discussion of possibilities because he seeks closure, predictability, certainty. He may also be unable to evaluate objectively the various possibilities. His agenda becomes primary, and his need for control can cause him to steer discussion, either overtly or indirectly, away from objective evaluation.

3. *Do I Tend to Try to Flee Rather Than Fight?*

Ever since I was a little girl, I wanted to be a lawyer. Both grandfathers had been lawyers. My parents were both lawyers. As the eldest, I loved arguing my case for greater expansion of childhood privileges, such as staying up later. Extremely idealistic, I was drawn toward politics and the chance to change society. It appeared to me that it was the lawyer/legislator who was best equipped for that. But when my mother died, my dreams died.

I determined to make a radical shift in the direction my life was taking. Up to now it strongly paralleled my mother's life. So, put the brakes on my career drive, and surely then I wouldn't be quite like her. I squelched the desire to take the law school admission test with the rest of my college classmates. "I know," I thought. "I'll be an American history teacher. I'll help high school students learn about the laws of our land instead."

So I escaped into the safety of a teaching position, which would provide meaningful work, I thought, while protecting me from any similarities with my mother. I literally hid out in the teaching field for five years, thinking that this decisive action on my part cut any tie I might have to my mother's life.

Adults from dysfunctional homes may find that they have fled into a career rather than chosen a specific field. It may not be a conscious decision, as mine was, but it will be driven by a need to protect themselves from what they perceive as possible harm. Some adults select careers in the same way they discovered hiding places as children. They find a comfortable, womb-like place to earn a living. It may be as subtle as investing yourself in a job that requires minimal effort from you so that you can be assured of success or discovering an insular environment for anonymity, such as the government or a large corporation.

Flight-or-fight responses to stress at work have been documented by numerous organizational behavior analysts. Both these underlying issues were present in the Hero's childhood. When the family got too crazy, the Hero would go into high gear trying to order the circumstances of the family so that the chaos was manageable. His intense need to control both circumstances and people later in life can be a pattern created by the conditioned reflex to the chaos and unpredictability of his childhood life. The other conditioned survival response, flight, caused him to escape into fantasy or activity to cope with the family problems.

When he enters the workforce and confronts job stress, his tendency is to respond with the same two conditioned responses, particularly if the job stress is prolonged and seemingly unrelenting. The Hero may exhibit a flight response through (1) conflict avoidance or (2) leaving the position or the job. Instead of fleeing, the Hero may fight the source of the stress by trying to control his environment, assignments, or personnel or by revamping the organization. The method he uses depends on how much latitude he has within the scope of his authority to effect those changes.[10]

4. *Do I Tend to Avoid Conflict?*

An adult from a dysfunctional home has spent a lifetime in conflict avoidance. This pattern may follow him into the workplace. Rather than confront a recalcitrant employee or coworker, he may avoid them. He may also attempt to avoid conflict by restructuring his work environment so that his interaction with those individuals is minimal. Why, I even structured my entire legal career to avoid conflict!

I had opportunities when I joined my firm after law school to pursue litigation in administrative agencies and federal courts as well as corporate work with nonprofit corporations. The combatant nature of most litigious proceedings was too close to home for me. Word wars. I had had enough of that as a child. I began subtly seeking more and more assignments in the nonprofit and preventive law side of the firm so that I could say, "Sorry, I've got more than I can handle right now" when the litigators came by my office seeking assistance.

Nonprofit corporations, needing counsel on various business or ministry issues—that's for me. Working to solve problems. Working together to advance their ministry objectives through the application of legal principles. Preventive law—establishing policies, procedures, and strategies that could minimize or prevent legal problems and conflicts from arising—was my chosen field. This felt right. No need to wage war here. Leave that to the litigators.

One of the most difficult areas in conflict avoidance is asking for a promotion or a raise. Issues of worth surround that request ordinarily, but for an adult from a dysfunctional home, it is easier to continue producing rather than rock the boat. This can create a potential for abuse. Patrick Gannon, in *Soul Survivors: A New Beginning for Adults Abused as Children*, found that

> many of you who have continued the caretaker role into adult life may have found that applying the same high control, problem-solving acumen used to survive your family ordeal has made you a manager's dream. You are used to hardship, so no task is too difficult. There is less fear of being abused, although the possibility for exploitation may exist in not being fairly compensated for all you do.[11]

5. *Do I Prefer Working Alone?*

Adults from dysfunctional homes are more comfortable working alone, and they typically have little skill in working together to resolve problems or accomplish an objective. They rarely, if ever, saw effective teamwork modeled in their homes. Yet teamwork is necessary in most businesses.

The Hero deals with this dilemma most often by avoiding businesses or career opportunities that require much teamwork. He is used to being a lone ranger and yet in so doing, accomplishing a great deal. He feels more comfortable working alone. After all, he can count on himself. The Hero may choose a field that allows him to work alone or that allows him a great deal of independence and autonomy. Instructors, doctors, lawyers, accountants, writers, editors, entrepreneurs all can work in an independent fashion.

I spent five years as a high school teacher thoroughly at peace in the classroom—my domain. Here I had total control and authority over all that was to transpire in six fifty-minute segments each day. I could plan out the course and each day's lessons. I executed those plans and I, alone, was responsible for the outcome of my efforts.

Law is not that much different. It requires long hours of solitude in work. Pouring over documents, reviewing cases, planning strategies are often done alone. Here, too, you could easily lose yourself in lone ranger thinking.

Fortunately, for me, I joined a small firm where my growth as a lawyer could take on a more apprentice-like relationship. I could be "teamed-up" with a more experienced, talented lawyer and work together on client matters. I often chafed at the rub that comes from that kind of close working relationship, but God was continuing to chip away at this particular aspect of my childhood patterns.

Working alone or independently is not a negative pattern in and of itself. However, when you find yourself unable to work with others when necessary, you may be reacting to unresolved childhood issues. Cooperative thinking, strategizing, and problem-solving are necessary components of any business. If the Hero is freed to operate as a part of a team, he can bring his extraordinary abilities and achievements to bear on the problem.

6. Do I Tend to Avoid Criticism and Reject Praise?

No one, I repeat, no one is harder on himself than the Hero. Due to his proclivity for assuming blame, his low self-esteem, and his incredibly high, almost unachievable standards, he is constantly berating himself for average performance. He must be the best. His work product must be outstanding.

So what happens when his work is criticized? Often the Hero will be unable to view his performance objectively. His personality and self-esteem have become so entwined with his work product that criticism of the product is taken as a condemnation of himself as a person. Emotions may well up as he hears a negative report. Inside he is churning. "How could you have made that mistake? You're so stupid. Don't ever let that happen again." The supervisor or boss giving the criticism may be even-handed, temperate, and encouraging in his approach to the review. No matter. The Hero will remember every comment and find twenty more reasons for self-flagellation.

The Hero could not afford to make a mistake in childhood. He had to be excellent at whatever he did. He must be the very best, but he is rarely pleased with his accomplishments. Just try praising him for a job well done and see what happens. "Thank you, but it was really nothing." "Well, I wanted to polish that last section but there just wasn't time." "Thanks, but if I'd had another day, I'm sure the results would have been better."

Praise makes the Hero uncomfortable for several reasons. First, there is a basic sense that the praise is not deserved. After all, even though he may be receiving praise for this particular project, he knows it was not up to his high standards. He feels as though he has defrauded the praise-giver. Second, he is afraid he will be found out. If this praise-giver only knew how far short the Hero fell from his own standards, he would not be offering these accolades. Third, the Hero distrusts the praise-giver, questioning his ulterior motives. He spent his childhood in heightened alert, trying to figure out what was going on in the family. He maintains the same vigilance now, questioning the intentions of each person he must interact with, trying to evaluate that person's ability to help or hurt him.

Learning to evaluate one's work is a difficult task for Heroes. So much of our self-worth is tied up in our activity at work, and yet it is so easy for us to condemn the work of our hands. We need to take our lumps, sure, and learn how to evaluate and incorporate criticism of our work. But even more difficult for us, we need to learn to accept praise—to accept our worthiness of praise. Most importantly, we need to learn how to praise our own work.

God Himself stood back from His work and paid Himself a compliment. He created day and night, oceans and land, and then He took a break and praised Himself. It was "good," He said. He created stars, the sun and moon, trees, and vegetation. Then He took another break, took a look at His work, and complimented Himself again. It, too, was good. He then created the birds and animals and took yet another break. Again, He proclaimed His work, "good." When He created man, He stepped back again, surveyed His handiwork and proclaimed it "very good." When our childhood issues are resolved, we can learn to practice this kind of evaluation of our work and in unabashed enthusiasm, praise it as "good" and "very good."

7. *Am I Able to Take a Break?*

There is a saying that the law is a jealous mistress. Many careers have time-pressure demands and ongoing production requirements. We get busier and busier and feel good about it. The work week, with its frenetic activity, keeps us pumped up. This adrenaline high of meeting deadlines, dispensing advice, and producing results has kept us moving during the week. When the weekend comes, without work, we crash. We feel depressed if we are not accomplishing something. If not work, then some personal project.

There is a principle in the Sabbath rest. Even God purposefully refrained from working! If He needs to take a break, then surely, we might consider it. When we grew up, we filled the anxious moments of our home life with activity, diverting our attention from the pain of our families. In adulthood, we continue to deal with our anxieties by becoming operational. These patterns remain established, unless we consciously work to interrupt them.

When we begin to set limits on our involvement in the workplace, we might feel anxious and attempt to fill up our time with activity in some other sphere. Here is where a close accountability partner can help us be honest with our use of time. When we lay our schedules before him or her and let them ask the scrutinizing questions, we come out of denial and face squarely our stewardship of our time and the motivations for our activity. Once we establish reasonable limits, we are going to need help to stay within them. We easily rationalize a few hours of work here or there, and by the end of the week, we have overworked once again.

Intense Loyalty

What happens to the Hero when he is in a destructive work environment? He stays. The Hero has amazing staying power, despite negative circumstances. When he was a child, he kept on producing those A's and honors, even though his family situation never changed. The transient interludes of peace in the family war were reward enough. When he gets into a negative work situation, he lacks the ability to evaluate when to move on. Perhaps this next project or program will be the one that makes the difference. His loyalty to the organization may keep him in a negative situation long past the time to move on.

Enjoying Success

Nothing the Hero accomplishes is ever good enough. He judges himself and his work product without mercy. His standards of excellence are tilted toward perfection, and he will demand nothing but his best. Yet he never quite seems satisfied with his work product.

There is a high cost to the aspirations that drive us. Because satisfaction of a job well-done is seldom enjoyed for any length of time, we continue to seek that which will deeply satisfy us. We set the next goal for success and soak it in high expectations. That then gives us something to shoot for, a new goal that, once reached, may fill up that aching void in our lives. When we arrive there, however, and accomplish that next level of success, we may find that we feel slightly depressed, perhaps even displaced:

> ...An uncomfortable listlessness overtakes them. They no longer feel rooted or involved, even in situations that were so vital for them before.... When people paint grandiose pictures for themselves of what it's going to be like on the next plateau, more often than not what they've envisioned doesn't materialize. Not because they don't reach the plateau. They do. But once they're there, the scenery isn't too different from the scenery lower down, and disenchantment begins to set in.[12]

If this listlessness and disenchantment leads us to pursue yet another rung of the ladder, another plateau, we will continue to be stuck in a self-defeating pattern despite our obvious successes and achievements. If there comes a point, however, that we become disenchanted with the emptiness of success piled upon success, we may discover that God intended more for us and, as a result, more for our work than we could ever have imagined. Remember, work was intended to be a part of the Garden of Eden—a wondrous experience of interacting with creation and the Creator.

Super-responsibility on the Job

When we have grown up in dysfunctional homes, we learned patterns of undertaking tremendous responsibility for others' actions and behaviors. We were there to rush in and rescue when needed. We were also there to take the blame for things that were not really our fault.

When we arrive in the workplace, there is also a tendency to blame ourselves for everything—giving ourselves little room for growth and change through mistakes. If you make a mistake in judgment or performance, you beat yourself up forever. "I'm sorry" becomes a constant buzzphrase. We also assume blame for failures at work that aren't our fault.

It is easy for us to assume blame for things that are not within our realm of responsibility. We have done it for years. We took responsibility for our parents' alcoholism or dysfunction. We believed the lie that if only we could do something different, then Mom or Dad would be okay. Maybe if we were good enough, our parents wouldn't fight. Now as adults, this burden of super-responsibility follows us into our relationships and into the workplace.

This is most often demonstrated by our enabling behaviors. We often play the role of the martyr, picking up the slack for inefficiency or nonproductivity elsewhere. "I'll just do it myself" becomes our frequent response. When we delegate a task to another, we rarely let it go. We manage our work by holding it close. We delegate but we take it back. Or if we manage to let another have the assignment, we may hover over them with the expectation that we will have to step in and rescue the project. Used to the many broken promises of our parents, we distrust a coworker's commitment to follow through on a project, and we tend to that individual in often suffocating ways. Yet in our apparently super-responsible way, we limit the growth of our employees or coworkers. They never have to face the consequences of work poorly done or not done on time if we are always swooping in to rescue the project. We say we do this for the sake of the firm or the client, but are we really more motivated by our need to bear the burden for a job well-done?

THE WORKPLACE AS HOME

You and Your Boss

Does your place of work surprisingly mirror your childhood home? Do the relationships you have with a boss or coworkers remind you of how you related to your parents as a child? Eliza Collins, a psychotherapist with the Center for Executive Development in Cambridge, Massachusetts, contends that people tend to view their bosses as they did their parents and attempt to recreate their parent-child relationship in their boss-employee relationship.[13]

Janet Woititz, in her book *Home Away From Home: The Art of Self-Sabotage*, examines what happens when Adult Children of Alcoholics enter the workplace. She notes that an ACOA boss, who operates out of unresolved childhood issues, has an extraordinary need to control, which can result in a demand for compliance. He will often be perfectionistic and will tend to micromanage. He finds it difficult to trust that others will do what they have agreed to do or that they will do it in a manner sufficiently acceptable to him.[14]

What happens to the Hero when he goes to work and has a boss like this, a boss like his dysfunctional parent in many ways? This negative work combination plays right into his self-defeating patterns. The two will feed off of each other. He will gear up, overwork, and overachieve, attempting to get the approval of this boss. The boss's unmet needs will make it difficult for him to grant that approval. Unless the

Hero has learned to stand back from his work and objectively praise himself for a job well-done from time to time, he will become increasingly discouraged. Isn't anything he does good enough? Yes, it probably is, but not if his only way of evaluating that is through the eyes of such a boss.

You and Your Subordinates

What if you are the boss? Does your high need for control and your inability to trust others create problems for you in working with employees? What if you, an adult from a dysfunctional home, are boss to employees who are also from dysfunctional homes?

In a recent *Personnel Journal* article, Dr. Michael Diamond and Dr. Seth Allcorn argued that "a better understanding of the often dramatic influence unconscious motives have on organizational behavior has become a managerial imperative."[15] In times of stress at work, perfectionistic bosses and self-effacing subordinates are caught in a double bind. The subordinates respond to stressful events by blaming themselves because they feel worthless. Perfectionistic supervisors have such high standards of excellence that they are able to blame subordinates for their inability to meet them.[16]

Manfred F. R. Kets de Vries and Danny Miller, both professors in graduate business degree programs, postulate in their book *The Neurotic Organization* that much of what has been written about dysfunctional families is directly relevant to superior/subordinate relationships in organizations.[17] The authors found that subordinates who idealize superiors are often looking for that parental approval they never had as children:

> They have faith and confidence in the leader, whom they do their very best to please. They are highly motivated and study the boss very carefully to see what they can learn in order to improve their own performance....

They are prone to be very flattered by a few words of praise from the leader and devastated by the mildest of reprimands. They thus become extremely dependent on the leader and very easy to control and manipulate.[18]

When the Hero is a boss and has unresolved childhood issues, he may find he attracts these types of employees. He is able to dominate them, fulfilling his own deep need for control. However, this results in a negative impact on the organization. This type of worker, although an excellent worker, has diminished independence and judgments. The employee's ability to be creative and to challenge assumptions is overshadowed by the strong desire to please his boss.[19]

Drs. Diamond and Allcorn urge bosses to be aware of the existence of these types of destructive interaction patterns:

> It is the responsibility of senior executives to recognize the effect of their behavior on subordinates. They should never underestimate the symbolic role that they fulfill for the people with whom they interact.[20]

Be that as it may, Heroes are unlikely to recognize how their behavior impacts subordinates unless they have previously recognized that their behavior itself may be motivated by unresolved childhood pain.

Whether boss or employee, Heroes may continue to re-create their home environment in the workplace or be drawn to work situations that provide an opportunity to repeat their family role. However, if we can become aware of the ways we carry our family relationships into our work, we can begin to identify the patterns, find their root causes, and change our behavior. Until we do, our work may become increasingly frustrating. We may change jobs, or even careers, but note that uncannily the same difficulties seem to reappear. At the root of our self-defeating patterns at work is our tenacious reliance on childhood survival techniques. We must be willing to lay down these once potent defense weapons if we are to find true satisfaction in the expression of our God-given abilities in work.

Chapter 8

The Glass Slipper

Man finds it hard to get what he wants, because he does not want the best; God finds it hard to give, because He would give the best, and man will not take it.[1]

George MacDonald
Unspoken Sermons (Series Two)

The dysfunctional home provides little preparation for the adult involved in romantic relationships. The inability to trust, the failure of intimacy, the fear of letting go, the need to control, and the overwhelming need to be affirmed are all part of the adult's character when she enters into a relationship. The confusion between the fantasy family and reality also creates an impossible barrier for most relationships to conquer. The adult is looking for bells and fireworks, or at least a crescendo of music, to signal that her prince (or his princess) has come.

The long history of fantasizing affects the ability of many women, in particular, to discern the reality about a specific individual. The character defects may be apparent to all her friends, but she continues on in the relationship, loyal to the end, because she fantasizes beyond that which is present to that which could be. Often, the adult from a dysfunctional home, and in particular, our Hero, is attracted to someone similar to the dysfunctional parent; she believes that with her influence and love, this person can change. Since she could not achieve that miracle with her own family, she is compelled to rework that past defeat into a present victory.

What is lost from a dysfunctional home is the basic model for a good relationship. The important variables that compose a healthy relationship include love, trust, intimacy, truth telling, communication, commitment, and acceptance. Adults from dysfunctional homes enter the world of outside relationships with this cavernous void from their families. They do not have any experience with true love and intimacy. They have not witnessed healthy confrontation on a variety of issues. Neither have they been involved in a realistic assessment of problems or an evaluation of appropriate solutions. In fact, they have learned to deny that there are any problems.

Heroes are well aware of their role to bring respect to the family and to seek the approval of the dysfunctional parent through their heroic activities. They take very seriously the responsibility to hold the family together. When they enter relationships, it is no different. They must hold the relationship together. How do they do this? The same way they did in their family: don't talk about the problems, exhibit an intense loyalty no matter how bad it gets, fantasize about how it will be better in the future if only their significant other will change, and then do anything in their power to make that happen. Six patterns of behavior from childhood haunt their present relationships: a need for love and belonging, a need to rescue, a need for acceptance, an inability to confront, a need to be loyal, and a search for perfection.

1. A Need for Love and Belonging

There is no deeper yearning, no more intense longing, in an adult from a dysfunctional home than to be loved. Years and years of rejection from a significant parent take a toll. The little child resides fully in the grown-up and still calls out to anyone who dares to come close, "Love me. Love me for who I am. Don't reject me. Tell me I am worthy of being loved. Never leave me."

This deep, agonizing desire to be loved crystalized for me as a young child in the desire to be married. Over and over I prayed, "Please, God, don't let me have a marriage like my parents." I recognized that they were caught in a destructive cycle, and despite my efforts to change it, their marriage was a disaster. But then there was yet to be my marriage. Maybe that could work out to be a good thing. Maybe there it would be peaceful, loving, caring, and happy. So I went out in search of the perfect mate.

Ninth grade, with all its adolescent hormones, is not the best measure of one's ability to relate well to men, but it did set the foundation for my pattern: If God really loved me, He would let Joe or John or Tom or whoever love me. A January 30, 1968, entry in my journal states, "God, why won't You help me! All day long Jimmy ignored me. He hasn't said a thing in two days! I can't stand it. Things have never been so bad in all my life! If there's a God in heaven, why won't He help me? Oh, I love Jimmy with such feeling. I could die at his cold shoulder. I don't understand why this is happening to me but God does. When in the world will something work out for me? I love Jimmy. Will he ever love me? God, please. Oh, God, PLEASE!"

From the time I discovered boys, I needed men with a vengeance. They had to satisfy a deep hungering in me for my father's love at the same time that they were to provide romantic love. It was a tall order for any man, but then I often chose to be involved with men who were most likely to reject me, as had my father. The self-fulfilling prophecy was made all the more complex because I spiritualized what had occurred. God was in control, or so I thought. He could make this man love me if He just wanted to. He could change that man to be an acceptable mate, or if he did reject me, He could make him love me again.

Pick a year, any year, from my journals and the theme is the same. As Vikki Carr sang, "Oh, please, dear God, it must be him. It must be him but it's not him. And then I die."[2] As my understanding of God deepened, the prayers became more temperate, but watch what happened to the incredible web of confusion I was building about how God works in a person's life, especially in the area of relationships.

In ninth grade in 1968, I wrote, "All I know is I like Jimmy very much and unfortunately nothing may ever come of it. I was feeling very low and prayed to God, something fierce. A passage popped into my mind and gave me hope. 'For truly I say to you if you have faith as a grain of mustard seed, you will say to this mountain, "Move hence to yonder place," and it will move, and nothing will be impossible to you.'" I was certain that if I prayed enough, "something fierce," and if I had enough faith, then this thing I desired could come to pass.

2. A Need to Rescue

Rick, my high school boyfriend, was moody and indecisive. We were on-again, off-again for the last three years of high school. I was never really certain we were right for each other until he revealed his drug problem. Now I knew he needed me. The pain associated with his erratic behavior toward me was bearable because I was needed. A June 1971 entry in my journal read, "I realize I've been doing all the giving, loving, and caring and that it had to fall apart someday because it was only one-sided. Rick is an A-1 rat, but I love him (or what he should be)."

At another point when Rick was caught for stealing money for drugs, I wrote, "Rick called me and told me he has been caught stealing money. Rick made me feel needed and he said he missed me and wanted me. I know he feels this way only when he's in trouble, but I like him to want me, to need me. I tried to help him. I told him I'd stand by him no matter what and pray." And stand by him I did. I tutored him daily for three months so he wouldn't flunk out of school. As his drug problem increased, his moodiness and his verbal tirades increased, and I made excuses for his behavior. After all, it wasn't him; it was the drugs. If I could just get him off drugs, then everything would be okay and he would love me again. I launched into the same patterns of rescue and redemption that I had used with my family.

I asked God to be with Rick and to guide his thoughts and feelings. I saw God as some sort of cosmic puppeteer who could pull the strings on Rick. There was no question that God was capable of so doing. It was simply a matter of my being patient enough to wait for God to accomplish it. But, of course, Nancy was not one to let God go uninstructed as to how He could accomplish this goal. Determined, I told God that if He would just get Rick straightened out with God, then he and I could grow stronger together.

The problem with "waiting on the Lord," as it is so often phrased, is that my personality was imbued with action. What Hero sits around on her duff and does nothing when a problem or challenge is presented? As I explained in my journal, "Please understand, God, I am not trying to hang on to the problems or to take over Your will. It's just that I can't see any results."

I took all the blame for the relationships falling apart. After all, hadn't I failed to bring my parents together? Now if only God could see how sincere I was to do better this time, if He would just give me the chance. I bargained with God: "God above, as sure as I'm writing this now, I will care for Rick if You restore our relationship. I promise. Please help."

Yet even at this tender adolescent stage, I wanted to believe that God could "fix things" if I could just turn them over to Him. My last entry in my journal before starting college in August 1971 showed signs of this growth: "I read part of *Beyond Ourselves* and it explained that giving over your problems to God is like giving a broken toy to your father. If you stand patiently by and only help when the father told you to, he could fix it much sooner. But if you get impatient, get underfoot, and then finally snatch it back saying I knew you couldn't fix it anyway, he doesn't have a chance to act. Oh God, I want to give You my broken relationship and I want You to please help me stay out of Your way. Help me to know You've got it and will fix it. I'm young at this, God, and my emotions and fears might try to overtake me. Please help me to believe in You and Your power and that You know best."

Other relationships were not all that much different. I never again dated someone so obviously like my father as Rick. However, I still managed to be drawn to those men who needed remodeling to be the men I wanted them to be.

I would involve God in my remodeling schemes to assist each particular man to be the right one for me. "Dear God, I enjoy being with Steven so much. He has many of the qualities I admire, but I see that he could not be the one for me because of his inability to commit and to love. I see that he lacks sensitivity and an ability to communicate. He does not have the ability to commit himself to a direction, a person, or to You. God, these are things that must be changed before he could be right for me. I pray with all my being for Your intervention in Steven's life to create and empower in him the desire to reach his potential."

This intense desire to remake a man to fit my image of a godly, caring husband was present in every relationship I had. I was constantly drawn to those men who were aloof and unattainable or who were in need of a savior, a redeemer, a rescuer.

This happens often in marriages. We believe that our happiness, our contentment, depends on how our spouse changes to be the person we think we need. As a result, we try to fix them ourselves, or to find them help. No one can do it as well as we. After all, isn't that what we learned from our families? Happiness was always right around the corner. If only Daddy would stop drinking. If only Mom would not be so volatile. If only this or that would change. Then our life in the castle would come to pass and we would all live happily ever after.

We endure the unhappy aspects of the present relationship because of the perceived future potential. No pain, no gain, right? Yet as long as we live with our happiness pegged to our ability to control another person and to change them to meet our needs, we take no responsibility for our own happiness or peace. Instead, we focus on the other person and his acceptability to us. Often all our efforts to change that person go unrewarded, leaving us with a repeated sense of failure and despair.

3. A Need for Acceptance

I dated men who were like my father in a number of ways: controlling, rigid, unable to communicate, or noncommittal. The more unattainable, the better. The challenge of winning their love became a test of my desirability. With God all wrapped up in my thinking, it also became a test of God's love for me as well.

Acceptance of another is at the root of a healthy relationship. An unhealthy relationship exists when the other person must perform to your specifications to be worthy of love and acceptance. Yet a performance-based love is often the only love adults from dysfunctional homes have known or are comfortable with.

We often are drawn to rigid individuals who equate performance to love. It is easier to satisfy a specific agenda for acceptability than to share one's soul. We learned early on to reveal only those parts of us that we think are lovable and acceptable. Few people really know us, and yet we have a deep hunger to be known and accepted for who we truly are. For example, in my sophomore and junior years in college, I dated Alan—a tall, good-looking man who played football for Georgia Tech. He had a heart for God and often spent much of his time caring for others. Alan also had strong beliefs about the place of women.

Although raised a Southerner, I had always been achievement-oriented, partly because of the role model of my mother, and partly because of the demands my Hero role placed on me. In the South in the early 1970s, an evangelical Christian woman was one who never worked outside the home and whose primary duty was to preserve the peace of the castle for her weary warrior when he came home from daily battle in the world.

So now I was dating someone for whom acceptance and love meant conformance to this standard. I tried hard to fit. In my journal in the fall of 1972 I wrote: "Today I was down because it's really hit me hard that I need to find out God's plan for me as a woman. I really want to know who am I supposed to be and where do I fit in relation to a man? It's hard to accept that God doesn't want me to be so achievement-oriented when it comes to a relationship. I grew up in a home where Mom was the head, the respected one. But I guess God didn't plan it that way. I want to know what His design is for me. I want to know how to be His woman. I feel better after realizing God is going to remake me into the woman I need to be." Implicit in that last statement was that God would remake me into the woman I now needed to be for Alan.

I denied myself and who God was calling Nancy Oliver out to be in exchange for the security of acceptance. If there was one thing I had learned from my childhood, it was how to adapt my behavior to be acceptable—whether to friends, teachers, or boyfriends. I needed to be the good one, the one who was acceptable in society and thus brought fame and honor to the home.

When I left the South after college in 1975 to attend

graduate school in Boston, I was perplexed by the difference in northern evangelical men. I thought I had gotten all this straight in college. Women, Christian women, were to capitalize on those qualities that gave them their "gentle and quiet spirit." But the Christian men I met in Boston had a different view—women should explore their God-given potential and their talents. I was so perplexed, in fact, that I tried to resolve this incongruity by writing my master's history thesis on the dilemma: "The Southern Woman: Saved, Sanctified, Submissive."

In my early twenties in graduate school, I fell in love with an accomplished, educated man. Rob had had many advantages—strong family relationships, money, the best education, opportunities to explore many avenues of interest. He was the most intriguing, well-rounded person I had known to that point. Surprisingly to me, he loved me. However, high on his agenda was to make me more like him. He liked to climb rocks, therefore I, too, should be exposed to rock-climbing. He loved music; I needed my lessons in the masters. He was athletic, an avid runner and skier, and started me on a running program. His theology was rooted in predestination; I should read the classics supporting this. This Professor Higgins self-image was tied up with his Eliza. Could he make me acceptable to him and to his family?

Did I question this Pygmalionesque plan? Of course not. I understood this all perfectly. I would be loved if I could meet these specific, declared objectives. I knew from my father that one was not loved for who one was but rather for how well one performed. Now if I could only run fast enough, dress appropriately, be interested in the right things, demonstrate competence in numerous fields ...

When he broke up with me, he stated that I was not spontaneous enough for him. Spontaneity? You want spontaneity from someone who only knew responsibility and performance? This breakup was harder than the rest. Possibly it is because I wanted to be that Renaissance woman he so desired. Failing to meet his standards for acceptability, I wondered if I would ever be acceptable to a talented man from a good family.

At the time I did not see how rigid an individual he was. People needed to march to his drumbeat. To be loved meant to perform. Instead, I took full responsibility for the failure of this relationship. After all, I hadn't been found acceptable.

He also explained as he broke off our relationship that he had aspirations for politics, and someone with my family background simply would not do. Not only was the poor flower girl thrown back in the streets; her hope for a future with any reasonably normal man was disposed of as well. My family background condemned me again. It was just as Catherine Marshall had explained to me several years before.

4. An Inability to Confront

When an adult from a dysfunctional home is involved in a relationship, he is handicapped by an inability to talk constructively about problems. Alan, my college boyfriend, had difficulty expressing his feelings. After two years of dating in college, Alan decided I was not the woman he wanted to marry. The way he broke off the relationship after two years of steady dating was simply to stop calling. No explanation, no letter, nothing—just disappearance.

The even stranger part, however, is how I responded. I waited. I prayed. I agonized. I theorized. I talked to others. But I did not call him for one month. I could not take the initiative and confront the obvious problem. I was too paralyzed; intuitively, I knew I had been rejected but I was too afraid to learn why.

After graduate school, when Rob broke up with me, he could only say that his feelings had changed. It did not occur to me to ask Rob why. I would figure out what was true instead by examining our years together. Why not confront him and simply ask or even more forthrightly, push for clarification of his feelings? My home life had taught me that confrontation was better to be avoided. Stand at the window and figure out if Daddy is in a bad mood tonight. Don't challenge him, don't push; just take it. But how can one get at the truth of a matter if one is afraid of confrontation? In healthy relationships, confrontation and conflict are opportunities for growth.

Rob came to see me in 1981, four years after we had broken up. Although we hadn't spoken in two years, my hope that we would one day be back together was still alive. We talked through many aspects of our relationship during the weekend. At the close of our time together, he said, "Things will be easier now..." He meant that there was closure in our relationship. Instead, I heard hope for a renewed relationship. I knew I needed to ask him what he meant. But I was too afraid to confront his statement and clarify the issue. So we parted with my hope alive. I spent much time in relationships guessing at what was happening.

5. A Need to Be Loyal

The amazing thing about children in dysfunctional homes is how intensely loyal they can be to the dysfunctional parent. Despite evidence time and time again of the parent's weakness and negative behavior, the child excuses the behavior. Much of this is learned from the Enabler who has made excuses to the children and to the outside world for the erratic behavior of the spouse.

When the children grow up, they are faced with a world of choices for relationships. Whether they are drawn to negative people to begin with or whether they draw out those traits in the people they date, invariably the character defects will begin to show. Others around them may see how destructive the relationship is and how damaged the other individual is. However, they will defend that person and the relationship. They remain intensely loyal, despite objective demonstrations that such loyalty is undeserved.

In my twenties and early thirties, I began to date a succession of two types of men. Either they were unattainable, due to an inability to commit, or they were of questionable character. It was not always obvious at first. Most had good pedigrees: good families, the right schools, good jobs. Mostly they were Christians. But invariably, they had obvious character traits that should have signaled trouble. Some lied, some juggled several women at a time as they proclaimed their allegiance to me, some could not maintain a job or had explosive relationships with coworkers. But always, when I discovered the flaw, I rationalized it away and stepped in to assist this wayward person to uncover his real potential.

Take Mark, for example, who began to demonstrate his inability to take responsibility for himself and his job commitments. He would frequently call in sick when deadlines for important projects neared. He blamed his boss repeatedly for his failures. Coworkers, he claimed, were out to get him. I jumped in to advise and, of course, to pray. My journal reveals that I saw these flaws, but rather than admit that objective piece of information, I pled with God to make him into the man he could be, for God, of course, and then for me.

I became career counselor, coach, job placement officer, resume typist—whatever was needed for his success, I had to offer. You name it, I was there to serve all in the name of love. If only I could polish this guy up, he'd be right for me. I could do it—with God's help of course. Mark, of course, eventually felt constricted by this able do-gooder at his side, telling him how to run his life, and left.

Then I became attracted to Michael, a nice-looking, well-educated, funny man. We had a wonderful time together. For awhile. Then he began to make excuses for not being with me—he had to work late, his car broke down, he had to go out of town on business. Then I ran into him at the movies with his other woman. We stared at each other in amazement. Each of us thought we were his special girl. Did this stop me from caring? No, I only desired him more since the rejection was so obvious.

Friends pointed out Michael's proclivity for juggling several relationships at once. I defended him. He was okay; it was my fault. As I recorded in my journal, "I am such a clinging person, wanting so badly to be married, that I try to make a relationship work. I'm driving Michael away to another relationship."

6. A Search for Perfection

This Cinderella was waiting for her prince to make up for her past. The man who could fit the glass slipper and win my heart became larger than life. The longer I waited for this man, the more amazing he got. This man would make up for all the hurt in the past. He would be a marriage partner who surpassed all others. He would love me for who I was and accept me. He would, in essence, be perfect at all times.

Unfortunately, when I found a potential Prince Charming, a knight in shining armor who would save me from all those awful dragons of my past, I measured this man against my glorious ideal. Of course, no man could ever measure up. I ended up passing over many wonderful men who did not seem appropriate.

How did I evaluate these relationships? By evaluating their character or the level of intimacy we had achieved in our communication? All these things might be positive, but the death knell for these poor men was that I didn't FEEL anything for them. Sure they were great guys, but I just wasn't in love. I might try to really like them but it didn't feel right. It didn't feel like I expected. Bells, music, fireworks—shouldn't these be present? Instead, there was nothing to signal that this was my prince. No, these were just ordinary guys. Ordinary, yes, but extraordinary in their ability to relate normally. Yet I passed over them, dismissed them out of hand, usually after only a few months of dating. Why?

I had built up my fantasy life so strongly that this normal relationship seemed to be a letdown. It was simply too normal for me to recognize it as anything but commonplace, certainly not something the char-covered Cinderella should receive as a payback for her good faith and long years of waiting. So I continued waiting.

LOVE IS A CHOICE

I did not begin to learn of love and truly know its characteristics until I understood that at the root of love is choice. I could not choose to love Jimmy, Rick, Alan, Rob, Mark, Michael, or any of the others until I understood I had the power to choose. And I could not choose a "nice guy" as long as I was waiting for my fairy-tale dreams.

I was well aware of the problem. In my senior year in college, on December 3, 1974, I wrote, "Lord, I don't know if I could ever discern the right guy at the right time. I know this—that I desire marriage and yet I fear two things: marrying second best or marrying at the wrong time. God please protect me from those two pitfalls, for I want Your best at Your best time. Lord, I know I can't ever really have my childhood and teenage years over in a love-filled, Christ-centered environment, but I hope my marriage will be so. I know, Lord, enough about myself to fear my choice. I want Your choice for me."

Little did I understand that to have God's choice, I would need to learn to choose for myself. I could choose a man who would replicate the pattern of death in which I had grown up, or I could choose a man who would bring life and wholeness to the relationship. I needed to learn to choose. It would take much work and many counseling sessions to break through the reasons for my bondage to love and to learn to choose to love a man. We will look at that process in part three: Laying Down Your Weapons.

God was not going to let me off the hook in my responsibility to mature in my choices, to take responsibility for the outcome of those choices, and to choose wisely. This area of relationships with men was my area of greatest weakness and thus greatest temptation. As Dag Hammarskjöld so wisely stated, "To say Yes to life is at one and the same time to say Yes to oneself. Yes—even to that element in one which is most unwilling to let itself be transformed from a temptation into a strength."[3]

PART THREE

The Surrender: Laying Down Your Weapons

Chapter 9

Risking Change: Discovering Our Dark Side

We shall not cease from exploration
And the end of all our exploring
Will be to arrive where we started
And know the place for the first time.[1]

> T. S. Eliot
> "Little Gidding" from the *Four Quartets*

I had almost finished teaching my fourth-period, eleventh-grade American history class when the door burst open and John strode in. A short man with jet black hair and glasses, he stood directly in front of me with his hands on his hips and exploded, "Just who do you think you are? In all my years of teaching I have never seen anything like this. Trying to take over my job, aren't you?" The students' eyes widened, and they leaned forward sensing that a battle was about to ensue. This teacher was known for his outbursts, and I had carefully avoided him during my tenure at this school.

I stood frozen. Mortified, I asked quietly, "John, do you think we could take this up after class?"

John continued on, pacing back and forth in front of my

students, gesturing wildly. His voice rose steadily with each sentence until he was yelling. "I'm the one the administration put in charge of this project, not you! You're undermining my authority, and I want it to stop right now, do you hear me?!"

I still didn't know what he was talking about. I tried once more to get him to stop. "John, could we take this up later?" I asked meekly.

Still he continued his tirade.

I stood frozen, unable to look him in the eye. I hated my reaction. Why did I just stand there and take his abuse? Why didn't I cry out, "Stop it!"? I saw a tear fall on my shoe. I blinked hard, fighting back the tears, but they began to pour down my face. I ran out of the room, embarrassed, defeated, and enraged.

That night I had a dream. I was swimming in a pool, when a man came up and placed an evil eel-like creature with a dragon's head and sharp teeth in the water. It began chasing me, and I swam furiously to the end of the pool trying to escape it. As I got to the end of the pool, a hand reached down to help me out, but when my fingers grabbed for the extended hand, the person drew back his hand and laughed. I woke up in a cold sweat, with my heart pounding.

I recounted the encounter in my classroom and the night's dream in my counseling session the next afternoon. As I shared how this reminded me of interactions with my father, I tried to analyze the situation. After all, John's behavior was John's problem, wasn't it? And I know I overreact to things like this because of my memories with my father. I know it was the little girl who stood there so frozen, unable to confront this inappropriate behavior of a fellow teacher.

But suddenly I hated this little girl because she would not cry out, "Stop it!" as John bellowed on and on. I blurted out to my counselor, "What's wrong with me, Bob, that I can't defend myself? I hate that part of me. Why do I just take it? I did that with my father too."

"Nancy," Bob suggested, "let's take a look at that dream you had last night. That's a very important dream, you know. How would you interpret it? What do you think the eel was?"

"I don't know," I replied. "I do remember the absolute terror I had when I saw it. I had to get away from it as fast as I could. I felt so hopeless when the one person who could help me out of the pool wouldn't."

"In dream interpretation, Nancy," Bob explained, "usually the people, animals, or objects that are in your dream refer to some aspect of yourself. They may represent parts of your personality."

"Oh, yes, I read about dreams in college and how they can provide insight about yourself. The eel must be a symbol—probably something I'm very frightened of since the eel was so ugly and terrifying."

"Nancy, that eel is you." Bob paused to let his words sink in.

I looked at him horrified. "Me?" I responded weakly.

"Yes, I know that doesn't fit into your expectations of yourself, but that eel is the part of you that is dark, ugly, fearful. My guess is it represents a number of deep emotions that you have buried and denied for years. Anger, rage, hatred, perhaps, even murder. These things are part of you too."

I shook my head in disbelief. *How could they be?* I wondered. After all, I spent most of my life being so good. Yet I was surprised by the intensity of the emotions that overwhelmed me when John had taken out his anger on me.

"Nancy, I believe that God is bringing you face-to-face with all that you are and all those things in you that frighten you. You will have to learn to accept the parts of you that are ugly, that don't fit into your expectations of who you are. Only when you can accept the good and the ugly can you begin to love yourself."

I pondered what Bob said for a moment. "I suppose that I swam so frantically to get out of the pool because I wanted to escape those ugly parts of me. Are you saying that for me to move on, to be healed, I will have to discover who I really am—stay in the pool—and meet myself head-on?"

"Absolutely. Emotions are powerful, Nancy. As God begins to bring these deep, hidden feelings to the surface, the intensity may surprise you. Remember that they have been buried for so long that when they emerge they may seem larger than life. Don't panic. Know that it is time to deal with them."

NECESSARY CHANGE, TERRIFYING CHANGE

I knew Bob was right. I knew that to change my self-destructive patterns I would have to acknowledge the dark side of myself. But it was terrifying. I had just tipped the lid of this Pandora's box and was surprised at the intense rage that had flown out. What else would be uncovered?

Therapy frightened me because it was an active step away from what I had been and the things that had bound me. My sickness was at least predictable; my sufferings, dependable. I knew me. Or at least I thought I did. I had spent so much of my life projecting an image of an accomplished, responsible, strong person. What would happen if I found out that wasn't who I was at all? Would I like this real me? Could I accept her? Would anyone else like her?

Searchlight on Our Secret Shame

Sandra Wilson, Ph.D., in her marvelous book *Counseling Adult Children of Alcoholics*, asserts that "discovery precedes recovery."[2] Change requires uncovering all the secrets, the denial, and the delusions that have sustained us for years. It means bringing our secrets out of the darkness to be exposed and transformed by the light. We each have written a family script similar to the litany that tumbled out of me in my first counseling session. It tells the world who we are. Often it involves asserting a passive victim role, which enables us to avoid taking responsibility for ourselves and our own sin, our own dark side.

It is part of our sin nature to cover up, to rationalize, and to minimize our shortcomings. Add into this a denial system that has been operational for years, and we tend to see ourselves as pretty good. We have been the Heroes for so long that we begin to believe the part. We then accept only those parts of ourselves that fit into that image and deny those parts of us which detract from that image. We make daily choices that preserve our roles. But the family role, which we take such great pains to perpetuate, is a mere shadow of the person we are. God knows it, and He looks past the roles we project to what is in our hearts. First Samuel 16:7 explains that "the Lord does not see as man sees; for man looks at the outward appearance, but the Lord looks at the heart."

Self-discovery is foundational for recovery. If we want to get well, we must first acknowledge we are sick. It takes courage to look at ourselves with exacting honesty, to call the curtain down on the family drama, and ruthlessly examine who we are now. My journey to expose my buried emotions involved five essential steps.

GOD'S PLAN FOR BURIED EMOTIONS

1. Examine Your Heart

The biblical understanding of people focuses on their heart. The heart is the center of our volitional will, the seat of our emotions, and the place of our spiritual response to God. To know ourselves and to begin our journey of recovery, we must get to know our heart. Proverbs 4:23 cautions us to guard our heart because out of it springs forth our very life. If we want to get at the root causes of the way we live, we must look within and be prepared to face all that is there—the good and the evil. God is a necessary journey-mate in this process.

2. Ask for God's Help

We need courage to be honest before ourselves and God. Sin and shame cause us to hide from the truth about ourselves. Fortunately, God loves us too much to let us wallow in our misery. If we are willing to begin this journey of facing our dark emotions, He will empower us toward recovery.

Scripture calls for an honest assessment of ourselves. King David prayed,

Search me, O God, and know my heart;
Try me and know my anxious thoughts;
And see if there be any hurtful way in me,
And lead me in the everlasting way (Ps. 139:23–24, NAS).

We can ask God to help us take this step of a searching and fearless inventory of our hearts. He can reveal the self-destructive patterns. He also can lead us out of those hurtful ways into the path that leads to life.

3. Identify the Emotions

When I began to look within, I discovered that my heart contained many dark emotions: rage, anger, loneliness, despair, terror, disappointment, abandonment, even murder. What I discovered in counseling was that God would use present circumstances and present pain to lead me to my past. I would experience something and know intuitively that my response was out of proportion to the event. It would seem that deeper feelings, more volatile than I would have expected, had attached themselves to the present event. That was a signal, a gentle nudge from the Lord, to look for a buried memory, a wounded feeling, long submerged and now ready for healing. Perhaps the most difficult emotions to get in touch with were the deep-rooted feelings I had of abandonment and anger toward my mother.

Many times in counseling, Bob asked me about me feelings concerning my mother and I would get angry. "Why is he mentioning Mom?" I asked myself. "It's Dad that is the problem." After a number of months of getting nowhere, Bob asked me why it was so hard for me to see my mom as having done anything wrong. I had no answer. I had written my family script where Dad was the mean and evil one; Mom, the kind and caring one. It frustrated me when things happened that didn't fit into that script. In a counseling session in 1979, I related a conversation I had with my father in which he was warm and honest, and I was hostile and angry. As I exploded about the way he had treated Mom, he had replied that he was under a lot of pressure to make money. I sniped back, "Oh, so you're blaming it on Mom?"

Dad replied, "Nancy, basically I am a lazy person. I didn't want to work. I wasn't ready for the responsibility of a family." As I continued on complaining about his abuse of Mom, he gently suggested, "Nancy, it takes two to make a marriage. I'm not going to demean your mother. I'm not going to put all the blame on her, but I'm not going to take all the blame myself either."

I was furious inside. Why was I so angry at him for acting "normal" in this conversation? Why did I want him to stay the mean and evil one? Was it to protect my image of my mom as the good and loving one? For some reason, I was afraid to ascribe any guilt to her at all for my home life. No matter how much we tried to get at this in counseling, I could not allow myself to uncover any emotions about my mom other than love and admiration.

Yet God was gentle. Three months later, He allowed a situation with a cat to bring up all the buried feelings I had about my mom. I came back to my dorm apartment from teaching a class and found our cat, Roo, an orange tabby named after a character in *Winnie-the-Pooh*, standing on three legs, wailing. I liked Roo, but Dale, my roommate, loved her. We both recognized that the wound was likely the result of some teenage abuse. On the way to the vet's, we decided to call a dorm meeting that night to encourage the kids to be nice to the dorm pets.

After dinner, however, Dale changed her mind. She laughed about dorm life and the nature of kids and said, "Well, what difference would a dorm meeting make anyway? That's just the way kids are."

An intense swell of rage rose up in me. The anger was fiercer than any I had ever felt before. I was angry at Dale for being so passive when she was the one who loved Roo best. I stormed out of our apartment for dorm duty. When Dale didn't even show up for the 9:00 dorm meeting, I became furious inside. Later, when she commented on poor Roo having to stay at the vet's, I screamed inside, "You have no right to be so concerned and caring..."

I knew that all this rage was indicative of some deep hurt, and I felt intuitively that it had to do with my family. I went to bed without saying anything to Dale. I had been in counseling long enough to know that there was much more here than being upset about a cat. I tried to understand my anger, but I could only surmise that somehow it was connected to Mom and Dad. As I went to sleep, I prayed that the Lord would use the next day's counseling session to unravel all of this.

And He did. "I just know it has something to do with my family," I explained to Bob at my next counseling session, "but I can't figure out what it is."

"Nancy, is there anything you are angry at your mother about?" Bob asked.

"No, of course not," I quickly replied.

Bob allowed a period of quiet for a few minutes as he prayed silently.

I shifted my position, suddenly uncomfortable.

"Nancy, think of the cat as yourself. Did you ever have a sense that your mom didn't protect you?"

I felt a sharp, stabbing pain in my heart. Then the sobs began to surface. "Well, she never protected us from Dad. She'd wake us up in the middle of the night and whisk us away to motels, but she never left him." There was silence in the room for a number of minutes while the full power of this emotion made itself known. Then deep within, excruciating pain seared my heart. I looked up in agony at Bob as I began to sob uncontrollably. Suddenly, I screamed out, "But she left me!!!"

The accusation hung heavy in the air for a long time as I continued to cry. Finally, I looked at Bob and said weakly, "All this anger at my mom surprises me."

"Nancy, whenever anyone dies and leaves us, it creates some anger in us, but it is especially powerful if they willfully leave us," Bob explained. "I think one of the reasons you have had to struggle so to get in touch with this anger is that you desperately needed to cling to your mother's love. Whatever it was, it was all you had. You probably redirected some of your anger toward your mother to your father because he was the 'bad' one. He deserved your anger and you knew deep down you had nothing to lose. Your father didn't love you anyway. But with your mother, you couldn't afford to lose her love."

Calmer now, I continued, "Bob, I wonder if that is part of the reason behind all of my achievements. My life seemed to parallel my mom's so much. I always thought I was trying to earn my father's love and attention. But perhaps I knew that was a lost cause. Perhaps I sought to preserve Mom's love for me."

We prayed for the release of this anger and the deep sense of abandonment I felt. On the way home from the counseling session, I grieved over the loss of my perfect mom. I felt so alone.

As we get in touch with our anger and loneliness, we

may find that feelings of abandonment emerge as well. When we were children, we may have been physically or emotionally abandoned. Parents so caught up in their own problems may have been unable to be there for us. Or, as in my case, we may have lost our parents to divorce or death. When we get in touch with these deep feelings of abandonment, they may frighten us because of the great sense of loneliness and despair that accompany them. We want so to belong and to be important enough to someone that they will commit themselves to us and not leave us.

As Christians, we know that Jesus said He will never leave us or forsake us, but we may doubt that reality in our own lives. We may have even read the assurance of David in Psalm 27 that "when my father and my mother forsake me, then the Lord will take care of me" (v. 10). It may take stripping away all of the things that have made us who we are—our rage, our hatred, our terrible fears of abandonment and loneliness—to discover that when there truly is nothing else, God is still there. This was a slow and painful process for me, made even harder because of my distortions about God's character. Yet this process would bring about the tilling of brittle soil in preparation for the planting of the truth about myself and about my God.

4. Validate the Emotions

We didn't have the natural safety of a healthy family where we could fly off the handle and then be helped to understand whether our response was appropriate in those circumstances. In the safety of a counseling relationship or with a trusted friend or pastor who has an understanding of emotions, we may need to sketch out the event and share how we felt and the intensity of the emotion. We can examine these new, untapped feelings and learn how to respond to them appropriately.

This may be difficult at first, since we don't often have a repertoire of emotion-language from which to draw. When

I was growing up, I could identify two emotions. I was either sad or okay. Yet there is a vast range of emotions, and we need to learn how to identify them when they arise. God made us emotional, feeling beings. He has acknowledged the presence of many emotions in His Word and especially in the book of Psalms. When I was first learning about my emotions, I found it helpful to let the Psalms express how I was feeling. I knew from Scripture that David was a "man after God's own heart" (Acts 13:22), and yet he seemed to experience a vast continuum of emotions and even express them to God in no uncertain terms without fear of losing God's favor. Perhaps I, too, could learn to express my feelings. Walk through some of these passages with me and check the ones that express your own emotions:

> I am troubled, I am bowed down greatly;
> I go mourning all the day long. . . .
> I am feeble and severely broken;
> I groan because of the turmoil of my heart.
> Lord, all my desire is before You;
> And my sighing is not hidden from You.
> My heart pants, my strength fails me;
> As for the light of my eyes, it also has gone from me. (Ps. 38:6, 8–10)

> But I will sing of Your power;
> Yes, I will sing aloud of Your mercy in the morning;
> For You have been my defense. (Ps. 59:16)

> Save me, O God!
> For the waters have come up to my neck.
> I sink in deep mire,
> Where there is no standing;
> I have come into deep waters,
> Where the floods overflow me.
> I am weary with my crying;
> My throat is dry;
> My eyes fail while I wait for my God. (Ps. 69:1–3)

Reproach has broken my heart,
And I am full of heaviness;
I looked for someone to take pity, but there was none;
And for comforters, but I found none. (Ps. 69:20)

For I am poor and needy,
And my heart is wounded within me.
I am gone like a shadow when it lengthens;
I am shaken off like a locust. (Ps. 109:22–23)

Do I not hate them, O Lord, who hate You?
And do I not loathe those who rise up against You?
I hate them with perfect hatred;
I count them my enemies. (Ps. 139:21–22)

Have mercy on me, O Lord, for I am weak;
O Lord, heal me, for my bones are troubled.
My soul also is greatly troubled;
But You, O Lord—how long? . . .
I am weary with my groaning;
All night I make my bed swim;
I drench my couch with my tears.
My eye wastes away because of grief;
It grows old because of all my enemies. (Ps. 6:2–3, 6–7)

I have set the Lord always before me;
Because He is at my right hand I shall not be moved.
Therefore my heart is glad, and my glory rejoices;
My flesh also will rest in hope. (Ps. 16:8–9)

You have turned for me my mourning into dancing;
You have put off my sackcloth and clothed me with glad-
  ness. (Ps. 30:11)

Have mercy on me, O Lord, for I am in trouble;
My eye wastes away with grief,
Yes, my soul and my body!
For my life is spent with grief,
And my years with sighing. (Ps. 31:9–10a)

5. Expose the Dark Emotions to the Light

The Light of Accountability

As children, we didn't learn to accept and identify our emotions or to express them appropriately. We learned to stuff our feelings. Don't talk, don't trust, don't feel were the three unspoken rules of our homes. If we are going to recover, however, we must invalidate these rules. We must now talk, trust, and feel. If there is a safe place to begin to talk about who we are as a result of what we experienced as children, such as counseling or within a confidential Twelve-Step Program, then we can develop the security we need to begin to trust and, yes, even to begin to feel. In the safety of these relationships, we find that feelings once repressed to avoid pain can rise to the surface to be healed.

Depending on the extent of the damage of our emotions, we may find that the intensity of these newly emerging emotions is too powerful to face alone. Admitting we need professional help, however, may be difficult. Sometimes, because our family role may have required independence, we might resist the need for outside help. We are notorious for getting the job done on our own. J. Patrick Gannon, in his book *Soul Survivors: A New Beginning for Adults Abused as Children*, notes that changing on your own, however, may be just another form of denial and that resistance to getting help may be simply a resistance to change.[3]

Fortunately, in the last decade it has become more acceptable for Christians to get psychological help. There are still those, however, who look askance at anyone who needs counseling. After all, aren't the Bible and prayer there to give guidance and point the way to salvation? Although this is true, it is important to remember that when we have been damaged in childhood, our confused images of God will often color how we interpret Scripture and who God says He is.

Christians may need to seek a *Christian* counselor or trained pastor for help. Secular psychologists may emphasize the need to reclaim one's past, but they often assert that uncovering the lost memories—reexperiencing the emotions of those memories—will in and of itself provide relief. A Christian counselor, however, understands that the discovery of our repressed emotions is not in itself sufficient. Neither is the most determined commitment on the part of the counselee to change. Although both these aspects are important components of a therapeutic relationship, the work of healing cannot be accomplished apart from the Cross. To think we can heal ourselves through reexperiencing these emotions alone is false. We reexperience the emotion to bring the sin pattern it created to the surface and to show us our need for the memory to be redeemed and transformed, not just relived. We must let Jesus accomplish His work in our lives by inviting Him into the dark emotion and asking Him to transform it through His resurrection power.

The Light of the Resurrection: Acknowledging Our Need

This is an imperfect world. We lived with imperfect parents. This is part of the legacy of a sinful world. John Bradshaw claims that 96 percent of all families are dysfunctional. To the extent that this 96 percent (I propose 100 percent) of all families suffer from the sin condition, I agree. Sometimes specific sins, as we know from Scripture, are handed down from generation to generation. We can trace our personal genealogies to determine what self-destructive patterns we may have inherited.

We must acknowledge this sin condition, but sometimes acknowledging this dark side of our hearts is difficult for us. We were the ones who always had to rise above the mess in our families and achieve great and mighty things. We were the little messiahs. We began to take on a belief system that makes it difficult for us to acknowledge our weaknesses or admit that we are really the ones in need of a messiah.

We also find it difficult to acknowledge our own responsibility for who we are today. We say we are victims. We say we were born into a family that sinned against us and caused us great damage. It is true that we developed self-destructive patterns as a result of our home life, but as adults we have a choice to continue to operate out of those patterns or to be transformed. We cannot know healing, however, as long as we shift the blame onto our parents and continue to deny our responsibility for perpetuating these self-destructive patterns. We must admit our need: that we are powerless over our own self-destructive patterns, which is the first step of the Twelve-Step recovery program of Alcoholics Anonymous.

Accepting the Solution

Why is a doctrine of the Cross important to our understanding of the healing of damaged emotions? Why can't we just get in touch with the emotion, use it to provide insight into our behavior, and then change our behavior accordingly? Why do we need Jesus to die for the dark side of our hearts?

Paul wrestled with this problem in the book of Romans when he spoke of being in bondage to sin:

> For I am not practicing what I would like to do, but I am doing the very thing I hate...For I know that nothing good dwells in me, that is, in my flesh; for the wishing is present in me, but the doing of the good is not. For the good that I wish, I do not do; but I practice the very evil that I do not wish (Rom. 7:15, 18–19, NAS).

Paul understood that this war between the desire to live rightly and the inability to carry it out was waged inside of him. We have also experienced this dilemma as we have recognized our own self-destructive tendencies and our feeble attempts to overcome them. We, too, could cry out with Paul, "O wretched man that I am! Who will set me free?" (Rom. 7:24, NAS). When our self-destructive patterns wage war with our desire for life, there is only one solution. Jesus Christ.

This dark side of our hearts must be exposed to the light of God's Word and the healing power of His forgiveness through Jesus Christ. The resurrection power of the Cross is critical for recovery. Otherwise, we would try to analyze our emotions, compensate for them, or overcome them, perhaps. Yet we would not be able to escape the tyranny of their control. We do not have the power within ourselves to transform this darkness into light but Jesus does. He took with Him to the Cross all sin and its damaging effects. His resurrection is the hope of our redemption—not only for eternal life but for freedom in this life as well. For those of us stuck in self-destructive patterns, that is good news.

When I realized that I was angry at my mother for abandoning me, I had to face a whole range of emotions that had been buried for years: bitterness, rage, disappointment, and terror. Most surprising, however, was the bitterness. I resented her thinking only of her own escape from my father and not seeking to release us from his tyranny as well. Completely unaware of my anger, I had nursed this bitterness for over a decade since her death. My counselor helped me realize that this deep-rooted bitterness was sin and I had to deal with it the same way I would any other offense against God. I had to ask God's forgiveness, forgive my mother, and with my will, invite Jesus to transform this newly exposed anger and bitterness by His resurrection power. The emotions didn't disappear immediately, but the power of the anger to poison my heart did.

Working It Out

For Christians who thought that once we asked Jesus into our lives the past would be wiped clean, it is surprising and sometimes quite defeating to discover we are still locked into these self-destructive old patterns. Once we accept what Jesus did for us on the Cross and we learn to invite His resurrection work into each dark emotion we uncover, we are well on the way to recovery. However, we also have to work out that which has been placed within us. Paul told us to "work out your own salvation with fear and trembling" (Phil. 2:12). How do we do this? First Corinthians 13 tells us that when we are children, we reason and act as children, but when we become adults, we should "put away childish things." The Greek word for the verb *to put away, katargeō* means: "to put away, to render inoperative, inactive, or powerless; to remove the meaning and significance from; to cause a person to be free from something that has been binding him."[4] This requires our active involvement and our conscious decision making to *katargeō* our self-destructive patterns that lead to death and choose responses that lead to life instead. These next few chapters explain some of the ways we can *katargeō* our childish ways.

Although the penalty for sin is paid for us by Jesus once and for all, our awareness of our self-destructive patterns and our discovery of our root issues is not just a one-time thing. These patterns have been part of us for many years, and they may not die easily. We may have to experience years of choosing to respond differently to our emotional tugs before the new patterns feel right and happen spontaneously. That's okay. Recovery is a process. Yes, and even more importantly, sanctification is a process. It takes time and we must be patient with ourselves.

It was years into counseling before I could listen to my father's tirades without either flying off the handle myself or being filled with rage as I silently "took it." It took practice, facing my father over and over again, messing up, talking with my counselor about how I responded, and role-playing how I would handle things the next time. The more I uncovered the darker side of my heart, however, and brought these painful and buried emotions to the foot of the Cross for healing and restoration, the more able I was to set proper boundaries in my relationship with my father and to evaluate what was happening in any interchange from an objective point of view.

When these self-destructive patterns reemerge from time to time, it is easy to get down on ourselves. We are so hard on ourselves anyway that when we see evidence of emotional struggles we thought had been conquered, we can despair. But, remember, God said He did not send Jesus into the world to condemn us but rather, to save us (John 3:17). It is very important, then, during this time of self-discovery that we not condemn ourselves either. God does calls this dark side what it is. Rage is rage; murderous thoughts are murder. But He has provided a way out for us. In fact, Jesus was sent to "those who sit in darkness and the shadow of death, to guide our feet into the way of peace" (Luke 1:79). God yearns for us to know His peace and to live in light, not darkness.

God wants to be a partner with us in this spiritual journey. He gave us the Holy Spirit to help us know how to pray about these things and to help our infirmities (Rom. 8:26–27). He is also active in our current circumstances to enable us to face things that otherwise would remain buried for years. Our damaged emotions and the patterns we have developed as a result are neither a mystery to God nor impervious to His power to uproot and transform.

Healing and peace await us in the light. Even more encouraging, so does an inheritance (Acts 26:18). God has a special plan to redeem the years the locusts have eaten in each of our lives.

TRUST AND OBEY: STEP INTO THE RIVER

Since I was twenty years old, I clung to a promise from Jeremiah 29:11, "'For I know the plans that I have for you,' declares the Lord, 'plans for welfare and not for calamity to give you a future and a hope'" (NAS). I felt as if my life had been one big calamity after another. Yet even though I was a Christian, I was skeptical. I had been distrustful of God's purposes and His intentions toward me for so long. Now in counseling, He seemed to be asking the unbearable: to get in touch with this teeming flood of emotions that had begun to surface. How could this lead to a "future and a hope"?

During this time, I remembered a promise God had made to the Israelites to bring them into the Promised Land. God told the Israelites to break camp, let the priests go first to stand in the river, and then the rest could cross the river. This plan seemed absurd. The Jordan River at this time of year was at the flood stage. Imagine the Israelites standing at the edge of the river. They looked out at the swirling, churning waters that kept them from reaching that place of promise. Then, just because God said so, the priests stepped into this mess. God held the waters back and enabled the entire nation to cross. The Jordan River, once a symbol of separation from all God meant for them, became a symbol of God's ability to move them from one point to another in fulfillment of His plan for them.

I thought about these brave folks and saw some principles for my own situation:

- The only way to the promised land was through the churning water, despite those awesome and fearful waters.
- It wasn't until the Israelites stepped into the river at God's request that God intervened to manage the turbulence.
- God didn't wait until they were standing in the river, neck-deep in the fierce flood, to control the waters. He was there ready to help as soon as their feet touched the water's edge.

We face our own Jordan Rivers. If we are willing to take the steps, yes, even come to the flooded waters of our past, we can trust God to control their awesome power. We may stand at the river's edge, frightened of taking that first step into those waters, but God can turn this churning flood within us into a pathway to a land flowing with milk and honey.

TRUST GOD'S TIMING

Especially with powerful emotions like hate, rage, and terror, we must trust the Lord in His timing for dealing with these feelings. Their initial appearance may frighten us. Years and years of events are attached to these feelings. We must allow Jesus to touch them in His time. I once asked Bob why God couldn't speed up my healing. After all, I was willing to have all this dark stuff out of me.

Bob explained, "Nancy, you're full of hate. You're angry at life, at your mother, your father, and God. You know you're not supposed to be angry or to hate, so you condemn yourself. Then you tell yourself you're not capable of being loved because there's so much hate inside, and you begin to seek out confirmations of that."

"Well, then, why doesn't God just come and take it all out?" I asked. "I want all this dark stuff out of me."

"Because if He worked any faster than He is now, you couldn't take it," Bob explained. "Over the years, Nancy, you so integrated hate and the condemnation that goes with it into who you are that if God were to come in and rip out all that hate, it would be like ripping off your leg. He has to chip away at it, a little at a time, and replace it with His love. Think of your life as a scaffold. The hate, rage, and condemnation are the scaffolding that holds up your life. If God were to take down the entire scaffold at once, the building would collapse. You think you feel shaky now. It's because God is very much at work, but if He were to do it all instantaneously, you couldn't bear it. He removes one prop in your scaffolding and replaces it with His love and then moves on to the next part of the scaffold."

"But it hurts so much, Bob," I said. "It is so painful. I don't think I can stand it."

"Yes, you can. It's God's timing. He has chosen this journey for you. Nancy, I know it is a lot of work, but it is a work for generations, and one day you will look back and give thanks."

Chapter 10

Laying Down the Cross: Quitting the Messiah Role

For we ourselves were also once foolish, disobedient, deceived, serving various lusts and pleasures, living in malice and envy, hateful and hating one another. But when the kindness and the love of God our Savior toward man appeared, not by works of righteousness which we have done, but according to His mercy He saved us.

Titus 3:3–5a

For so long we have spent much energy and creativity in attempting to control our families' destinies. To be told we must stop carrying this enormous burden for our families does not relieve us as one might suspect. Rather, we are terrified. Our personalities and identities are defined by our messiah role. We don't even know how to stop controlling others because we have done it so subtly, so well, for so long.

Claudia Black urges that in learning to give up control, we give up "some control."[1] There is great wisdom in that. We can begin to take small, but measurable, steps to letting go of our role as savior for our families. Six practical steps helped me to diminish my role in my family's lives.

1. Break Out of Isolation

We grew up in a closed system. The family disease was never discussed, and we learned to keep the family secrets. We rarely had friends over. We felt alone and isolated. We have for years been the sole savior of our family. Now it is time to break out of this isolation and realize that we are not alone.

One of the best ways to do this is through the Twelve-Step programs. There are specific programs now, Adult Children of Alcoholics as well as Codependents Anonymous, that address the needs of adults who have grown up in dysfunctional homes. When Janet Woititz wrote her groundbreaking book, *Adult Children of Alcoholics* in 1983, support groups for this contingency were just beginning. Now, nearly a decade later, the recovery programs for adult children and others have proliferated with some fifteen million adults attending the meetings each week.[2] I am fortunate to be in the Washington, D.C., metropolitan area where there are over seventy ACOA meetings each week. Yet even in smaller communities, one can find Twelve-Step programs.

By participating in a Twelve-Step program, we can learn tools to deal with the effects of our families. We may find that this is the place where we learn to trust, to talk, and to feel again. In the safety of the confidentiality of such groups, we begin to let down our defenses. In the shared experiences of others, we learn we are not unique, and sometimes that fact alone can bring great hope. We hear in others' stories bits and pieces of our own, and it helps us to recall events, reexperience emotions, and admit we need help. We learn to share. We may even learn to laugh at ourselves.

Many churches now provide their own adult children Twelve-Step programs. In a recent article in *Christianity Today* on the church and recovery, Charles Sell notes that many adult children of alcoholics who are Christians feel that their problems should have been resolved when they became Christians. As Sell acknowledges, "By supporting the ACOA movement, church leaders can help correct this attitude and give permission to ACOAs to enter a recovery program. For this reason, pastor Charles Swindoll promotes his church's New Hope program in various ways, even appearing at the beginning of a staff-produced video to endorse the program."[3]

I attended an Adult Children of Alcoholics group sponsored by my church in 1985, which was specifically geared toward Christians, with an emphasis on education, prayer, and Scripture as key elements of our group experience. Recently, helpful books such as *The Twelve Steps for Christians* and its companion workbook, *The Twelve Steps—A Spiritual Journey*, have helped Christians to integrate their faith in their recovery experience. If not a Twelve-Step program, perhaps counseling, or some other form of accountability group or relationship will be necessary to assist us in shifting from being so intimately involved in the salvation of our families to taking care of ourselves and leaving our family's future up to God.

2. Pray Differently or Perhaps Not at All

Often my prayers were one-sided. Begging. Pleading. Beseeching. Earnestly seeking a response. Perhaps prayer was even used as a way to keep myself enmeshed in my family's lives. Since their well-being was so essential to my own, I had to feel like I was doing something to help.

One summer evening in 1974, the summer before my senior year in college, I learned my brother Sam had holed himself up in a motel room, threatening to kill himself. I immediately went to God in prayer. My journal confirms: "I know I pray in His will, for God says in Matthew 18:14 that it is never the will of the Father in heaven that a single one of these little ones be lost. God, bring Sam salvation.

Free him from Satan's clutches. Heal his mind. Lord, destroy all the bitterness and hatred that is killing Sam. Save him, Jesus, save my brother. I am so afraid he will shoot himself. I cannot believe that it is Your desire to have my family kill themselves one by one. Lord, please save my brother."

Sam did not die that night, but over the course of the next few years, his mind deteriorated as he spent months and months in various psychiatric facilities. My prayers continued: "Father, I ask again for salvation for Sam. He is heavily influenced by drugs, mental illness, and the occult. I am concerned that Satan has a strong grip on him, and I ask that You free him. I am fasting today for that purpose. You said in Your Word, 'Is this not the fast that I choose? To loose the bonds of wickedness and to set the captive free?' God, You have the power and the wisdom to answer these requests. I expect great things from my God."

But Sam only got worse.

The same was true with prayers for my father and my mother. Over and over I had prayed as a young girl, "God, please help Daddy. God, please protect my mama." As I matured and I became a Christian, my prayers became more fervent. "God, I just know You could change my dad. Help him want to get better. Don't let him yell at Mama so much and be so mean. Help us to know how to show him we love him and care for him. God, I just know You can help us."

But Daddy didn't change; in fact, as the years progressed, his attacks increased.

Especially after my mother's first suicide attempt, I turned to this all-powerful God in prayer: "Lord, Mama really needs Your help now. She is so lonely and confused. She needs to know You care. Show her in ways only You can that she is loved by You. Don't let her feel that hopeless ever again. Let her know You are her loving Father and that You can heal her and take care of her problems."

But she died anyway.

Deep down, I didn't believe God loved my brothers or my parents more than I did or that I could trust Him to care for them. My prayers were like deposits I was making in the bank of heaven. I figured that when enough collateral accumulated, I could secure action on the part of God.

The shadow of my mom, my father, and my brother lingered over my prayers and over my relationship with God for years and years. I summed up my confusion in my prayer journal this way: "Lord, I have never quite ached this much inside in a long time. I don't understand what is going on. I can't rejoice in my circumstances right now. I can't praise You like I'm supposed to. I don't even feel You're there or care about me and all my hurt. I am so confused. I have been constantly trusting You with this, believing You would help. But Lord, nothing's changed. In fact, it's worse. I feel like You are just laughing at me. That You like to see me hurt and confused and begging for help. Where is the truth to Your promise that those who wait on You will not be ashamed?"

I fell easy prey to comments from well-meaning Christian friends. "Nancy, if you would just pray more, I'm sure God would act." So pray I would. In fact, I had to make sure I prayed right, so I would devour books on prayer to learn how to pray more effectively. Others suggested that since my family situation was so dire, this might need prayer coupled with fasting to secure God's action. I tried one-day fasts once a week. Three-day fasts. Seven-day fasts. Even twenty-one day fasts—all in hopes of convincing God to act. Others suggested there must be a lack of faith on my part. Faith? I could drum up faith, couldn't I? If there was anything I knew, it was believing for the best despite impossible circumstances.

Yet, even in the midst of all this activity to win over the heart of God, I knew that I did not know God. "Father," I wrote in my prayer journal in my senior year, "if the point of prayer is to know You, then I have a problem. I've been so busy telling You what I desire because I don't know You well enough to believe You'll give me good things. I keep spending time in prayer asking over and over again because I don't really believe You care. I am afraid of You, God. I can't seem to grasp the fact that You long to be gracious. I want to know You and be able to trust You."

Prayer, fasting, faith all became tools to earn God's favor, to convince Him to act on my behalf. When nothing happened, I often redoubled my efforts. More prayer, more fasting, more belief. The blame had to be with me. After all, for God to be God, He must be good and loving. If there was a reason why He could not respond to my heart's cry, it must be because something was wrong with me.

I felt great responsibility for protecting God's reputation. As the Hero, I made sure my family looked good to all outsiders. Now I made sure God looked good. I assured myself, and my Christian friends, that God would meet my needs. If He didn't, then the blame must be mine.

There are times in our lives when we might find it wise to stop praying for our families or any other object of salvation. If we find that our prayers have become manipulative, instructive, and that we are extremely frustrated as the answers to the prayers we pray are not forthcoming, then it may be time to step back and not pray for a while. We can ask another person to pray for our fathers or mothers or siblings for a time while we step back and examine our relationship with God and deal with some of these control issues.

3. Relinquish Your Past to God

Many of us are making our present do double duty for our past, and we are very frustrated. Perhaps we are in a relationship now that seems disappointing. Is it because it isn't making up for our past the way we thought it would? Are we asking our spouses to love us now as spouses and as little children at the same time? Is their love having to do double duty for our parents? We despair because we feel empty and disappointed that our present relationship isn't enough to fill all the holes in our hearts. Our spouse or companion is frustrated and wants space from us because our demands are too great for even the most loving and well-meaning individual to provide.

It's time to relinquish our pasts to God. Grieve over them. Mourn their loss. But let them go. I wanted so much for my future hope and dream of being happily married and having a loving family to be reality. I wanted this husband and children to be all the things that I had never known. I wanted God to make up for my past—to balance out all of life's unfairness. By clinging to these incredible needs for my past to be redeemed, I sabotaged many relationships. No man could love me enough for now and for the past as well. Only God could heal those deep longings of my past and make me whole.

It was up to me to relinquish my past to Him and let Him work it out as He would. Giving up my control over my past was the key to giving up my control over my future. Yet even as I relinquished control of my past to God in prayer, I felt empty. My deep longing for a happy family had sustained me for so long. When I gave it to God, I did so out of obedience and not because I really expected that He could redeem those years. I had a lot to learn about this heavenly Father.

4. Affirm God's Role in Your Family

Very important in letting go of control is to affirm that God is the true Messiah. We can do this in two ways. First, we can stop acting like we are the messiah. We have to scrutinize any action we take to "help" our families. Perhaps we hear of a new program or a counselor in their area. We rush to the phone to tell them about it. Or perhaps we meet a dynamic person who lives in their town. "If only Joe could meet my father, I know my father would respond to him and get help." We begin to scheme and orchestrate. Now how could I get Joe to talk with my father?

Watch out when this happens. It is easy for us to rationalize sending another in our place to save our families.

Second, we can start affirming that Jesus is the only true Savior for our lives or the lives of our families. John the Baptist had a strong ministry to proclaim the coming of the Messiah, but he realized that when the Messiah, Jesus, did come, it would be time for his own ministry to fade away. "He must increase, but I must decrease" (John 3:30). The same thing must happen in our own lives. We must consciously affirm that God is the only one with the plan of salvation for our parent or any other person we desire to see helped.

5. Establish Boundaries

As part of this process, we need to learn to establish new boundaries in our family relationships. Before, it was confusing where we began and our parents ended. Our families came to expect us to be there for them. In an odd way, the abusive parent came to depend on our willingness to "just take it" when he dished out his blows—verbal or otherwise.

Now we must learn to establish boundaries and set limits on the behavior of others. "No, you can't do that to me." "No, that is not a proper way to talk to me." These are new concepts for us and can be very frightening. Sometimes we may need help in establishing these boundaries.

On May 30, 1975, a week before my college graduation, I wrote in my journal, "God, please, only You can do this. Please help Dad be glad, not mad, at my graduation. Oh Lord, I am scared because I feel so out of place with my family. Everyone else will be hugging and happy and glad to be with their families. I am so afraid my father will fight, make a scene, and ruin it somehow for me. I am afraid I will feel very, very lonely. Please, God, I need Your help."

My worst fears came to pass. My father came to the baccalaureate service that bright June morning of graduation day with a heavy scowl on his face. He was angry and I didn't know why. "Please, God, please don't let him make a scene. Not today!"

I introduced him to my friend's parents, Reverend and Mrs. Woodward, who had taken me into their home for many Christmases and holidays. He snapped at them and turned and walked off. I stood there horrified. I made a hurried apology and ran after him. We stood in the quadrangle and talked.

"Your mother was a demanding woman," he snapped. "I could never satisfy her. All she wanted was money. And for what? To send you kids to college so you could parade around in some cap and gown and think you know everything? Well, let me tell you something, young lady, you don't know nothing. I've had the school of hard knocks teach me a few things, but you're just full of book knowledge. You've got a lot to learn, and I can't wait to see you get your comeuppance."

I was in tears. The quadrangle was filled with activity as families walked back from the baccalaureate service. Suddenly, out of the corner of my eye, I spotted a professor, Mary Boney Sheats, coming toward us. "Oh, no," I thought. "Please, Dad, be nice to her." Dr. Sheats had known my mother and was coming to greet my father. He snarled at her in the same hangdog way. I was mortified. In absolute graciousness, she wished my father well and then pulled me aside. With her hands on my shoulders, she looked deeply into my eyes and said, "Nancy, this is your day. Do not let him ruin it for you. You have worked hard for this, and you deserve to enjoy it. Now tell him to go home, get himself together, and you'll expect him not to come back for the graduation service unless he can act responsibly."

I looked up at her in surprise. What she was telling me to tell my father seemed so authoritative and so presumptuous. Somehow, I did exactly what she said, perhaps because of the strength of the peace in her eyes. No one was more surprised than I when he reappeared at 5:00 P.M., as civil as anyone could be.

This was my first taste of setting boundaries. I needed more practice, however; and under the guidance of my counselor, I began to establish new boundaries for my relationship with my father.

My father often threatened suicide. When he did, I always came to his rescue either by physically being there or by verbally talking him through that period. Then one night after several years of counseling, he called again, abusive and threatening suicide unless I did something he wanted.

"Well, Dad, I love you," I responded, "but I am not going to allow you to blackmail me emotionally anymore. I will be glad to work on a relationship with you if you will get help either from AA or a counselor. But otherwise, don't call me and talk to me this way."

"If you don't move back to Atlanta, I'm going to kill myself!" he screamed into the phone.

"Dad," I said, "I am not coming to Atlanta. I can't make you want to live. It's not fair that you are trying to manipulate me."

"Well, you'll have to come to Atlanta anyway for the funeral," he retorted and hung up.

Two days later, he called back to apologize. As I recorded in my journal that night, "My father may always try to use words to blackmail me emotionally and manipulate me, but it is my responsibility to tell him when he is doing that and to tell him to stop."

6. Honor Your Parents

One of the Ten Commandments is that we are to honor our fathers and mothers. I struggled for years with how to live out this command. When my father called, drunk and abusive, should I try to help him, listen to him, and wait for a moment to interject some thoughts? Should I just let his tirade go on while I prayed? What if I told him that if he continued to talk in this manner, I would have to hang up on him? Was that honoring my father?

The command to honor father and mother appears two times in the Old Testament and six times in the New Testament. It is the only commandment with a promise: "that it may be well with you and you may live long on the earth" (Eph. 6:1–3).

The key to understanding how to honor our fathers and mothers is found in the verse preceding the command to honor them. In Deuteronomy 5:15, the commandment to honor a sabbath rest is given, where the Israelites were told to do no work, to rest, and to reflect on God's personal, redemptive actions on their behalf in the past.

There is a reason, I believe, that God gave us that commandment first before He told us to honor our parents. We often resort to two methods of dealing with our parents: we either try to do everything in our power to change them, or we don't want to have anything to do with them. However, this sabbath perspective helps us to set proper boundaries. If we recall that it was God's power that got us out of our enslavement, we are less likely to assert our role as savior in their lives. We are not their God. We are not even God's little helpers. We are fellow strugglers who have had the benefit of an awareness of our problem and the gift of mercy to accept God's solution. This same God has the power and the ability to set our parents free from their bondage. That should give us hope.

We should never forget what it was like in our own

"Egypts"—how we struggled, how demoralized we felt, how there was no rest. Proverbs 15:33 states that "before honor is humility." If we can remember our own enslavement, we may be more willing to have our hearts turned toward our parents. For those of us who have been abused by a parent, and perhaps are still abused even now in our middle adult years, this is difficult, but not impossible. In the last sentence of the Old Testament, a prophecy is given about the coming Messiah: He will "turn the hearts of the fathers to the children, and the hearts of the children to their fathers" (Mal. 4:6). We can ask the Lord to turn our hearts toward our fathers or mothers—something perhaps otherwise humanly impossible.

That said, how do we practically set biblical boundaries in dealing with our parents? Several suggestions are made in the Bible about honoring our parents.

Don't Speak Evil about Them

Twice in the New Testament the command to honor our parents is linked together with another law from the Old Testament: "He who speaks evil of father or mother, let him be put to death" (Matt. 15:4; Mark 7:10, NAS). How do we keep from speaking evil of our parents? For those of us in recovery, one way is to take responsibility for our own self-destructive patterns. We don't need to indulge in blaming. Yes, horrible injustices were done to us as small and defenseless children, but when we continue to recite our litany of woes to anyone who will listen, we dishonor our parents.

Peter, one of Jesus' disciples, helps explain what it means to forgo speaking evil of our parents: "To sum up, let all be harmonious, sympathetic, brotherly, kindhearted, and humble in spirit; not returning evil for evil, or insult for insult, but giving a blessing instead" (1 Pet. 3:8–9, NAS). The King James version states we are not to return "railing for railing." How often has our parent been able to hit just the right buttons to stir up our anger? Yet now we are not to return that anger. In fact, as we grow, we may learn to give a blessing instead. Again, we must not be too hard on ourselves in getting to this place; it is a growth process. Peter reminds us of this in an earlier portion of his letter when he tells us to lay aside all malice and "evil speaking" and to desire, like newborn babes, the pure milk of the Word to grow in our salvation (2:1–2). It may take time and practice, but we can learn not to speak evil of our father or mother.

Live Wisely

Proverbs 10:1 tells us that "a wise son makes a glad father, / But a foolish son is the grief of his mother." Proverbs 17:21 states that "the father of a fool has no joy." In contrast, "The father of the righteous will greatly rejoice, / And he who begets a wise child will delight in him" (23:24). The verse before that tells us to seek truth, wisdom, instruction, and understanding. Whether or not our parents act glad or joyful, we honor our parents when we begin the process of recovery and live in truth, not denial. We also honor our parents when we determine to learn how our family backgrounds have affected our lives today. When we respond to our parents' continued abuse, not on the basis of survival techniques, but identifying our self-destructive patterns and transforming them, we live wisely and honor them.

Avoid Strife

Proverbs 20:3 states that "Keeping away from strife is an honor for a man" (NAS). Practically speaking, this may mean that it is appropriate to say no to abuse. The dictionary defines strife as "violent dissension; bitter conflict." There were times when I could tell that a telephone conversation with my father was rising to the level of a violent dissension. At those times, I would tell him quietly but firmly, "Dad, I want to talk to you, but I won't be able to if you continue in this manner. If you cannot calm down, lower your voice, and refrain from verbal attacks, I will have to hang up on you." Many times I had to do just that.

It was very, very difficult. I felt as though I was dishonoring him by hanging up on him in the middle of a sentence. Yet I couldn't go by my feelings. I knew that I had to set limits for proper behavior that would honor our relationship. Some counselors suggest establishing written family contracts that outline specifically what behaviors are to be expected in the relationship. Clarifying proper actions up front can be helpful for the dysfunctional parent as well. Sometimes they are not aware of the inappropriateness of particular behaviors. Also, they need to discover that there are reasonable consequences to wrong behaviors to help them learn to face their own problems. Otherwise, we keep enabling them and providing more opportunities for strife.

Share Your Message

The Twelfth Step of the Twelve Steps of AA is "having had a spiritual awakening as the result of these Steps, we tried to carry this message to others, and to practice these principles in all our affairs." When we have experienced the realization that our self-destructive patterns lead to death and have learned to make choices that lead us to life instead, we have something to share. Perhaps the hardest person to carry this message to is the one who has most offended us—our abusive father or mother. Yet Proverbs 25:25 tells us: "As cold water to a weary soul, / So is good news from a far country." Jesus instructed a man who had been healed from great demon possession to "go home to your friends, and tell them what great things the Lord has done for you, and how He has had compassion on you" (Mark 5:19).[4] Paul, too, admonished us to remember that when we come though suffering we have a commission now to "comfort those who are in any trouble, with the comfort with which we ourselves are comforted by God" (2 Cor.

1:4). We have a message of hope to share. Are we willing to tell our parents?

Several years ago, I wrote to my father to share my healing with him. Surprisingly, as I wrote the letter, I felt great compassion well up in me. I spoke of coming to terms with my family in counseling and being able to forgive both him and my mother.

"Each of us in our family suffered the effects of the pain with which we grew up. You need to understand that the pain did not begin in 1972 when Mom committed suicide. That pain began long before. Probably in Mom's life, it began in her own relationship with her parents and was exacerbated in her relationship with you. And for you, as well, I'm sure your pain did not begin in 1972. I'm sure your pain goes way back as well. Perhaps the pain of trying to earn your parents' love and approval, or the pain of losing your own father. I do not even know you well enough to understand the pain you may have grown up with that was so deep that it caused you to need to dull it with alcohol and pills. But I know now that many of your acts and words were due to the violent mood swings that an alcoholic experiences.

"For several years, I have been learning more of what it means to come to terms with being raised in an alcoholic home. I understand that a person drinks to quell an unbearable pain and as he drinks, his personality changes, his acts and words can become violent and abusive, and he can drive away those who are closest to him. The family itself becomes oriented around that chemically dependent person and alters its actions to try to keep things on an even keel."

I continued explaining how the alcoholic family operates, how I saw us fitting into these roles, and how growing up in our home had affected me. Then I shared with him my good news. And I wished the same for him. He wasn't able to hear it then. He wrote back that he had used alcohol for a brief period after my mother's death but that he had not used it before or since. His denial system was clearly functioning at high gear. To my surprise, I understood. As I wrote back to him: "I appreciate that you may not know how to respond to what I said in that letter. It took me a long time with a lot of help from a dedicated counselor, Al-Anon, and Adult Children of Alcoholics meetings as well as inner healing to be able to face the reality of the effects of growing up in a home with a chemically dependent father. It's okay not to respond to what I said right now. I just ask you to think about it and my request that you go to AA."

I didn't hear from him again for two-and-a-half years, but I continued to pray that the Lord might help him realize that hope existed for him too. I wasn't promised that my father would change if I shared my recovery with him. I did know that I was honoring him by doing so, however, and that was enough.

Chapter 11

Mirror, Mirror on the Wall: Redefining Self

As [a man] thinks[1] in his heart, so is he.

Proverbs 23:7

When we let go of control and begin to define proper boundaries, we discover a new self emerging. The family Hero role is fading and we are searching in the mirror now to see the reflection of who we are becoming. It takes courage to look in the mirror honestly. We must examine the various ways our family role has determined who we are and choose now to think differently about ourselves and to act in accordance with these new thoughts. We have to redefine who we are in the important spheres of our lives and cast the inaccurate pictures of ourselves—as martyrs, as second-class persons, as potentially perfect wives and husbands, mothers and fathers—aside.

AS MARTYRS

How do you think of yourself? When someone says, "Tell me about yourself," what do you say? For years, I responded to that question by pouring out the litany of my family experiences. Invariably, people responded in amazement. "Aren't you strong to have gone through all of that!"

I was defined by my suffering. I found my identification, my sense of who I was, in suffering. I began to think of myself as a martyr. I would remain strong, loyal, and faithful to God no matter what happened in my circumstances. I was the "strong Christian," an example to others, because I could bear up so well no matter what God allowed. I made an idol out of my suffering.

The problem with idols, of course, is that they misrepresent the truth about God. James 1:17 states that "every good gift and every perfect gift is from above, and comes down from the Father." My idol of suffering stood in the way of my receiving anything good. That wouldn't fit into my theology. My counselor once asked me what would happen if God suddenly got my brother out of prison, changed my father, and brought me a wonderful man to date. I laughed and said, "I wouldn't be able to cope!"

Suffering is what we do best. We rise to the occasion and demonstrate once again how strong and courageous we are. But what about good times—times of blessing? This is uncomfortable. At best, we struggle through it; at worst, we sabotage it. Just as the Israelites had to smash their idols if they were to see the true God and know themselves in relationship to Him, so we have to smash any idols we have set up in our lives. Mine was suffering. What is yours?

AS SECOND-CLASS PERSONS

No one is harder on myself than I am. My journal is full of self-recriminations:

- "I hate myself. I don't know why I am this way. Why do I cling so to a guy? I feel so bound up and I don't see any way out."

- "What's wrong with me? Why am I always so lonely and afraid?"
- "I feel so rejected. God, I don't measure up to what You want. I'll never be pleasing to You. I feel real love is a blessing too wonderful for me."

This self-hate was evident in my struggle with overeating. My journal recorded resolution after resolution to conquer this problem. I just knew that if I were diligent enough, I could control my eating. I constantly berated myself for my weak will. Finally, in my journal, I concluded, "I must submit myself to a discipline strong enough to break a lifelong habit." Then I would undertake some program or another to lose weight. Invariably, I would fail again, which only gave me more concrete evidence that my self-hatred was deserved.

Much has been discovered in recent years about the connection between eating disorders and growing up in an alcoholic or dysfunctional home. We know now we must get to the root issues behind the need to eat. Otherwise, the core issues continue to fuel the battle.

I wanted to talk to Bob about my self-hatred, but it took many months before I could raise it with him. I ventured out a little and shared this incredibly embarrassing but difficult area of struggling with overeating. He didn't respond at all like I wanted him to. He seemed unconcerned and said, "Weight is a defense mechanism, Nancy. It builds walls between us and others. It's also a way of punishing yourself. When you discover the things that bring on the need to overeat and God heals them, this problem will lose its power. This next week, I want you to think about why you condemn yourself so harshly."

That's all? A cut-and-dried psychological response to something that so bound me, so confused me, so desperately frustrated me? Why was he so unconcerned? He acted as if this whole need to eat compulsively would just disappear one day. Didn't he understand how much this thing had me bound up? I just confessed to an awful sin. Shouldn't he dispense absolution or something?

I was very angry. I wasn't sure what I was looking for, but I felt my money was being wasted this week. The entire next week I plagued myself with Bob's question: Why do I condemn myself?

The same week I talked with Jenny, a teenager who ran away from home to live with a guy in another state. Jenny and I had been close friends for years. On four occasions, I tried to get her to come up to stay with me and think things out. This guy was really bad news, drunk and fighting with her on a daily basis. Yet she seemed unable to break away even to come up here for a few days. Some inexplicable pull kept her with him. That Tuesday night when I called, they were having a huge fight. I could hear him throwing things around. Our phone call was cut short when he pulled the phone off the wall. The next day when we talked again, she told me he had held a gun to her head. I pleaded, "Jenny, why do you stay with him when he treats you like this?" She had no answer.

I related some of this when I came to counseling that week. Then I burst into tears as I told Bob, "I've been miserable since last week. All I have thought about is your question, 'Why do I condemn myself?' I don't have any answers for that." As I talked, there was a gray silence hanging in the room. It was the first time I had been to my weekly appointment since the time had changed, and although it was 5:00 P.M., it was dark outside. The darkness only served to heighten the silence. I felt very, very alone as I sat there wanting to understand why I condemned myself so harshly.

Bob said, "Let's talk about Jenny. There's more there, Nancy."

"Well, the thing that bothered me so much this week was that she is in a bad situation, really bad, and can't seem to get out. It bothered me personally because I see myself in her. I worry that I like negative situations; that I enjoy getting hurt...but why?" I almost shouted. "I'm afraid my whole life will be one bad thing after another and that I can't, I won't escape."

"Why wouldn't you want to escape?"

"I don't know. I don't know. I get into relationships where I know they'll reject me, or when I am in a relationship where the guy loves me, I bring on its downfall. I do things to attract rejection, even from those who are trying to love me."

"Nancy, you don't consciously desire negative experiences. But the self-hate and condemnation you have incorporated into your personality cause you to be drawn toward them as an affirmation of who you are. God is going to heal this. That will involve letting Him love you and replacing your self-hate with self-acceptance and forgiveness."

A number of sessions later, I related a dream to Bob. In the dream, I was in the dining hall at the boarding school where I taught, when one of the faculty children came in and killed himself with a gun. I rushed to the parents to offer comfort. After all, I knew what it felt like to lose someone that way. But the father simply responded, "It's okay, Nancy, we're just thankful the Lord is in control. Praise the Lord."

Bob explained, "Nancy, picture yourself as that little boy as well as the person who was going to talk to the father. That's you, committing suicide by overeating. Everyone in your family has been self-destructive. They have each chosen different means of destroying their lives. Yours is very subtle and will take a long time. You'll just eat yourself to death.

"When you went over to the parents and tried to express your real feelings, you didn't get any response. You just got clichés—Christian clichés. You have become a Christian cliché yourself, Nancy. You can say all the right things, and yet at the very root of your relationship with God is your refusal to let Him have your life. Are you going to control your life or is God? Your control is self-destructive; you overeat. You, Nancy, have a choice."

That night I recorded in my journal my thoughts about this session. "This desire to take control and destroy ourselves pervades my whole family. Now it is at the very core of my healing. I suspect, too, that it is at the very core of giving myself to another person. I can't bring this self-destructiveness and self-hatred into a marriage. God, please heal me. Begin to work on this incredibly strong need I have to destroy myself through my own devices. Teach me how to choose Your way which leads to life."

At the core of my poor self-image was self-condemnation and self-loathing. Not only did I hate myself, I wanted to destroy myself. Only I was the good girl who wouldn't use drugs or alcohol to dull my pain. I would use food. Whatever the means chosen, the end was the same: destruction and death. But God had a plan for wholeness and blessing, and it first meant getting honest with myself about the reasons for why I overate.

I had a very good married friend in another state who I saw about twice a year. Usually right before I visited her, when we talked on the phone to arrange our plans, she would ask me if I had lost weight. Invariably, I replied yes. However, when I visited, she would see I had been lying. Then I would have to listen to her plea: "Nancy, you're pretty, sharp, and intelligent. If you'd only lose weight, you'd be married."

I told Bob this when he asked me why I was so reluctant to go on this trip. Bob asked, "Do you always gain weight before you go to visit her?"

"Yes," I replied.

More sharply than I would have liked, he said, "Nancy, you've got to stop lying to her."

"What do you mean?" I asked.

"Don't you see what you're doing? You're trying to tell her you don't want to be married. So stop lying and tell her that directly." I was astonished. Of course, I wanted to be married.

Bob continued, "Why don't you ask her what's so great about marriage anyway?"

I thought about that for a few minutes and then asked, "How can I have such an intense desire to be married and fight so hard against it at the same time?"

Bob explained, "Nancy, nothing in your family background suggests that marriage is good. So although you intuitively desire marriage, a part of you sees it as a harmful thing to be avoided."

So I was afraid of the one thing I wanted more than anything else in the world. So afraid that I built up a wall of flesh around me to keep others away. My homework assignment that week was not to join Weight Watchers. It was to stop lying, stare my fears in the face, and invite Jesus into my fears of marriage so He could transform them. The disciple John explained how this works: "Whoever confesses that Jesus is the Son of God, God abides in him, and he in God. And we have known and believed the love God has for us.... There is no fear in love; but perfect love casts out fear, because fear involves torment" (1 John 4:15–16a, 18a).

AS POTENTIAL WARD AND JUNE CLEAVERS

At some point in our recovery, we have to let go of our fantasy family. Otherwise, when we marry and have children, we set up ourselves and our spouses and our children for failure. As long as we uphold an image of this perfect, loving family that we have gleaned from many years of fantasizing, we will constantly be disappointed. We need to redefine what it means to have a good, loving family.

Most of us have to get "up close and personal" to a realistic marriage and family. The greatest benefit to my three years of teaching at The Stony Brook School was its boarding school environment. All faculty lived either in dorm apartments or in houses circling the campus. Single faculty were assigned to a dining room table where a faculty couple and six boarding students sat. We were to have at least two meals a day in the dining hall. It was there, in this fishbowl existence, that I began to know the Gustafsons.

Rob and Beth Gustafson were willing to live their lives in front of me. Over several years, I observed their marriage. I saw conflicts arise but not escalate to violence and watched them be resolved in a healthy manner. I saw them turn together to God when confusing questions arose. I found myself drawn to them, often hanging around the edge of their marriage, wanting to soak in all that I saw demonstrated there. I was intrigued. Perhaps marriage wasn't a death knell after all.

When their son was born, I found myself in great conflict: I had always been afraid of children. Many times in counseling, I talked about my fear of having children. I was afraid that I would warp them somehow. After all, my mom had loved me very much, and yet here I was in counseling, trying to make sense of my life. If I was going to continue to be a part of the Gustafsons' life, however, I would have to get to know Robbie.

Robbie, a towheaded toddler, began to steal my heart. He didn't know of my background; he didn't understand my struggles. My successes didn't matter to him. I was simply his friend. One day his parents came out of the dining hall after lunch with Robbie in tow. He saw me coming up the path from the classroom building and he ran toward me, arms outstretched. I knelt down and scooped him up, and he said enthusiastically, "I love you." Rob and Beth shared that I was the first person outside of them to hear those words.

Those simple words, unconditionally given, washed over

my soul in waves of healing. I was often feeling discouraged and unlovable, as I peeled away layer upon layer of negative patterns, yet this little boy was affirming that he liked me. No, he loved me! Perhaps, there was hope. Perhaps, one day, I would be a good mom.

Because there was so much yelling and anger in my house, I especially needed to see Rob and Beth discipline their children in love. I needed to see modeled before me the way a parent builds up a child's self-esteem, sets limits on his or her behavior, and protects their childlikeness. Reading about it in books was not enough. Too many counterexperiences were indelibly printed in my mind.

None of these experiences would have happened without the willingness of the Gustafsons to live so vulnerably before me. We need role models of solid marriages and families to help us set aside our fantasies. We then can discover that a good marriage need not be perfect. Problems do not need to be presented, discussed, and resolved in thirty-minute segments as on television. Families can disagree and yet still love one another. Family members can express deep emotions and yet not damage another. They can love each other, yet hold each other lightly, letting God have the right to develop each of them according to His plan.

What are the characteristics of a functional, healthy family?

- Openness and vulnerability underlie their communication with each other. For those of us from dysfunctional homes, we will often be naturally drawn to these families because of the lightness and upbeat approach we see in their interactions with one another. We will feel surprisingly at peace in their homes.
- Laughter, at themselves and at life, will abound. There will be an ability to roll with the ups and downs of life. Crisis times will draw them together in dependence on one another.

- Discipline is consistent. In healthy homes, the families will from time to time need to enforce family rules that are flexible, clearly explained, and take into consideration the differences in family members. However, children are not punished for being children. Accidents happen. Willful behavior, however, that violates the family rules is punished, but the punishment fits the crime. There is clear communication about the rules, and parents work with the children to help them understand the reasons for the rules.
- Feelings may be expressed without condemnation. Children are taught how to express feelings in appropriate ways. Susie may be boiling angry at her younger brother, but she is not allowed to punch him out.
- Forgiveness is requested and dispensed when needed. Parents as well will from time to time ask their chilren's forgiveness for mistakes or inappropriate behaviors. Short accounts are kept. When they forgive, they forget. Grudges are not borne or scores kept for purposes of one-upmanship.
- Disagreements or painful issues are not swept under the rug in a peacekeeping fashion. Even though it is difficult, family members will work together to express feelings or talk out a problem.
- Praise is given freely; praise for just being, not just for doing. A good effort is sufficient; perfection is not required.
- Honesty is a part of the family dynamic. If the father loses his job, for example, the children will be told in ways appropriate for their age levels. Children are not expected to bear the burden of this family problem, however. Parents will not keep secrets, but not overload them with inappropriate information, either.
- Children are not asked to side with one parent against the other.
- Children are encouraged to try new things and given parental support for their efforts, regardless of the results.

It is also important for those of us who have come through these experiences to open up our homes and our marriages. Once we have experienced this for ourselves, we can bring a great gift to others by sharing our families with them. For me, one so terrified of marriage and of repeating my family history, the Gustafsons gave me a new reflection of wife and mother when I looked in the mirror of family.

Chapter 12

You Meant It for Evil: Forgiving Your Family

Every one says forgiveness is a lovely idea, until they have something to forgive.[1]

C. S. Lewis
Mere Christianity

In the first six years after college, I lived in four cities and seven different houses, and whenever I moved, I was confronted with what to do with "the box." This brown cardboard shipping box contained over one hundred letters and other documents written to me by my father, including a legal complaint served on me for $808.37, which my father said I owed him. Periodically, I would gather up the letters I received and dump them into the box. Most were stream-of-consciousness versions of the verbal abuse of earlier years. Others were lengthy statements of his philosophy of life, with long sections implicating my mother's role in destroying his life and career. Many were only half-read. When I would receive one of these diatribes, I would begin to read it, feel my anger rising, and then scan the rest of the letter for any hope of decent communication. Finding none, I would toss it in with the others. Over the years, this large box was reaching capacity.

Each time I moved I would question the wisdom of transporting this box again. Why not just get rid of it? My cool, rational side argued that these papers were evidence if I ever needed to procure a peace bond to keep my father away from me. But my heart knew better. I hung onto these papers to fuel my unforgiveness.

Each time I considered throwing out the box, I would reread some of the letters. My anger would stir up inside me. Then, in great indignation and self-righteousness, I would pack up that box once again. Dr. Susan Forward, in her recent book *Toxic Parents*, makes the claim that it is not necessary to forgive your parents to be healed and that forgiveness is only appropriate when "parents do something to *earn* it."[2] I believed that for years. I had been the offended party. My father should come to me, repentant and humbly seeking my forgiveness. Certainly, I should not forgive him while he continued to act abusively.

Then one very hot summer day in 1985 I was confronted with the challenge to forgive my father. As I read my Bible on the banks of the Potomac, I understood that forgiving my father was the next step in my healing. I didn't understand fully how it would benefit me. I did understand that holding onto my unforgiveness and bitterness was only going to destroy me. Hebrews 12:15 explained that letting bitterness take root could damage me and others. I had to let it all go—let go of the hatred, the anger, the desire to get even. So I stared at the sluggish waters as they moved wearily past the bank where I was sitting, and I said simply, "I forgive you, Dad."

That part was easier than I thought. But then, as I continued to watch the river, and felt the August sun beat down on my head, I heard God say, "Now get rid of the papers."

I jumped up as if I had been doused with a pail of ice

water, looked up at the sky and said, "You've got to be kidding, Lord! I need those papers. What if I have to go to court for a peace bond?"

For several weeks I bargained with God. "What if I promise not to read them again?" "How about if I put them in a safety-deposit box?" "Okay, I won't add any new letters to it; I'll just keep the old ones for a little while longer." For weeks I struggled with this. I argued with myself. "If I have really forgiven him, why do I need to hang onto the papers—these reminders of his ill treatment of me? But let's be realistic, Nancy. This is America. You have to have proof. You can't just go accusing someone of something without evidence."

Quietly, but firmly, God said, "Who are you trusting for your protection—Me or those papers? Get rid of them."

The issue at this point was not forgiveness. That had been accomplished on the banks of the Potomac that summer afternoon. The issue was justification for continued bitterness. Those papers represented my right to nurse my wounds. Now I had to decide whether to let all this go.

Finally, one night I hauled the box out to the backyard and lit a fire in the grill. One by one I placed those pages into the flames. I was tempted to glance at the papers one more time, just to refresh my memory. To truly forgive my father, however, meant to give up any right to nurture bitterness by revisiting his hurtful deeds, either in print or in my memory.

It also meant accepting responsibility for my own choices. I had a weapon—my righteous indignation and justified bitterness—to use against my father. By passively withholding my forgiveness and nurturing my bitterness toward him, I could get back at him. I had become just as spiteful and vengeful toward him as he had been toward me.

The physical act of burning those papers sealed my forgiveness and helped me let go of my bitterness and resentment. To forgive my father for his acts and to ask forgiveness for my own sin was another step in breaking the cycle of destruction in my family.

WHY FORGIVE?

A powerful example of an individual having to forgive his family for abuse is found in the Old Testament story of Joseph, the favored son of Jacob, who lost his mother at a young age. His brothers despised Joseph for the obvious favor he received from their father. They plotted together to kill him but on reconsideration decided instead to sell him at the age of seventeen into slavery. For the next thirteen years, Joseph suffered. Enslaved in Egypt serving in the home of Potiphar, the chief guard of the Pharaoh, he had no contact with his family or his beloved father. He was falsely accused of rape by Potiphar's wife when he refused to sleep with her and was then thrown in prison. While in prison, he assisted one of the Pharaoh's officials by interpreting his dream and predicting his freedom. Yet, once the official was freed, he forgot his promise to remember Joseph and seek his release. Joseph had for nearly half his life at that point been mistreated horribly and had every right to be bitter.

Several years later, when the Pharaoh had a disturbing dream that none of the magicians and wise men of Egypt could interpret, the Pharaoh's official whom Joseph had previously helped recalled that Joseph had correctly interpreted his dream years before. The Pharaoh sent for Joseph, who interpreted the dream and predicted that seven years of great harvest would be followed by seven years of famine and instructed the Pharaoh to designate a wise man to administer the Pharaoh's affairs during this period so that there would be a reserve of food stored up for the years of famine. Pharaoh determined that Joseph was that wise man and placed him second in command in his government.

Just as Joseph had predicted, the seven years of abundance were followed by a severe famine. Because of Joseph's wise administrations, Egypt became the purveyor of grain to people from many lands. In fact, Joseph's father sent his ten sons to Egypt to buy grain for their family. When they came to purchase the grain, Joseph recognized them but did not reveal his identity until later. When the brothers understood that this great Egyptian leader was their brother, Joseph, they were greatly disturbed: "What if Joseph should bear a grudge against us and pay us back in full for all the wrong which we did to him!" (Gen. 50:15, NAS). However, Joseph promised to provide for them and their families and told them, "You meant evil against me, but God meant it for good" (v. 20, NAS). How could he say this? Where were his bitterness and his spiteful revenge? Why, now that he was in a position to help, would he do so with such willingness?

Joseph had already worked through his feelings and had forgiven his family. How else could he have responded this way? We have a clue about this in the names he chose for two children born to him in Egypt. Joseph named one son Manasseh, which meant "Making to forget" and said it is because "God has made me forget all my trouble" (41:51, NAS). He said of his second son, Ephraim, which means, "Fruitfulness," that "God has made me fruitful in the land of my affliction" (v. 52). From Joseph we can learn the keys for us to forgive:

- Recognize that God is in control of all circumstances.
- Acknowledge that, despite the circumstances that have resulted in our bondage to negative patterns, God can heal us.
- With God's help, forget the pain and trouble of our past.

- Receive God's perspective as to how all this evil in our lives can be used for good.
- Be willing to confront our offenders with how they have harmed us.
- Be willing to forgive.

If we are willing to begin a process of forgiveness, we will find that it validates and draws upon much of our recovery experience. In the beginning of our recovery, we had to learn to break out of denial and be honest with ourselves and with God. Forgiveness requires honesty and a willingness to address objectively the wrongs we have experienced. As we progressed in our healing, we learned to release our tight control over other people and circumstances. When we forgive, we must trust God's sovereignty over all circumstances, even those which are painful and harmful. Otherwise, our desire to get even prevents us from being able to forgive. Since forgiveness is based on obedience to a higher standard than retaliation, it frees us from bitterness which assumes we have the right to nurse our wounds. Finally, we discover that the end result of all our pain, introspection, and earnest questions and struggles as we journey toward wholeness is blessing. The process of forgiveness lays the groundwork for growth not only in our own lives, but potentially in the lives of those who have been our worst offenders.

Forgiveness Is Honest

Forgiveness of the abusive parent is probably one of the most difficult things any of us will ever do. It requires great courage; it is not a sentimental act. Most importantly, it requires recognition of the truth. Joseph told his brothers, "You meant it for evil...." He did not minimize their wrongs or excuse their behavior. They meant him harm and he restated that hard cold fact to them. If we are to forgive, we must first acknowledge the "evil" that occurred. Facing the truth about what happened to us is the initial phase of our recovery where we break through denial and face our feelings, and it lays the foundation for forgiveness.

After I burned the box of letters from my father, I expressed that forgiveness to him in a letter. In that letter I spelled out for him exactly what it was I was forgiving. I talked about the impact his drinking and his verbal abuse had had on me, providing several specific examples of his actions. Explaining clearly what I was forgiving him for might help him break through his own delusions about our family life. My responsibility, like Joseph's, was to shoot straight. You meant it for evil, Dad. And then to forgive.

When we are honest about what it is we are forgiving, we are walking in our recovery and may even help others on their journey. For my father, that journey had not yet begun. Other than one six-month period in his life, he could not recall ever drinking to excess. As he explained in his letter to me, "Although we had alcohol in our home, I believe it was never used to excess prior to 1972. I freely admit that subsequent to 1972, I used it to excess for a short period of time. I soon realized that I had an inborn negative affinity for its consumption and discontinued its use." His denial system was working at full tilt. However, when we are honest ("You meant it for evil"), we don't perpetuate the denial system through quick forgiveness that skirts the real issues ("That's okay, Dad, it doesn't matter"). This may help our parents challenge their delusions about how family life was and begin to break their own cycle of secrecy and shame.

Forgiveness Recognizes God's Sovereignty

It takes great courage to forgive someone who has emotionally, physically, or sexually abused us and not resort to bitterness, hatred, and spite. Something in us naturally wants to see the scales balanced. They should get their due, their just rewards. When we attempt to balance the scales, keeping their evil acts on one side and our bitterness, resentment, and hatred on the other as their punishment, we play God. We have judged them and now are meting out just punishment. It may even give us a sense of power or control over them. Perhaps now we finally have something they want or need—our forgiveness—and we can get back at them by withholding it. To forgive means we release this desire for vengeance and permit them to go, perhaps from our perspective, unpunished.

If we recognize God's sovereignty, however, and His right to be God in the lives of our parents, it puts a new twist on our desire to see the scales balanced. We step out of our judicial robes and relinquish to God the right to punish or to grant mercy. If we are honest, we may have difficulty giving up this role of Supreme Judge because some of us are afraid God might do just that—grant mercy. We may think we deserve God's forgiveness, but no one as awful as our father or mother deserves His forgiveness. Forgiving our parents is an act that recognizes God's control of circumstances and our parents' ultimate fate.

Forgiveness Releases Us from Bitterness

Unforgiveness breeds bitterness, and bitterness makes us miserable. Sometimes we enjoy that state. For a long time, I blamed my father and God for my current struggles. If my father loved me, he wouldn't have treated me like that. If God loved me, He wouldn't have let my father treat me like that. I was bitter toward both. Repeated acts by my father only served to provide additional support for my bitterness.

It may come as a surprise to us that we may need forgiveness ourselves. We may have sinned against our parents through our continued resentment, our bitterness toward them, perhaps our own brand of "evil" thoughts about them. When we are ready to take responsibility for our own self-destructive patterns, we need to recognize that bitterness can be just as destructive to us as the acts that caused the bitterness. Whether or not our parents change, forgiving them releases us from the destructiveness of bitterness and resentment. We will be free inside even if nothing else changes in our relationship with them.

Forgiveness Releases Blessing

Forgiveness often occurs further along in our recovery because we first have to break through our denial systems to confront the harms done to us by our parents. We need to experience and receive healing for our feelings and let go of our desire to have power over our parents by hurting them. Forgiving our parents comes in its time as a part of this growth in our spiritual journey toward life. As we walk through this process of forgiveness, it releases blessing in our lives. We mature in our ability to confront the evil that happened to us and as a result, learn healthy patterns for confronting ongoing abuse. We also begin to see our own weaknesses and tendencies to retaliate.

For Christians, forgiveness is also an issue of obedience. We don't have to feel like forgiving, but we must forgive. Why? Because we have been forgiven. Jesus paid the debt of our sin in full with the price of His life. He expects us to forgive others in the same manner. When Jesus taught His disciples to pray, He asked that God "forgive us our debts, as we forgive our debtors" (Matt. 6:12). He then told a parable in Matthew 18 to help us understand this cyclical pattern of grace and forgiveness:

A king decided to bring his accounts up to date. One of his debtors who owed him an enormous sum of money had no ability to recompense the king for his debt, so the king ordered that he be sold into slavery to pay for the debt. The man fell down before the king, begged for mercy, and promised to repay the debt. The king was so moved, he released him and forgave all of his debt.

This man then left the king, and went to a man who owed him a small sum in comparison to that which he had owed the king. He grabbed him by the throat and demanded instant payment. This man fell down on his knees, begged for mercy, and promised to repay the debt, but he was thrown into prison until he could pay the debt in full.

The king heard about this and called the man whom he had forgiven before him and said, "You wicked servant! I forgave all that debt because you begged me. Should you not also have had compassion on your fellow servant, just as I had pity on you?" Then the king sent the man to be tormented until he had paid the entire debt.

As Christians, we have been forgiven an enormous debt. Jesus Christ has paid up the account in full with His life. Now when we need to forgive an offender that we'd rather throttle, we can call to mind this extension of grace to us and forgive our parents on the basis of our being forgiven. This is not to say that the hard work of forgiveness is not costly. To secure the debtor's forgiveness, the king had to absorb the financial loss of that debt. To secure our forgiveness, Jesus gave up His life. We may find that we, too, pay a price when we forgive. We have to face the reality of the harm that happened to us and the emotions that accompany that realization. We have to relinquish our right to seek to balance the scales. We have to get down from our high seat of judgment and recognize our own need for forgiveness. And when we are forgiven for our hate, bitterness, and anger, then we can forgive.

Forgiveness is a process. We won't forgive once. We will forgive many times—as each memory surfaces. We need to be patient with ourselves and give ourselves time in this process. Forgiving our families is an important step in our recovery and includes many important mini-steps of honesty, confronting the abusive behavior and setting boundaries, taking a moral inventory ourselves and discovering where we are bitter, and recognizing God's control of our lives and the lives of our parents. Let's not shortchange the process. It may not simply mean saying, "I forgive you." It may also mean burning the papers.

Chapter 13

But God Meant It for Good: Knowing God as Father

Our real idea of God may lie buried under the rubbish of conventional religious notions and may require an intelligent and vigorous search before it is finally unearthed and exposed for what it is. Only after an ordeal of painful self-probing are we likely to discover what we actually believe about God.[1]

A. W. Tozer
The Knowledge of the Holy

LET GO AND LET GOD

Early in my counseling, Bob challenged me to consider letting God have control of my relationship with Him. I also heard in the Twelve-Step programs that I should, "Let go and let God." That sounded reasonable until I tried it.

"You know, Bob," I explained, "I became a Christian when I was fourteen because someone who knew my family situation said God could help. That sounded wonderful, and I worked very hard to develop faith in a God who could do this kind of a miracle. But nothing happened. I think I'm afraid it is all a great hoax. So, if I give myself up to God like you suggest, and find out He isn't there, then I have really lost out." I shifted in my seat and looked at Bob directly, hoping for an answer to a predicament that had shadowed me for years.

"Nancy, you exude a great deal of energy to win over God's favor. You strive to be faithful. You struggle to trust God in the midst of your circumstances. You work extremely hard to be good. You think that by operating in this way, you can win God's action on your behalf. The end result is that you are in control of your relationship with God," Bob responded. "God wants to take you on a deeper walk with Him. He wants to give you the hope and the faith and the love you so desire, Nancy, but He wants it to be a natural expression of your relationship with Him. God wants you to understand what He is really like. You can't know that until you are no longer dependent on your own beliefs about who God is and how He will work in your life."

"But, Bob," I asked, "what if I give myself up to God and He is not there?"

"That's the risk you'll have to take. Either He is there for you or not. But you can't discover that while you continue to be in control."

Bob challenged me to face this very difficult question head-on. He knew it was the key to faith and to knowing God loved me. But I was too afraid at this point to find out if God was really there or not. I was too comfortable with my ineffective, but predictable, God and too secure in my independence.

Several years later, this issue arose again. In order to complete my financial-aid application for Georgetown law school, I needed a sworn statement from my father that he had not claimed me as a deduction for the last three years. I argued for weeks with the financial-aid office. Why did I need him to sign anything? "I have been on my own now since I was eighteen," I said. But despite the ten years of emancipated financial status, Georgetown held firm. No signed statement from my father meant no financial aid from Georgetown.

I knew that one rarely got anything from my father without paying a price, but when I called him to ask if he would complete the financial-aid form, he surprisingly agreed. Over the next few weeks, however, I suffered through a series of increasingly abusive phone calls, which harped on the same thing over and over again—how much we children had cost him. Finally, he changed his mind about completing the form and said I would have to get along without any more financial help from him. I tried to explain that I didn't need his money, just a signed and notarized statement. No matter, he was on a roll now. He had something I needed and he knew it. He relished the cat-and-mouse game we were playing. I was furious and my anger spilled out in the next counseling session.

"I hate having to depend on my father for anything. I'm twenty-eight years old, and I am at his mercy, just like when I was a child. This has been so frustrating." I paused for a moment and continued, "Bob, I feel like there's got to be more to my anger than just this. Every time my father called to toy with me about whether or not he would provide the form, I would hang up from talking with him and cry for a long period of time. I was furious at being so beholden to him and yet I felt so lonely at the same time."

"Why do you think you felt lonely, Nancy?" Bob asked.

"There's a part of me deep, deep down that wants desperately to trust key people to be dependable. But there is a part of me that is cynical, guarded, and cautious. It is as if I am constantly preparing to be let down again. I know this carries over into my relationship with God. I want to trust myself to God and leave the most important aspects of my life, particularly marriage, up to Him. Yet, each time something like this happens, it just steels my resolve to never be in the position of depending on anyone for anything. Besides, although depending on God is a nice idea, I'm not so sure He's dependable."

"Of course you don't think God is dependable," Bob explained. "You have been let down by so many people in your life that you have closed yourself off, determined that no one, God or man included, will hurt you like that again. Yet you desire to be married. Nancy, do you realize that to be in a relationship with a man, you will have to learn how to be vulnerable and how to be dependent? If you can learn to depend on God, you will find it easier to make yourself vulnerable to a man. God can teach you that He is dependable, if you are willing to let Him."

"How can He do that?" I asked.

"To build dependency, God will have to strip away your independence. He has started to do this already by bringing up these situations in your everyday circumstances that seem larger than life to you. He does this to help you remember all the other hurts, betrayals, and disappointments that occurred in your life. As these memories resurface, you feel deeply that sense of mistrust, loss, and betrayal that you felt before. At this point you have a choice. You can shore yourself up again, garnering your own resources and tackling the job yourself, saying once again, 'I knew I shouldn't have depended on him.' Or you can enter into this fresh experience, embrace the pain, and ask God to heal the deep hurt. Only as you begin to see how God faithfully heals you, memory by memory, will you begin to understand that He is dependable even when others are not."

Bob had a special insight here. He was not asking me to uproot this independent spirit of mine overnight and cast myself unflinchingly into the arms of God. He knew I didn't trust God enough for that yet. He was suggesting that I choose to trust my past pain, which had now attached itself to a present disappointment, to God for healing. If I would be willing to forgo my natural response of shutting down this memory and, instead, embrace the pain of it, I

God was faithful to heal that memory. Then a foundation from which to go forward the slowly, I would build up a storehouse of experi- ere God was operating in my life for good. Then when painful times occurred, I would have some place in my history to go and to select a reminder or two that confirmed His love and His care.

I needed a new history with my God. He was willing to rebuild my understanding of Him, bit by bit. Letting go and letting God was not an overnight occurrence but a determined effort of almost a decade to replace my wrong conceptions of Him and to build a new history. It would involve learning to be honest with God, exploring surprising feelings of anger and fears that I had toward Him, and practicing ongoing choices about what I would believe about Him. I would discover, however, that God would return again to this basic question at the root of any authentic relationship with Him: Was I willing to let go of my control and let Him be God?

RELATING TO GOD AS FATHER

When Jesus prayed to God, He used the very familiar form of the word *father*. In essence, Jesus called God His daddy. Yet adults from dysfunctional homes find it difficult to know God in this way. This deeply personal relationship with God suffers from the same problems as our relationships with our parents and others. Our ability to make ourselves vulnerable to another is crippled by past rejections. We build stone walls around our hearts, closing others out and keeping ourselves safe. Or so we think.

The fear of rejection or abandonment is so strong that it causes us to throw up barriers that make it impossible for intimacy to occur. There may be moments of self-revelation, but sustained intimacy is impossible without trusting that the risk of revealing oneself is outweighed by the benefits of a deeper relationship. We know this, but we are not sure that this risk is worth it.

We learn to cordon off our innermost self from God in many ways. We may reject God completely before we can be rejected by Him, or we may cloak Him in so many commandments that we spend a lifetime trying to measure up to an impossible standard. Or we may busy ourselves with service for Him to the exclusion of being with Him. Or as in my case, we may fill that aching void for intimacy with a consuming intensity for human love that devours every man that comes along.

My father broke his promises, destroyed my trust, ruined my childhood, and discounted my worth. This caused me to hang back in the shadows, skeptical and unsure about the intentions of this heavenly Father toward me. I wanted to believe that "God meant it for good," but nagging doubts plagued me. I was as skittish about my relationship with my heavenly Father as I was with my earthly father.

OUR DISTORTED VIEW OF GOD

The parent/child relationship has a natural imbalance of power and authority. How our parents handled that power imbalance shapes how we respond to God. If they used their power and authority to hurt and abuse, we respond to God with fear and distrust. Sandra Wilson, Ph.D., observed six major distortions of the character of God that were common to Christian adult children of alcoholics.[2]

1. The Cruel and Capricious God

This view is most commonly held by adult children who suffered severe abuse, especially if the abuser was the father. Adults most often respond to this God with terror and fear.

If we have become Christians as children growing up in the dysfunctional home, we may turn to God to change our family situation, as I did. Maybe the child even asks God for protection from the abusive parent. If God is really a caring God, a loving Father, He'll help, won't He?

Not only does this make sense theologically, but it is what we are taught in Sunday school, church, or Bible study. God knows your every need. God cares individually for you. If you were the only one left on earth, He still would have sent His Son to die for you. Not a sparrow falls to the ground without the Lord knowing. He has numbered the hairs on our heads. Surely He will help now.

I used to love to read the Psalms. Here I had assurance over and over again that God was powerful enough to protect me and to help me, no matter how difficult the circumstances. Psalm 91 promised He would be my refuge and fortress. Important word pictures for one on the front lines of daily battle in the home.

> You will not be afraid of the terror by night,
> Or of the arrow that flies by day; . . .
> A thousand may fall at your side,
> And ten thousand at your right hand;
> But it shall not approach you. . . .
> "Because he has loved Me, therefore I will deliver him;
> I will set him securely on high, because he has known
>   My name.
> He will call upon Me, and I will answer him;
> I will be with him in trouble;
> I will rescue him, and honor him" (v. 5, 7, 14–15 NAS).

Yeah, Lord. Do it! I just knew God could help . . . if He wanted to.

Sometimes, it does appear that God is helping, that the family is getting better. There may be up times in the cycle of family life where you begin to believe long-hoped-for changes are occurring. These lulls in the storm cause us to begin to trust that God really does care about us and is at work in our deepest concerns. Then, inevitably, the stormy times reappear. Where is God in the thunderclouds? He appears capricious—willing to help in some moments and distant and silent in others. Who is this God? Is He dependable? Does He care? I feared this capricious God.

2. The Demanding and Unforgiving God

This view is most commonly held by adult children who experienced neglect or emotional and verbal abuse, frequently the family Heroes who perceive God as requiring much and forgiving little.

Since the time I became a Christian in the ninth grade, service to God became a venue for earning God's favor. Choir, leadership positions in youth and young adult church groups, involvement in an inner-city children's ministry, and Young Life became places to demonstrate my faithfulness and commitment to God. Why? So He could deem me worthy of His attention and help.

Service to God should be the outward expression of faith in a loving God. It is responsive, not manipulative. When God is viewed as demanding, however, Christian activities can be an attempt to meet the perceived high standards necessary to be acceptable to God.

As a child, I used my achievements to demonstrate to my parents and to outsiders that I was okay. As a Christian, my activities were aimed to prove to God I was worthy of His love and help. When things didn't change in my family, I presumed it was my fault and redoubled my efforts to win over this demanding God.

3. The Selective and Unfair God

This view is most commonly held by those adult children who believe that God is not cruel, capricious, demanding, or unforgiving with all His children, but only with them.

Andrea, the network broadcaster whom we met in chapter 2, viewed God like this. Because of her sense of her own unworthiness, she could understand a God who withheld His blessings from her while He dispensed them to others. She didn't even challenge this perspective as unfair. Of course, God singled her out for His disfavor; she was so obviously deficient as His child. Whereas others might rail out at God and challenge this seeming inconsistency and unfairness, Andrea accepted God's perceived actions toward her as logical and justifiable. This demanding, unforgiving God had specially chosen her for His displeasure.

4. The Distant and Unavailable God

The last two views of God are also common to children who had parents who were inaccessible, too busy, or unable for whatever reason, to love and nurture their children. Adult children view this God, like their parents, as inaccessible. Chronic parental unavailability reinforces this distorted view of God.

When Jim, whom we also met in chapter 2, became a Christian, he discovered that he rarely brought many concerns to God in prayer. Why bother God? His troubles were his own, and surely God was too busy to care, anyway. So he learned to bottle things in. When his business began to fail, he carried his pain inside. He was competent. He could manage. He didn't think that God would help if asked. In fact, Jim didn't even think to ask. Years of cool parental interactions had taught him otherwise.

5. The Kind but Confused God

This God remains aloof and distant. He is perceived as weak and ineffectual, unable to help with the world's problems or those of the adult child. Dan didn't begrudge God His powerlessness. He accepted it. For years Dan had tried to help his family change, and yet they remained the same. Dan was aware of how hopeless it was, so why should God have any more success?

Dr. Wilson found four statistically significant differences in the spiritual perceptions of evangelical adult children of alcoholics, compared with evangelical adults from nonalcoholic homes. Adult children of alcoholics had significantly more difficulty in experiencing God's love and forgiveness, trusting God's will, believing biblical promises, and forgiving others. For example, 44.8 percent of adult children of alcoholics had trouble experiencing God's love and forgiveness compared to only 4.8 percent of those adults from nonalcoholic homes.[3]

I also saw God in one other distorted image—that of a fairy godmother.

6. The Fairy Godmother God

The amount of fantasizing we did as children affects our relationship to God, so we become stuck in fairy-tale thinking. We begin to view God as the fairy godmother who waves His magic wand, makes good conquer evil, and delivers the happy ending.

One of the underlying assumptions of fairy-tale thinking is the juxtaposition of good and evil. Rarely are the fairy-tale characters a complex enigma of good and bad traits. Rather, there typically is an evil protagonist: a witch, an evil king or queen, or a wicked stepmother. There is also a good hero or heroine, often portrayed by children or adolescents. When we carry that thinking into adulthood, however, and into our relationship with God, we see ourselves as victims of some wicked agent and often do not take responsibility for ourselves. We view the dysfunctional parent as someone from whom we must escape. But have you ever noticed how that person reappears in others' clothing? That parent is surprisingly similar to a boss, a coworker, or perhaps a spouse.

With fairy-tale thinking, we learn to wait for the fairy godmother to arrive and change our circumstances. In fairy tales, people are rescued from their circumstances. Dragons are slain. Wicked people killed, banished, or at least put in their place. We often view God in the same way. However, when we wait on God to intervene and change our lives so that they are bearable, we lose the opportunity to experience His faithfulness in the darkest situation.

A third aspect of fairy-tale thinking is how we view ourselves. Not only do we tend to focus on the wicked or evil agent that is ruining our lives—seeing that person as someone from whom we must escape—not only do we wait for the fairy godmother's intervention, but we also begin to believe that we must be good enough to deserve this intervention. Cinderella was the good but mistreated stepdaughter. Snow White was the purest, fairest of them all. Perhaps to get this fairy godmother to act on our behalf, we must be good enough to deserve this special dispensation of grace.

This misdirected belief about God puts the burden on us to be worthy enough of His help and His merciful dispensations. Yet this aspect of our relationship with God is not foreign to us either. We feel comfortable trying to be pleasing enough to earn acceptance, love, and favor. It is how we have operated for years. But, ah, there is the dilemma. We must be the good person who deserves the action of an omnipotent being, but at the very depths of our souls we are convinced of our unworthiness.

It is easy for us to believe we are unworthy of God's favor and assistance. At the core of our being is self-rejection and lack of self-worth. We accept without question that we are unworthy sinners. The shame that surrounds our souls since early childhood condemns us daily: who would want to love you? You are not worthy. It is tough for us to accept that God loves us, not because of who we are, not because of what we do, but because God has decided to love us.

Even so, we do not jettison fairy-tale thinking. It is the basis of our hope.

A child from a dysfunctional home can wait a lifetime for the fairy godmother to intervene and change the little cinder-covered girl to a princess. When she becomes a Christian, she transfers that type of belief into her relationship with God. No one has a greater capacity for hope and endurance in spite of difficult circumstances than our Hero.

What are her hopes and dreams? For me it was first for my family to be restored to health and wholeness. When it became apparent that that would not be happening, I asked God to give me an extraordinary husband. For others, it may be changing a spouse or providing that long-awaited breakthrough in a job situation. The dreams may differ, but the technique is the same. We live in the future anticipation of what God could do. If He would just act and change this or that, we would be happy. Then we apply all of our efforts to convince God how He should act to bring about this dream. It becomes more and more perplexing when the circumstances do not change. We question over and over whether God really cares about us. We equate His love with His action, and without evidence of it in our circumstances, we begin to doubt.

But we must not doubt. We must have faith! So we buck up and call from deep within our own incredible reservoir of endurance, yet one more day of belief in this reluctant God. After all, you never know when He might appear and grant our heart's desire. And so the merry-go-round goes on and on.

A GENUINE VIEW OF GOD

Did my relationship with my heavenly Father have to be doomed by my experiences with my earthly father? No, but I would have to work harder at it than others. Much of the hard work I did to correct faulty thinking and poor choices in my earthly relationships had to occur in my relationship with God too. I would have to learn to trust God, to get in touch with my feelings toward God, to relinquish control, and to give up my performance-based understanding of His acceptance of me.

Identify What We Think about God

We need to confront our view of God. To renew our minds, we must first take stock of our basic beliefs about God no matter how counter to standard Christian thought they might appear. For example, I saw God as capricious. He would get me to trust Him and then just when I had, He would pull the rug out from under me with great pleasure. It wasn't until I was in counseling that I had the courage to share this perspective, because as a good, strong Christian I wouldn't malign God like that.

Once I identified a conflict about the way I thought about God and the way God is presented in the Bible, I would search my personal experiences for those events that gave me support for this view of God. I remembered praying to God over and over to help Daddy not yell at Mom so much, for instance. But nothing changed.

How Do You Feel?

As this personal experience came to mind, I would ask myself how I felt about it. Did I feel abandoned? Let down? Angry? I asked myself why I felt that way. "Because God shouldn't be like this; He should be like that," I'd respond. We need to trust our intuitions about what the character of God should be like. Those thoughts may be more accurate than we realize. Many of us will learn of God as Father, not by example, but by contrast. As J. I. Packer explained in ther; they belong to His family; they may approach Him *Knowing God*:

> To those who are Christ's, the holy God is a loving Father; they belong to His family they may approach Him

without fear, and always be sure of His fatherly concern and care. This is the heart of the New Testament message.

Who can grasp this? I have heard it seriously argued that the thought of divine fatherhood can mean nothing to those whose human father was inadequate, lacking wisdom, affection, or both.... The thought of our Maker becoming our perfect parent—faithful in love and care, generous and thoughtful, interested in all we do, respecting our individuality, skillful in training us, wise in guidance, always available, helping us to find ourselves in maturity, integrity, and uprightness—is a thought which can have meaning for everybody, whether we come to it by saying, 'I had a wonderful father, and I see that God is like that, only more so,' or by saying, 'My father disappointed me here, and here, and here, but God, praise His name, will be very different'.... The truth is that all of us have a positive ideal of fatherhood by which we judge our own and others' fathers.[4]

When I took an honest look at what I thought about God and how I felt toward Him, I was shocked to uncover deep anger and rage. I was angry at Him for letting me be born into my family. I was mad at Him for not changing my father. I hated Him for not caring enough for my mother to give her hope to live. I was furious with Him for not taking care of my brothers when I begged Him to all these years. I buried all these feelings, however, because Christians don't get mad at God.

Bob helped me understand that my rage, at work in my other relationships, was also operative in my relationship with God. As with my love for my mom, I couldn't acknowledge that anything was wrong in my relationship with God. Somehow I needed His love too much. If I acknowledged my true feelings about God—these dark emotions of anger and rage—I might lose His love.

I was trapped in a vicious cycle, however. Something

would happen to cause my anger at God to rise up within me. I would be afraid to acknowledge my feelings to myself or to God. That anger, boiling within, would whisper over and over, "I told you God is not to be trusted." Then I would steel myself further to rely only on myself.

I learned from my family to tiptoe gingerly around the house, trying to make everything appear fine, stuffing my feelings about my pain. Now God wanted me to be honest with my feelings, but I had had few natural experiences that told me it was safe to share them. I was comfortable locked in my pain, playing out my role as a strong Christian, but God was not. He jealously yearned for me to know Him as Father, to trust His work in my life, and to enjoy my relationship with Him. He would work in my individual circumstances to bring me to the place where I would speak honestly with Him.

Be Honest with God about These Feelings

Knowing God is relational. He deliberately made it that way from the beginning. When Adam and Eve hid from Him out of fear as a result of their sin, God called out to them, "Where are you?" He does the same thing for us today. He understands the damage that has occurred to us as a result of our families. He understands that our fears cause us to want to retreat into repression or denial and distance ourselves from Him. He calls out to each of us, "Where are you?"

This invitation to honesty is often turned down because we are afraid God can't take it. Or that we will offend Him and catch even more of His wrath. Or we will lose whatever minimal interest He had in us in the first place. The same honesty that is required of us in our personal recovery to break through our denial systems, however, is also required with God. It takes great courage to answer Him honestly. Once I did that, I could begin to have a genuine relationship with Him.

A GENUINE RELATIONSHIP WITH GOD

To have a genuine relationship with God, I had to trust in the person of God. In Hebrews, the great epistle on faith in God, it states: "Without faith it is impossible to please Him, for he who comes to God must believe that He is, and that He is a rewarder of those who diligently seek Him" (Heb. 11:6). Coming to know God as Father crystallized for me into two distinct phases: (1) learning that He loved me and (2) learning that He intended good for me.

When people learn of all that I have faced in my life, they invariably respond, "You're such a strong person to have gone through all that." I received a lot of feedback over the years that I had value because I was strong and because I could go through anything. Yet as a little girl, the one thing I wanted more than anything else was the love of my father. I observed that my father valued someone who succeeded in school. Therefore, I applied myself diligently in school to succeed, hoping to secure his love.

My relationship with God was no different. For some reason, I understood and accepted the fact that God had paid the penalty for my sins in the death and resurrection of Jesus and that His act enabled me to have a relationship with Him. But once I was in that relationship, I did the same thing I had with every other man in my life. I placed the burden on myself to stay in His good graces. Then, in the summer of 1983 in three distressing events in the space of four months, my ability to rebound and rise above my difficulties as usual was shattered.

All three situations had to do with relationships with men. These were not the three most important relationships I ever had with men. Nor were these the three most devastating blows I ever had in my life. But there was no time to recover from one disappointment before the next hit. At the end of my second year in law school, I met and dated David, an attorney, for several months. As the summer drew near, however, he told me he didn't know where I got the idea he was interested in a long-term relationship. He was not; he was simply being nice. I was hurt by this but shrugged off the pain.

After all, Steve, a man from law school whom I had been close friends with for two years, had recently written and called and said he wondered if there was more to our relationship than just a good friendship. He thought we should date when he returned to Washington that summer. So I thought, "Well, maybe this relationship will finally take off." The day after he arrived in Washington, at a party, I introduced him to a very good friend of mine and they talked for a moment. The next day Steve called me for her phone number so he could ask her out. I was shocked and hurt and confused.

Years before, I had dated Rob during my graduate school years, a guy that I loved very deeply. Despite his intensive efforts to shape me into the woman of his dreams, an acceptable politician's wife, he had broken off our relationship. I always thought we would get back together, however, someday. We stayed in touch off and on over the years and shortly after the summer began, we talked again. He told me that he had never stopped loving me and that he, too, had always thought we would get married. Since he was about to move from the east to the west coast to begin a new job, he asked if we could get together in a month to talk about where we would go from here. Encouraged, I wrote him that week, but I did not hear back from him.

Six weeks later, I received a letter from his best friend. I raced upstairs to my room, tearing open the envelope, my heart beating fast. I scanned the letter quickly until I got to these words, "Rob married earlier this summer." The wind knocked out of me, I sank onto my bed and held the letter tightly as my eyes filled with tears. Married! "God, why are You doing this to me? I don't understand." I felt numb and empty and so very lonely.

By this time I had nothing left in me to regroup. This was the KO punch. I couldn't recover from it. I couldn't just get up off the mat and stagger on to the next round. This time, I was left with nothing. I felt abandoned.

Bob was out of the country when I received this letter. On his return, he found a letter from me waiting for him:

> I tried to think what you would tell me if I could have called you. Remember last time? I remember you telling me this is bigger than David, bigger than Steve. So, I said to myself: "This is bigger than Rob." But I felt so empty. So what if it is part of God's plan and He wants to use it to heal me? I can't take God's methods anymore. Bob, I am scared. I can't seem to hang onto my faith this time. I feel so very alone . . . betrayed even. Why get up and try again in this trusting God stuff? All it gets me is one more crisis, one more disappointment, over and over again. No wonder my mother killed herself. How many times can one person get knocked down and still believe God cares? I feel so afraid; like a pawn in some cosmic game. I know I will see you on Friday. I am so frightened, please help me.

When I saw Bob that week, he explained, "Nancy, I know that there is a lot of pain. This deep-rooted fear of being alone and of being abandoned has been a part of you for so long, but you have covered it up for years by being a good Christian. Be still now for a while and let God nurture you. The pain is necessary so your heart can be open to God the Father's love. Let Him love you as His daughter."

I couldn't respond to Bob. I was so despondent, I left his office quietly. That night I wrote in my journal:

> I am afraid
> of being alone
> rejected

abandoned
I am afraid God will leave me too
that when I most need Him, He won't be there
I am afraid I will never be married
that there is no good man for me.

I want so much to know deep love
to have the longing of my heart satisfied by God
yet I do not know how to make that happen.

So all this pain is Your love,
Your mercy?
I can't see that now.
I am afraid of You.
What if You are not there?

My despair was so deep that for several counseling sessions, I couldn't get past expressing my pain to Bob. I recorded in my journal, "Jesus must have known how hard it is for some of us who have never known this kind of intimate, unconditional love to really accept God's love for them. In His last prayer for us, Jesus defined eternal life as knowing God and pleaded with the Father that the love with which He loved the Son might be ours as well" (John 17:13, 26). That thought began to break through my darkness with a glimmer of light. Jesus was interceding for me to know the Father's love as He had experienced it.

The next counseling session, as I was expressing the agony in my heart once again, Bob said, "Nancy, I want you to trust me. I have some very important things to tell you and I want you to hear me. You are experiencing God pulling up out of you all the loneliness, fear, and abuse you have ever experienced. That's why you feel so shaky now. Listen to me very carefully, Nancy. I know with the depths of my being—now this is not psychology or intellectualism or spirituality; this is the conviction of God—I know that God is preparing you for His love, that all of this loneliness and pain you are going through now is His love too. You cannot see it; I don't expect you to, but I will go through this with you as much as I can. God has stripped you of every resource of your independence to get you alone with Him. Because you've been hurt so often, you have built up quite a reserve of resilience and stubborn persistence. It is that reserve that God has had to empty. You will never know that you can really trust God until He is all that is left."

"Bob, in Romans 8 it says that nothing, absolutely nothing is capable of separating us from the love of God. I want so much to believe that is true for me. Yet I see God right now as a tall, strong man with arms folded across his chest, looking disdainfully down at a child who is pulling at his pant's leg, clinging to him, saying, 'Please love me.' I guess I need to know God won't just respond to me with tolerance. I wish my mental picture was of Him hugging me and laughing and being excited to see me. I have so many fearful thoughts about God. But right now, all I can trust is you. And if you tell me that all this loneliness and pain is God's love at work in me so that I can know His love, then I will trust that."

Over the next several months, almost imperceptibly, a peace began to fill my heart, an assurance of God's love that I had never known before. As I went about the ordinary activities of my final year in law school, work, and time with friends, I began to believe that God was there, loving me without any action on my part. Now I was coming to believe in Him in the midst of disappointments and to accept the fact that God loved me because He chose to do so, not because I had proven myself worthy. God's Holy Spirit was at work patiently during these months. I could finally understand why Paul said that as Christians we don't have to be "like cringing, fearful slaves, but we should behave like God's very own children, adopted into the bosom of his family, and calling to him, 'Father, Father.' For his

Holy Spirit speaks to us deep in our hearts, and tells us that we really are God's children" (Rom. 8:15–16 LB).

In a counseling session at the close of 1983, Bob reflected on what had happened over the last five months and said, "Remember, several years ago I told you that when you could relinquish your independent nature to God and let Him love you, you would be in a position to receive the gift of marriage? I want to encourage you to begin to pray for this now. You are more ready for marriage now than you have ever been in your entire life. All that is missing is the gift of a husband from God. There's nothing else you have to do except wait for this free gift of God. Go ahead now and pray for being married."

"But Bob," I complained, "I am afraid to do that. I'd almost rather live with an unfulfilled desire than to express it to God and not have it be fulfilled."

"Nancy, this may sound strange to you now, but I think God wants to begin to demonstrate His provision for you. He is a Father who gives good gifts. I think that one of the ways God will demonstrate His love for you is through a man. For so long you have desired marriage and wanted God to create for you that new family. That desire goes hand in hand with your desire for God, but you need to come to this desire of your heart fully. God's love is going to come to you in even a deeper way, and I believe it is going to come to you through another person."

THE REAL GOD ASKS YOU TO CHOOSE

God designed us so that we have the privilege of participating in our own recovery: He gave us the ability to choose. When God created the earth and mankind, He purposefully limited Himself and His control over His creation by giving us free will and the privilege of making choices. We often view ourselves as determined by our home life. Our fate seems sealed from the beginning. We can resort to the "if onlys" of regret. "If only I hadn't been born into this family, I wouldn't be so anxious and fearful now." "If only I had another father, I wouldn't be so driven." "If only I had a loving family, I could relate easily now to God." These are excuses for staying stuck in self-destructive patterns.

But we do have choices. We can choose to blame our pasts for our present problems, or we can choose to examine our pasts for connections to present problems and change as a result. The good news is that we can become transformed people. We do not have to repeat our families. At any point, we can begin to choose to live according to new patterns of relating to ourselves, to others, and to our God.

Choices Have Consequences

We not only have the privilege of making choices but also the responsibility of making choices. Our choices have consequences. "Do not be deceived, God is not mocked; for whatever a man sows, that he will also reap" (Gal. 6:7). We reap the consequences of poor choices as well as the benefits of good choices. Over time our choices measure our lives. Each choice we make becomes foundational for the future as we develop patterns based on our choices.

Sometimes the negative effects of our choices are felt generations later. This is especially true in family life. Those families that are nurturing tend to produce men and women capable of nurturing their own children. Dysfunctional families tend to reproduce their own kind.

Central to breaking the cycle of dysfunction in my family was to learn how to make choices that would result in life and health to me. Bob explained to me the principle of choice making that God laid out in Deuteronomy 30:19–20:

I have set before you life and death, blessing and cursing; therefore choose life, that both you and your descendants may live; that you may love the Lord your God, that you may obey His voice, and that you may cling to Him.

Life and blessing or death and curses. These were the two distinct paths I could choose. Bob explained that my family had conditioned me to choose those things which were death to me. Each one of my family members had chosen death—a physical, moral, or spiritual death. Three of them had either threatened, attempted, or committed suicide. I had grown up with these people and incorporated these tendencies toward choosing death into my personality. It would take conscious choice making on my part for my life to go counter to these natural tendencies. In counseling, I learned that I had a responsibility to participate with God in determining my future paths. I was not at the mercy of my past. I could make choices that would give me hope for a different future and leave a legacy of life for my children.

When Faced with a Choice, Make the One That Leads to Life

I learned, with Bob's help, not to respond so impulsively to decisions but to step back, examine the choices, trace the consequences that might flow from each of those choices, and then choose the path that led to life, blessing, and health. Nowhere was this more problematic for me than in relationships with men. I was naturally drawn to men who were unable to commit or who were untrustworthy. Stable men who were able to express their feelings and make long-lasting commitments did not interest me. Learning to choose life in this area would be the greatest challenge in my recovery.

I also needed to learn how to choose life in my relationship with God. I had to learn that it was possible to begin to choose to believe what was true about God despite my natural proclivity to believe otherwise. As I uncovered what I believed about God—distorted or not—I could then decide whether to affirm or refute these beliefs.

Take Your New Beliefs about God to Another for Validation or Correction

I took these discoveries to either Bob or to my good friend and running partner, Elaine Griffith, to help me evaluate the truth of my beliefs. This next step was very important. Otherwise, I could stay stuck in my anger, disappointment, or fears about God by mulling over those experiences that gave credence to my distorted view of God. Without validation or correction of my distortions by someone who had already worked through a biblical understanding of God as Father, I would only distance myself further from God, convinced He was just as untrustworthy as I originally thought.

Elaine and I often ran together along the W & OD Railroad bike path in Virginia. One brilliant June day a few weeks after I had graduated from law school in 1984, I explained, "Elaine, I am so confused. I feel like God has stripped me of everything I have depended on these last few years. Last fall, I lost my long-held hope that Rob and I would get back together and be married. I don't see how God could bring anyone into my life that would measure up to him. I leave tomorrow for San Francisco to study for the bar exam. After that I move to San Francisco and start all over. I leave my church and all my close friends here. It doesn't feel right. I don't have any peace at all about this decision I made six months ago to join a San Francisco law firm. But God did not provide an opportunity to stay here in Washington." We kept running, but my pace slowed as I labored to breathe steadily; I felt a tightening in my chest from my fears about the future.

"Nancy," Elaine said, "God knows exactly where you are at this point. He knows your fears and He can help. It's alright to be confused now. You don't have to push so hard to understand."

I suddenly stopped running and turned to Elaine and said, "But I can't seem to trust Him with this. I want so much to stay in D.C., but I don't see any way to do that. My school loans come due in six months. I'm scheduled to take the California bar exam in seven weeks. It's impossible to get a D.C. job at this late date."

Elaine put her hand on my shoulder and said, "So don't trust Him with it. Say instead, 'God, I trust You to give me what I need to know to trust You. You show me the next step.' He'll do that for you, Nancy. Ask Him to show you the next step."

I cried gently now, brushing the tears away from my cheeks with the back of my hand.

Elaine continued, "Nancy, you are very capable. I think God wants to show Himself to you in a way you have never seen before. I think He wants to show you His power and His ability to work on your behalf. But He's getting you to the place where you can't see how to work it all out. Remember, God is not devastated because He has all the power and all the solutions. He wants to demonstrate this to you, if you'll let Him. Nancy, remember what it says in Ephesians 3:20: God 'is able to do exceedingly abundantly above all that we ask or think, according to the power that works in us.' Ask for this; watch for this. God knows you can't uphold the burden of this. He says He will do something marvelous for you on the basis of His power at work in your behalf. Can you believe this?"

I looked off into the field of wildflowers by the bike path and blinked hard, fighting back the tears. "It's okay," Elaine gently said. "Just ask Him to show you how to trust Him. Tell God, 'Okay, You've brought me this far; I know You love me. It's new territory, however, to believe You want to act on my behalf. Just open the door a little and help me receive.'"

Replace Old Thinking with Truth

As I flew off to San Francisco, I had the verses Elaine shared with me on an index card. Over the next several months, I would look at them over and over, reminding myself what the Bible said was true about God. He was a rewarder of people like me who sought Him. He would make it clear what He wanted for me. He wanted to accomplish it based on His love for me and His desire to act on my behalf.

I discovered that the key to knowing God was to replace distorted beliefs with the truth. This did not happen overnight. I had spent many years in contrary belief patterns, and these perspectives were ingrained in my thinking and my response to God. It took me quite some time to sort through my wrong thinking about God and replace it with the truth. I found I didn't have to plan out an academic journey to do this. God used my present circumstances to help me learn the truth about His character.

Shortly after I arrived in San Francisco, I received a phone call from a Georgetown law professor who wondered if I might be interested in a job with a Washington firm. The firm had called him, and he had called the law review office to ask for some names. It so happened that a friend of mine answered the phone and suggested he call me in California. I was thrilled. Here it was! God was about to act on my behalf. Hallelujah! I hurriedly got off a resume in the mail and waited anxiously for his reply.

I struggled with the waiting. As I wrote to Elaine, "It is difficult to wait. I get so anxious when nothing is happening. This firm has my resume and I haven't heard anything for three weeks now. I can feel that old habit creeping up. I have a tendency to say, 'See, I knew God wouldn't do it.' Oh, Elaine, please pray for me. I want so much to believe that God is at work on my behalf. It's as if God is trying to build into my experience things for which I have no reference point. I knew neither a father's love nor a father's provision. Is this how faith is born—pushing through the familiar, but wrong, concepts to trust the unfamiliar but true? I stand at the threshold of faith and my past, my common-sense logic, my experiences tell me I am a fool. Where I stand now, there is no turning back—it's just hard to leap over. Will a small step do? For me, today, that step is just admitting to you and to God that this is where I am. Please pray with me that Isaiah 64:4 becomes real in my life: 'For since the world began no one has seen or heard of such a God as ours, who works for those who wait for him!'"

A few weeks later, the professor called. The firm was not interested in interviewing me. I was devastated. My emotions swirled around me and I clutched the telephone receiver tightly. Now I had a choice. I could let this experience confirm that God loved to toy with me, getting my hopes up and making me trust Him and then pulling the rug out from under me. Or I could choose to believe what was true about Him despite my circumstances.

I grabbed the index card, went out the door to run, and in cadence with every step, repeated the verses. I told God I chose to believe those verses were true even though my feelings were screaming otherwise. I asked God to make His faithfulness, love, care, and mercy real to me.

The day after the bar exam, I went to San Diego—my three-day reward for the last six weeks of intensive study. I still desired to stay in the Washington area, but it was now three weeks before my scheduled move to California. I took long walks on the island of Coronado and shared my thoughts with God. Over the next three days, as I walked and talked with God, I discovered He had much to teach me, too, about my original decision process to move to San Francisco.

I realized that I had sought my own success. Like many others on law review, I bought into the theory that I should go to a big firm in a big city. These plum jobs were usually reserved for law review graduates. The wisdom around the law school was to go to the big firm, big city first, and then work your way down to a smaller firm, if you wanted. To do the reverse would keep you stuck at a small firm. That sounded reasonable to me, and I had only sent my resumes out to large firms in five major cities. As I prayed, God revealed these words: "Moses, Joseph, Paul, and Jesus." I continued to wait on Him in prayer asking what He meant. After a long silence, He spoke again: "Forty years in the wilderness first, a slave in Egypt first, fourteen years of preparation first, a carpenter's son first." I was deeply humbled. I had sought my own success, and so often God's way is the opposite of how I would accomplish my goals.

I also prayed about marriage. I was thirty-one years old and still unmarried. I seemed to get into one unfulfilling or destructive relationship after another, and yet I yearned to have a marriage of deep, committed love. What was wrong here?

As I prayed about these things, I received assurance from God that these desires—to return to Washington and to be married—were from Him. I received a clear word to trust Him and *to wait on Him*. Yet when I returned to Washington, I spent the first week running around, researching law firms, reworking my resume, printing up 150 copies, arranging to borrow a memory typewriter for cover letters, and other such frenetic activities. After all, God had said I could trust that my desire to stay in Washington was from Him, hadn't He?

As I was rushing out of the house to mail the letters, God brought me up short. "Where are you going?" He asked.

"God, You know where I am going; I'm going to get a job."

"Nancy, you're seeking your own success again. I want you to go back inside and wait for Me to act."

"So, God," I retorted, "I suppose You just want me to wait for the phone to ring?"

"That's exactly right. Do not take any initiative; only wait for Me to bring you the contacts."

"Right," I said halfheartedly and turned out of sheer obedience to climb the stairs to the house. "Sure, with just a few weeks to go before I am supposed to move to California, You want me to just hang out and wait."

And wait I did, even though it struck at the very core of my nature. My emotions were running high. Bob shared with me at the close of a counseling session that I should watch my feelings and not fall back in the trap of letting them take me off the track of trusting God. "The Father wants to do good to you, Nancy. The Father wants to give you good gifts. He knows the future and He wants what's best for you. Don't give in to your feelings of anxiety and become operational once again. Let Him be your Father."

Two weeks before I was to move, the phone rang. Kim Colby, an attorney with the Christian Legal Society who knew of my desire to stay in Washington, said, "Nancy, I don't think this firm is looking for an attorney, but the managing partner, Chip Grange, is on our board and has a lot of wisdom. Why don't you call him and see if you can meet with him?"

Four days later, I was in the law offices of Gammon & Grange, sharing with Chip my spiritual journey this last year and how it had brought me to waiting on the Lord. Within one week after that, I had met all the partners and they had extended me an offer to join their firm. I would be working in a small firm with other attorneys, learning the ropes of nonprofit law to serve the needs of tax-exempt organizations, including Christian ministries. As I left their offices after accepting the offer, I asked, "When did you know you needed an associate?"

Chip responded, "I began praying for God to bring the right person three months ago in June." God had begun to put into place all the circumstances necessary for me to stay in Washington early in the summer. It was the process of trusting God's love for me in His provision of my needs, however, that was His ultimate goal.

All of these principles from counseling—facing self-destructive patterns, choosing life, and believing the truth about God—were soon to coalesce in my greatest desire—to be married. It is one thing to learn principles in the abstract; it is another to apply them in the areas that have always been your greatest struggles. I knew that my understanding of God's love for me had gotten all wrapped up in whether or not He would provide me a loving family of my own. I had unraveled much of this in counseling, but it was not until I was faced with choosing His plan for me over my own natural desires that I would be able to understand God really had intended it all for good. I was about to experience my greatest challenge to all I had learned about myself and God in counseling: the choice of a marriage partner.

PART FOUR

The Victory

Chapter 14

Someday My Prince
Will Come

*They often have difficulty figuring out why they ever allowed
themselves to get involved in these painful relationships in
the first place. They feel victimized, and yet they consistently
seek out men who make them unhappy. Nobody wants to
be miserable, right? Wrong! Misery and anguish can feel
delicious, while the predictability of steady, supportive love
can get tiresome.[1]*

Dr. Connell Cowan and Dr. Melvyn Kinder
Smart Women, Foolish Choices

In 1985 at the age of thirty-two, I was yet again very
committed to someone who wasn't committed to me. Richard, thirty-eight, managed his own financial services business. An Ivy Leaguer, tall and quite attractive with dark
brown hair and eyes, he had fascinating stories of his exploits in other countries prior to settling down in the Washington, D.C., area. We had dated off and on for over a year,
with the relationship undergoing growth and then retrac-
tion, but never really moving beyond a certain point. He
said he loved me, but then he'd pull back. Despite a few obvious character flaws, I was loyal to Richard. I could help

him, I thought. I believed in him. I knew he had the potential to be a very dynamic Christian man. I encouraged him. I stood by him through his business ups and downs. And, without fail, I prayed for him. God and I together could bring out the best in Richard. The repetitious nature of that plan still seemed to escape me.

Then, on a warm spring day in early April, as Richard and I returned from a weekend visiting his parents in Massachusetts, I learned the reason for his inability to commit to me. We pulled in front of his house and parked the car. As he began to pull out a suitcase from the trunk of the car, another car drove up beside us and stopped. A beautiful woman with striking features and long blonde hair called out to Richard and then stopped short. She looked at me with as much surprise as I looked at her. It was then I met Ellen, his other girlfriend.

Richard fumbled for words, trying to engineer some excuse that would satisfy both of us. Ellen spat out a nasty remark and then sped off. Richard jumped into his car and took off after her. I stood alone, staring in disbelief as both of them drove down the street.

This was not the first indication I had had that Richard was unreliable and dishonest. Yet I so wanted the relationship to work that I had ignored obvious character defects. Instead, I envisioned Richard as I knew he could be. If there was anything I knew how to do well, it was to wait with great expectations for miraculous change. Since Richard was a Christian, I had a powerful accomplice in God, didn't I? Didn't He want Richard to be the kind of man I envisioned as well?

But meeting Ellen face-to-face was something even I, with all my fairy-tale thinking, just could not ignore. Although Richard told me that he would never see Ellen again, I knew it would just be a matter of a few months before there would be another, different Ellen. I told Richard I needed some space, some time to think things through. Surprisingly, although my head and my friends were telling me to jettison this relationship, my heart couldn't let go.

Painful, confusing relationships were no stranger to me. I was learning in counseling that my relationship with God was intimately tied up with my relationships with men. I began to see that I was looking to God to redeem my family and my mom's life through my own relationships with men. I was strangely attracted to men who were incapable, for a variety of reasons, of loving me in return, just like my own father.

I heard from Richard several times during the next few months. He appealed to me to give him another chance. He seemed earnestly repentant, and I wanted to believe in him so much. Maybe God was really working in his life to change him. Maybe now, since he had almost lost me, he would be open to committing himself to me. So I agreed to go out to dinner with him, just once.

He was as charming as I had ever known him that evening as he entertained me with tales of his time in Kenya. He thanked me for sticking by him, despite the number of times he had hurt me, and he shared with me all the changes that had occurred in his life during the last few months we had been apart. He had made a renewed commitment of his life and his business to the Lord. He was reading his Bible daily. He had not dated anyone else, he claimed, during the time we were apart.

I was thrilled. All this pain had not been for nothing. Now we could be together again, only this time, I knew the relationship was headed toward marriage. But as the weeks went by, I began to realize that this was not a new Richard, it was the old Richard. The time between dates grew longer and he became vague and noncommittal about when we would get together again.

On July 22, I received a phone call from Jeff LeSourd. A mutual friend, Bill Brown, a Navy pilot whom I had met

I spilled out my account of what had happened that weekend and concluded, "I'm not sure your mom would be thrilled with you taking an interest in me now."

"Yes, she would," Jeff said confidently. "I know that if she were alive today, she would enjoy spending time with you again. Nancy, you've been through a lot, that's true, but how you have handled all this is what makes you so special. I have only recently begun to appreciate the courage it takes to look squarely at your past and admit your need for help. You know, Bill had told me about you for several years. He was always prompting me to call you when I was in Virginia."

I laughed and said, "And you never did. Meanwhile, every time Bill came to Washington, he'd talk about you. Jeff LeSourd. Jeff LeSourd. That seemed to be his constant theme. A great guy, he'd say. Would I get together with you when you came east to visit your family, he'd ask. Finally, I got so tired of hearing about you. I remember the last time Bill was here. We were walking along the Mall and stopped near the Washington Monument. Once again, he talked about his friend, Jeff. I said, 'Bill, I really don't want to hear about this guy again. I promise you that if he ever calls when he's in Virginia, I'll talk with him; but I'm sick of hearing about him!'"

Jeff laughed. "Bill made the mistake of telling me all about you. I mean, ALL about you. I heard about your family, your struggles, your years and years and years of counseling."

"Oh, come on, now. It wasn't that bad!" I said.

"Oh, but Nancy, it was. You see, I was very stuck up. I was the son of Len LeSourd and Catherine Marshall. I deserved a woman with a pedigree. Then Bill tells me about you and your counseling. She's a Christian, I think. She has the Lord; she doesn't need counseling. She's obviously not the right one for me, so why even meet her?"

"The joke's on you now, I suppose," I laughed.

"Well, I do think God has a sense of humor. I never expected to like you. I called you just for job contacts. You were so warm and funny and upbeat. I thought, 'This doesn't sound like a depressed lady, dragged down by life.' So I called back. You know, I don't think this could have happened without my new stepmother, Sandy."

"Why is that?" I asked.

"Well, Dad met Sandy a year ago, and they just got married last month. I had a very hard time accepting Sandy into the family. You see, like you, she had a messed-up background. Before she became a Christian, she was an alcoholic, had tried to commit suicide, spent time in a mental hospital and halfway house—definitely not the type of woman the man who had been married to Catherine Marshall should marry. Because I was not really over Mom's death, I felt I had to protect her memory and it was hard for me to let Sandy in."

"But your dad married Sandy in June. How did you cope with that if you felt this way?" I asked.

"Right before they married, God really humbled me about my proud attitude. Here was this living example of a woman whose life had been transformed by God's grace, yes, but also by hard work on her part too. A month before Dad and Sandy married, I wrote her a letter, apologizing for my attitude and welcoming her into the family. Writing that letter, I felt the release to let God be God and bring whomever He wanted into my life, even if it was someone with a less than perfect background."

"Well, if that is me, you certainly got what you asked for!" We laughed together, and I said, "So, let's see, next weekend I'll be meeting the LeSourd family all at once. Oh, and yes, I'll be meeting you, too, for the first time. It's going to be an interesting weekend."

We hung up from that phone call, each with our own separate thoughts. Jeff was amazed at the Lord's goodness to him. One of the thoughts that kept coming back to him during the year after his mom's death was how discouraged he was that his mother would never meet his future wife. She had been there at Linda's and Chet's weddings but could not be there at his. Yet, if I was the one he would marry, God had completed that detail years before in 1974.

I thought, "I've got to be crazy. I have never even met this guy and I am going to spend the weekend with his entire clan. What if it is a disaster?" I really liked him. It was ironic though. It was clear his family was very committed to one another. They had strong personalities, strong relationships, and a strong faith in God. This was exactly the kind of family I wanted to be a part of, but would my past be too much for Jeff to handle?

The day Jeff was to fly out to Washington, I was nervous and scared. What had I done? It is one thing to meet someone for the first time, but did I have to tack on meeting his entire family too? I stared at the computer keyboard on my desk. Come on now, Nancy, complete that letter to the client. Concentrate. Concentrate? I couldn't sit still. I jumped up and paced in my office. Over to the window to stare out and try to calm a racing heart. The phone rang. I jumped.

"Hello, this is Nancy."

"Nancy, Jeff. Are you a wreck? I am. Only a few more hours until I catch my plane. This is going to be the longest day in my history."

"I've tried to work. It's hopeless. I would go home early but then all I would do is pace around the house."

"I know what you mean. Uh, the family is looking forward to meeting you, Nancy."

"Jeff, I wonder if that was such a good idea. I mean, meeting them just an hour after I pick you up at the airport?" I began to hedge and felt my heart pounding in my chest. What had I done? I felt confused and excited all at once. Why had we put so much pressure on ourselves to meet in this way at this time?

"Nancy, you're scared," Jeff said in his matter-of-fact way. "So am I. It's okay to be scared. This is a scary situation. Here we are, two people who have determined that they like everything they know about one another but who wonder if the chemistry will be there. This will either be an amazing story, or this will be the biggest disaster in romantic history."

I had to laugh at his abrupt but accurate assessment of our weekend ahead. "Jeff, I just want us to meet and get it over with. It's like this stupid physical test we both have to pass. There is so much warmth and caring already in our relationship, and I want all the romantic feelings to go with it."

"Nancy, whatever happens tonight, this weekend, we will continue to be friends. The bond we have formed these last few weeks is built on honesty and acceptance and God. So, what's the worst that can happen? We determine that it isn't right for us to date and we'll be great friends. That's not so bad, now, is it?" Jeff stopped suddenly and then continued, "Hey, Nancy, I just realized, I don't have any idea what you look like. How am I going to recognize you?"

"Just look for the blonde in a blue dress," I laughed. "Besides, at 10:42 at night, how many people are going to be meeting a plane from St. Louis?"

After we hung up, I left the office. I went home and took my time getting ready. I wanted to look especially nice. I had hardly slept the night before. Jeff had called at 11:00 and we had talked until 4:00 A.M. I was nervous, not so much about being with Jeff as about finding out if I would be attracted to him. I noticed that my neck had taken the brunt of this tension. It had only been five months since I had been in a car wreck, and I was still healing. On my way out of the house, I stopped to take a muscle relaxant that the doctor had prescribed to see if I could get my neck and shoulders to loosen up some.

I arrived at National Airport much too early. I paced the

halls trying to burn off this nervous energy. I kept checking the overhead monitors: TWA Flight Number 576 was scheduled to land on time. Good, I thought, I don't think I can wait much longer. As I began to walk back toward the gate, I noticed there were only a handful of people gathering to meet the plane. That should make it easier, I thought, and then I spotted the only other woman there—a blonde in a blue dress. "Oh, this should be fun. I can picture it now. 'No, not her, Jeff, over here, here I am.'" The passengers began to deplane and come up the ramp to the gate. Fortunately, the other blonde met her party immediately and walked off. Now it was just me. As I stared at the men walking up the ramp, I noticed one man with a huge grin on his face. He gave me a quick wave and I knew this was Jeff. Average height and broad shouldered, with dark brown hair and light blue eyes framed by horn-rim glasses, he was dressed in a navy pinstriped suit and crisply starched white shirt accented by a navy-dotted red tie. With his briefcase in one hand and *The Wall Street Journal* tucked under the other arm, he came toward me. I took a deep breath. "Jeff?" I asked.

"Nancy!" he exclaimed. "Finally!" He gave me a hug and we both began talking at the same time as we walked toward baggage claim.

"How was your flight?" "Did you have to wait long?" "Can I carry anything?" The words tumbled out of both of our mouths as we searched for common ground in this awkward situation. We talked for a long time as we waited for Jeff's suitcase. Finally, Jeff pierced through the formalities with one statement. "Nancy, you passed the physical test." He saw me blanch and then lower my eyes. He hurriedly added, "Let me explain what I mean by that. I mean that if I were at a party and I saw you across the room, I would be attracted enough to you to want to go over and meet you. Could you say the same about me?"

Jeff got his answer in my silence. I didn't want to hurt

him, but I felt no physical attraction to him at all, even though he was nice looking. I didn't understand it. It was the most disappointing moment of my life.

It was certainly no picnic for Jeff either. As we walked to my car, Jeff reminded me about what he had said earlier. We would be great friends. But we were both sad. He put his suitcase in the back seat and opened the door for me. As he came around to the driver's side, I realized I was so very tired. Jeff shut the door after him, and I said, "I know we have a long way to go to Evergreen, but Jeff, I can hardly keep my eyes open. I took a muscle relaxant before I came to the airport and I had forgotten that it makes me sleepy. Please wake me up before we get there so I can make myself presentable for your family. I'm so sorry."

I laid my head back on the headrest, closed my eyes, and fell sound asleep. Jeff eased the car out of first into second, exited the airport parking lot and headed west to Evergreen. "Oh, Lord," he prayed, "here I am about to take Nancy to meet my entire family. Why did I do this? I should have waited until we had met first. But I just felt so strongly that this relationship was right. Why is she cutting me off like this? The Nancy I met tonight is not the one I have shared so deeply with these last few weeks. Help me, Lord, and help Nancy know her own heart."

Fortunately, our delay at baggage claim had kept the family from waiting up. When we arrived at Evergreen, the lights were out and we were able to come into the farmhouse in silence. I was grateful. I just couldn't face meeting his family. They would probably be, like Jeff, very nice. It would make me feel even more like a creep.

The next morning, the sun streamed into the guest bedroom on the first floor. I looked out the window on the expansive lawn and the huge boxwood in the dell. Huge tall trees sheltered a small stone springhouse. *Evergreen.* An appropriate name. I glanced over at the white wrought-iron bench under a deep burgundy Japanese maple tree. So peaceful.

Okay, Nancy, this is it. Let's go meet Jeff's family. I emerged from the bedroom to find kids everywhere. Sons and daughters, cousins and friends all seemed to be heading in a million directions. Edith, the wife of Peter Marshall, Jeff's stepbrother, came up and looked me over with her clear blue eyes. She introduced herself, flashed her brilliant white smile, and in her most commanding voice said, "Nancy, dear. We've all been waiting to meet you. Come on. Let me introduce you." I was then whisked away to the kitchen. They were each as warm and accepting as Jeff had told me they would be.

Later that day there was to be a large gathering of friends from the Washington area. Soon we were all swept up into activity to prepare for the event. It enabled me to get to know the family without too much scrutiny of Jeff's and my relationship. However, Susan, Jeff's sister-in-law, wasted no time in making her position known. After the picnic tables were set up and the food prepared, Susan, tall and slim with light brown hair, elegant in a simple cotton jumper, called over to me. "Nancy, I'd like to talk to you a few minutes." We sat down on a stone wall near the patio and Susan began. "Nancy, Jeff is very special to me. He has been very committed to Chester and me and our family. He takes time to encourage us in our marriage and in our time with our children. So, tell me, what are your intentions with Jeff?"

I was shocked. Susan was so straightforward. And yet I was also touched. She obviously loved Jeff a great deal and wasn't about to let any woman who had captured his heart trample all over it. It was a direct question; it deserved a direct answer. "I wish I knew, Susan. I really like him, but when we finally met last night, I felt like I was meeting a dear friend, one with whom I could be very comfortable and safe. But I just didn't feel anything romantic. I wanted to. I really did. But it just wasn't there."

"Is there someone else, Nancy?" Susan asked.

"Well, there is this guy, Richard. We've been seeing each other off and on now for about a year, but recently I began to realize that his character is lacking some key strengths that are necessary for a committed relationship. I have chosen not to see him anymore, but I have to admit, the romantic attraction is still there."

"An attraction that is missing with Jeff?"

"Yes."

"Nancy, right before Chester and I married, I was involved with a guy like Richard. Deep down I knew he was not the right guy for me, yet there was a strong attraction to him. His inability to commit to me kept me waiting for him to change. I finally realized that he was never going to change. I've been married to Chester for five years now, and do you know, that guy is still not married?"

That caught my attention. I realized that last night when there was no attraction to Jeff, I had begun to think about Richard again. I knew Richard was wrong for me, but I couldn't seem to let go of my feelings for him. "Susan, what made you realize Chester was right for you?"

"Oh, Nancy, if you only take the time to get to know Jeff, you'll realize there is something very special about these LeSourd men. They care deeply. Family is very important to them. They make great husbands and wonderful fathers. Their characters have been strengthened and built over many years of faithfulness to values and principles that the family holds dear. You'll never have to play games with them. Most importantly, Nancy, they know how to love a woman. Give Jeff time. You'll see what I see. No one would make a better husband or father. Trust me."

I looked over at Jeff, laughing with his dad and Chet as they fired up the grill. The LeSourd men. Standing together, their warmth, humor, and ease with one another depicted years of love and commitment to each other. Perhaps Susan was right.

The next afternoon, a steamy August Virginia day, Len LeSourd rounded up some of the family for a croquet game. Jeff, always ready for a competitive game, signed up immediately. Jeff's older stepbrother, Peter Marshall, and his two teenaged children, Mary and Pete, joined in. I signed up too. I'd never played before, but croquet seemed harmless enough. Just tap a big hard ball around the grass with a mallet. Oh, no. Not the way the LeSourds play croquet. They play to win. In fact, so serious are they about their croquet game, they have an entire field edged in boxwood and hyacinths, neatly manicured and reserved exclusively for croquet. Forget making an impression on the new girl. And Len, or Poppy, as the grandchildren call him, was the worst of all.

Jeff and I teamed up against Poppy and Mary. I could feel the excitement in the air as Poppy and Jeff teased each other about who was going to whip whom. Peter and his son, Pete, made an imposing pair, our third team. Peter, at six feet, four inches, was a humorous sight as he bent over the croquet ball with the three foot mallet. His son, Pete, only eleven years old but already five-feet, seven-inches tall, was also raring to win. Poppy, Peter, and Jeff took their first shots to see which team would go first. Poppy, of course, won. He took his first shots one-handed and with great ease, making it through two sets of wickets on the first turn. I knew I was in trouble. Where were the card games?

After Mary took her turn, Jeff looked at me and said, "We're up." With great patience and encouragement, he led me through the paces of getting the croquet ball through flimsy white metal wickets. Then he took his turn. With his eye on his father, he skillfully guided his ball through the wickets, placing a perfect set-up shot for the next wicket, and then tapped his ball through the wicket. "Look out,

Pops!" he shouted and then he slammed his mallet against the croquet ball and with a large crack, the ball shot across the lawn and hit Poppy's ball, knocking it out of its previously well-placed position in front of the next wicket. "Ah, Pops, sorry!" Jeff exclaimed. But he wasn't one bit sorry.

I suddenly realized what this game was all about. So what if Peter, Pete, Mary, and I were playing? This was a match between father and son. A good-natured, fun, high-spirited, but determined match. As the game progressed, I watched Jeff playfully bait his father, compliment his dad on good shots, and encourage the younger children and me on our sometimes flailing efforts at moving that croquet ball through its paces. I thought about what Susan had said. The LeSourd men.

After the game, as Poppy rounded up Susan, Peter, and Chet for a tennis match, Jeff suggested we take a walk instead. He wanted to show me the farm. We walked down to the century-old stone barn. Huge trees shorn of their limbs provided the beams of support to a two-story structure. Bales of hay were piled high on the second floor. He pointed out the five foot hinges, original from the pre-Civil War period, on the barn doors. "When I worked summers on the farm, the toughest thing was trying to find replacement hinges. You just can't replace history."

We walked down by the pond and through fields of hay. Some fields had already been hayed, with large rectangular blocks of hay baled and drying in the sun. "That's tough work," he said and told me what goes into baling hay. We passed a creek and Jeff told me stories about Evergreen and the care his grandmother gave to clearing the creeks of all sharp stones and glass to make it safe for them to play as children. As he talked, I saw his love for Evergreen, for preserving tradition, and for simple values like keeping creeks safe for children.

We walked through one field to the top of a hill and admired the view of the Blue Ridge Mountains as the sun glinted off the tin roof of a nearby farmhouse. Cutting through another field, we came out onto a gravel road and walked along it until it intersected with Route 722, the road the farmhouse was on. As we walked, I began to share my feelings.

"Jeff, I admire you so much. I can see how special you are and what a heritage you have. You have a wealth of love and joy to give to some woman. I just don't think it is me."

Jeff was quiet and we continued walking.

I kicked a small stone into a rivulet and continued, "I have observed the way you interact with your grandmother, your father, your siblings, and the children. You are amazing with people. As I have watched you, I have tried so hard to muster up romantic feelings for you. I mean, it seems so right. You are exactly the kind of man I should be involved with, and I do appreciate your friendship. I really do. It's just that I don't feel anything more than that."

As we neared the intersection of Route 725 and Route 722, Jeff suddenly turned to me, put his hands on my shoulders, and looked me straight in the eyes. "Nancy, I understand what you're saying, but I think you're wrong. Your life is at a crossroads. Yes, you can continue caring for people like Richard. Or you can make a different choice. You've shared with me how at every point in your journey you had to forcefully turn your back on your natural inclinations and choose that which seemed foreign to you at the time. Yet, as you saw the consequences that flowed from those choices, you felt free and less constricted by your past. Am I right?"

"Yes," I replied. My eyes filled with tears as I knew he was speaking the truth. Was God calling me to choose life now with Jeff? Was moving on in our relationship despite my lack of feelings for him something that would result in good and life to me?

"Nancy," Jeff said firmly, "you have a choice now. Do you want Richard and all the other Richards like him that you could date? Or do you want me? It really is your choice, you know."

I began to cry softly. Jeff drew me close and I put my head on his shoulder. As we stood there together at the edge of Routes 722 and 725, I knew he was right. I did have a choice. Jeff was steady, consistent, and committed, and for some reason that didn't attract me at all. Richard was aloof, noncommittal, and incapable of loving, but I was inexplicably bound to him. I felt miserable. Would I be able to choose what was best for me even if it didn't feel right?

Jeff lifted my chin with his hand and looked directly in my eyes and said, "You don't have to choose today. Let's just see what develops for awhile. Nancy, it's your decision. I am not going away. This time, you'll have to be the one to end the relationship."

Chapter 15

Choices

Where is the man who fears the Lord? God will teach him how to choose the best.

Psalm 25:12 (TLB)

Jeff and I saw each other every few weeks and kept the long-distance phone carriers in business. One weekend, we both flew to New York City to visit good friends of his family, Clyde and Norma King. Clyde, general manager of the New York Yankees at the time, and Norma had been married for thirty-nine years. It seemed that not only Jeff, but many of his friends, had the secret to strong relationships and happy marriages: an abiding respect for the deep worth of the other. Over the weekend, I watched the mutual support and encouragement the Kings gave to one another. One night, as Jeff and Clyde eased into overstuffed chairs to talk baseball, Norma and I went to the kitchen for coffee and talked about Jeff. She had only good things to say about him.

It was that way wherever we went. Whether it was on Jeff's turf or with his friends in other cities, no one could say enough good things about Jeff. "Jeff is so generous." "Jeff is such a committed friend." "Our kids love Jeff." It was the same with my friends. No matter how many people I made him meet, they all said the same thing, "Jeff is a good man, Nancy."

The next day we took a Circle Line tour around Manhattan. We sat on the upper deck of the boat and let the early fall sun counter the cool wind on our faces. As the tour guide continued his monologue about the city in an unenthusiastic monotone, I told Jeff how Norma had sung his praises. "Jeff, everyone who knows you thinks you're wonderful," I said.

"But you, right?" Jeff teased.

"Jeff!" I protested. "I think you're wonderful too. I do. It's just that..."

"I know, Nancy. You don't have to say it." He watched the shoreline for a few moments. Then he continued, "Nancy, you're waiting for your knight in shining armor, aren't you?"

I laughed, "Yes, I guess I am."

"And I'm not he, am I?" Jeff asked seriously.

"No, Jeff, you're not."

"Well, let me tell you something, Nancy. I may not be your knight in shining armor, but you're no fair maiden either!"

I stared at him in shock. He had touched a nerve in me, though. He was right. I certainly was no fair maiden. What made me think I needed a knight with no chinks in his armor?

I pondered this question the next weekend when some friends and I drove to Rehobeth, our favorite beach located in Delaware, about a three-hour drive from Washington. A friend who had known my agonizing over Richard and had recently met Jeff put a book in my hands and said, "Read this book this weekend, Nance. I think it will answer some of your questions."

I loved late September at the beach. Although we spent many summer weekends here, I liked the early fall the best. The water was still warm, the sun strong, but the crowds gone. It was a quiet, contemplative time. I settled down on a large towel on the sand and picked up the book, *Smart Women, Foolish Choices*, and began to read. I could not put it down. When I got to chapter 5, I read the following:

> Women who confuse longing with love find it difficult to feel "in love" if their feelings toward a man are reciprocated. They associate love not with "having" but with "wanting".... Unless they recognize and change this pattern, they continue to play out this no-win game.... Women may resolve such internal conflicts by continually seeking out men who are unavailable. Because their love for such men is not reciprocated, these women can remain in that exquisitely miserable state of longing.
>
> Nice men are not elusive, unknown, or mysterious. They're right there. They are predictable. They call when they say they will. And yet these men are often passed over because they don't stimulate that sense of longing so often linked with the feeling of being in love.[1]

There I was. In black and white. They could have been writing about me alone. And about Jeff. He let me know exactly who he was, what he had to offer, and, even more, that he wanted to offer it to me. There was no mystery. No game playing. Jeff was guileless. Yes, he was predictable because you could trust what he said.

The *Smart Women, Foolish Choices* authors made a case for women turning to "diamonds in the rough" instead of their usual dates:

> In fact, the diamond in the rough is quite special. He has developed qualities of personality and character that are more substantial than flashy. If he appears less aggressive and more sensitive than other men, it may be because he's less defensive and cocky, more comfortable with openness. He is the kind of man about whom you might say, "I felt safe and comfortable with him, but I

don't know, there's just no sizzle." What some women fail to understand is that what they call "sizzle" is really nothing more than uncertainty and nervousness about their place in a man's affection. There is really nothing terrific about feeling anxious. And there is really nothing wrong with feeling safe and comfortable with a man. After all, that is what a good, stable relationship is all about.[2]

I jumped up from the sand and began to jog down the beach. I had to think. Was it, like Jeff had predicted, really a simple choice to love him? Would the feelings follow? What if I never had any feelings for him? Could I marry him without feelings? I didn't think so.

As I waited to talk with Bob a few weeks later, I remembered what he had told me several years before when I was bemoaning the fact that I seemed to get into one painful relationship after another. "Nancy, God is using situations with these men to show you that you did not escape the family pathology of addiction. Your addiction is to relationships. When the deep deprivation in your life, the loneliness and fear, resurfaces, you can't deal with the pain. Instead, you become operational and look to a relationship to stop the pain. God is going to bring it up over and over to get all this pathology out in the open so He can touch it and transform it."

"So you're saying I am probably going to go through more of these painful relationships?" I asked.

"Probably. Until your patterns are healed. I have seen a pattern in the men you are attracted to, Nancy. These men have feelings for you, but they have their emotions and feelings well under control. At the point the relationship should move on to intimacy and commitment, they block off their feelings."

"Why do I go for these types of men?"

"Because they are the opposite of your father. You saw

your father as irrational and highly emotional in his displays of anger and rage. So you are drawn toward the cool, rational guys who have a tight control on their emotions. These men are not in touch with their feelings, but you see them as strong and controlled. You'd be afraid of an emotional man because to you an emotional man is equivalent to an abuser."

"But what attracts these men to me? I don't see myself as cool and detached. I am usually the one in the relationship who is open about my feelings."

"Exactly. This type of man is attracted to you because you are sensitive, affectionate, and emotionally vulnerable. They want to be like that themselves, but they are threatened by this part of them. They deny that part of them, and in so doing, deny you, and eventually have to push you away."

"So I have really messed up, haven't I."

"No, absolutely not. Nancy, it is not an issue of what is wrong with you. This whole process of healing and change is a step-by-step path. Your life is much broader than this or that man. God is at work to heal much of the pain and loneliness in your life. But two things must occur. First, you must open yourself up to being loved by a sensitive man. Pray that God will open you to receive more love from a man and to be in the position to accept a man who can be open. Second, you have to wait. Wait and trust in a loving God who desires to provide good things for you. Don't get operational, Nancy, during this waiting period. Let God be God."

As I reflected on Bob's words to me over two years before, I began to wonder if I was shutting off God's choice for me. Jeff was a man who could express his feelings unashamedly. Richard, on the other hand, was cool and controlled. Was I perceiving Richard as strong and attractive because he was unemotional and Jeff as weak and unattractive because he was a sensitive man?

I told Bob about my response to Richard when he had recently called. I could see that perhaps that was more anxiety than chemistry, but I still couldn't work up any romantic feelings for Jeff, no matter how well-suited he appeared to be for me. As usual, Bob cut to the heart of the matter.

"Let's talk about feelings, Nancy. You can't go by your feelings. They have been damaged for years. Severely damaged. They are unpredictable barometers of what it is you are really thinking. In fact, often they will lie to you. You can't trust them. You shouldn't trust them."

"But certainly I can't marry Jeff without being in love with him," I protested.

"Why not?" Bob asked.

"Why not?" I repeated. "Bob, surely you wouldn't expect me to marry someone without loving them!"

"That's not what I said. You said you couldn't marry Jeff without being 'in love' with him. You were talking about your feelings about Jeff. I think it is perfectly reasonable to expect that you could marry someone without feeling you were in love."

"Oh, come on, now. These aren't biblical times with childhood betrothals. We have choices now. And we shouldn't marry without really loving the other person."

"Nancy, that is exactly right. You have choices. You have a choice now. You can choose to love Jeff and to marry him—despite your feelings." I shook my head, trying to get a handle on what Bob was saying to me. Bob continued, "You can't trust your feelings, Nancy. This area of your life—your relationships with men—has been the hardest one to conquer. So many men have been death to you, Nancy. Now here is Jeff—healthy, caring, and willing to commit himself to you. He is life to you, Nancy. Your feelings will tell you otherwise, but he is life to you."

"Bob, are you saying that if I choose to love Jeff, my feelings will follow?" I asked hopefully.

"No, I'm not. You have to decide if Jeff is the man God has for you—to bless you, Nancy. If so, you may have to walk down that aisle with absolutely no romantic feelings whatsoever, strictly out of obedience to what you know is right. It may be years into the marriage before you are able to discern that you have romantic feelings for Jeff."

"Bob, you've got to be kidding!" I exclaimed. "How can I marry someone without the confirmation of feelings?"

"Nancy, isn't it true that if Jeff were to clam up, become aloof and mysterious, not be so open about his love for you, you would begin to be drawn to him emotionally?"

"Sure! Isn't that how I have always operated?"

"Exactly. But God doesn't want you to do that now. And He has brought you together with a man who refuses to play into your pathology. God loves you very much, Nancy. He is trusting you with a great gift, if you can accept it."

"You know, Jeff and I talked about this last week. I told him that he could 'make' me fall in love with him, if he wanted. He agreed but told me he refused to play any games. He told me it would be a hollow victory to have me fall in love with him because he mimicked these other men in my life."

"He's right, Nancy. This is the first man who has the potential for providing you with a deep intimacy and un-ion. This throws you into terror and the terror causes you to squelch your feelings. You knew it was safe to feel deeply toward the other guys because subconsciously you knew they would never commit to you.

"Despite your strong desire to be married and have a family, you fear it as well. You see the possibility of severe abuse, even death, as it was for your mother. Nancy, the terror you face is the terror of going into life. You have a choice, here, and the choice to choose commitment over feelings is a step forward."

"But why does it have to be commitment over feelings? Why can't it be commitment and feelings?" I pleaded.

"Nancy, it is going to be very difficult for you to have appropriate feelings in this situation. Realize, however, that you just need to get started in the process of saying yes to this commitment."

I tried to do what Bob said. In late November, when Jeff was visiting me, I told him that I loved him. Jeff saw the terror in my eyes after I said those words and watched as I began to withdraw and shut down once again. Within minutes after my declaration, Jeff asked gently, "Nancy, would you like to take that statement back?"

"Yes," I replied and began to cry. "I'm sorry, Jeff. I'm so sorry."

"It's okay, Nancy. It's not time yet. I don't know why I am committed, but I am here for the long haul."

I was so frustrated with myself after that weekend. When I told Bob about it, I once again talked about my lingering feelings for Richard and my lack of feelings for Jeff, despite my feeble attempts at commitment to him. Bob pointed out that if God was preparing me for marriage to Jeff, I would have to remember that part of the process of cleaving to a marriage partner is leaving your original father and mother. "Richard represents your family, Nancy. To move toward commitment with Jeff, toward marriage, you will need to leave Richard, and all that your feelings for him represent, behind."

Bob continued eagerly, "Nancy, I want to share something with you. Before you called, I was praying for you and our session. The Scripture in Deuteronomy came to mind again which has been so much a part of your healing. God has set before you choices: life and blessing or death and curses. He tells you that you have the right and the power now to choose life. He is trusting you to make that choice, but He is also saying that 'I, the Lord your God will bless you in the land in which you are entering.' You have the choice now, Nancy, but He's also right here ready to give you the healing you need to propel you forward into life."

The next few months I struggled with this decision. Jeff remained true to his promise to me. He listened to me agonize about my lack of feelings and my confusion. He prayed with me and for me. And he waited.

Jeff was on business in Chicago for two weeks in February, and we planned for me to visit him on Valentine's weekend. The day before I left for Chicago, I went to a business luncheon. I felt a hand on my shoulder as I was talking to several people after the program. I turned to see Richard smiling at me. My heart began to beat fast and my mouth got dry. I hadn't seen him in several months, now, although we had talked on the phone a number of times. He began to talk to me about his work and a recent trip to Paris. His warm brown eyes held mine as he talked. I found my mind racing. "This is not love, Nancy. This is not chemistry. Don't give in to his charm now, Nancy. Choose life. Come on. Don't pay attention to your feelings; they can't be trusted here."

Suddenly, my mind snapped back as I heard him say, "...and I have really missed you, Nancy. I know you've needed some space from me, but I wonder if we could get together and talk about our relationship." He seemed genuinely caring.

I felt my heart pound even harder as I struggled to answer him. "I don't think that would be appropriate, Richard. I am glad to see you here, but it would not be right for me to be with you in any other context. I have to go now. I hope you can understand."

I walked away from him and out into the unusually warm winter day. As I approached my car, I realized what I had done. I had said no to Richard, something I had been unable to do before with Richard or any other guy like him. I threw open the car door. As I put the key in the ignition, I laughed out loud. I did it! I said no to a bad relationship. The power of that choice, despite contrary feelings, was exhilarating. As I drove to my office, I began to wonder if I could now say yes to Jeff.

I boarded the plane for Chicago later that evening with a spring in my step. I was going to see Jeff. Yet after he dropped me off at my hotel room the first night, I realized that although I was very comfortable with Jeff, I was still not "in love" with him.

The next night we went to see the movie, *Out of Africa*, the story of Karen Blixen, who wrote under the pen name, Isak Dinesen. As the movie ended with Meryl Streep's lilting voice repeating one of the movie's opening lines, "I had a farm in Africa...," I suddenly began to sob uncontrollably. Jeff put his arm around me and let me cry, despite all the odd looks from people leaving the movie theater. I was the only one crying in the whole theater. We sat there until all the patrons had left, the lights were up, and the ushers were sweeping up popcorn. I was still sobbing.

"I don't know what's wrong, Jeff," I said in gulps between sobs. "I've never done this before."

"It's okay, Nancy, it's okay," he said gently and just kept stroking my hair. The ushers moved around us quietly, giving each other quizzical looks.

Finally, I stopped crying and said, "Let's go." As we opened the side exit door to the parking lot, the biting wind hit our faces. We ran to the car and once inside, I started crying again. This time from the pain. Salty tears, now trapped in constricted pores on my face, stung sharply. I cried and we laughed. "Chicago in February!" I exclaimed. "Delightful!"

We drove to a nearby restaurant for coffee. After the hostess seated us, I said, "Jeff, I have no idea why that movie affected me so much. The portrayal of Isak Dinesen's life disturbed me."

"What did you want to happen in the movie?" Jeff asked.

"I don't know." I sipped my coffee and replayed scenes

from the movie over in my mind, searching for what troubled me so. Perhaps she reminded me of myself. Her strong will and determined spirit kept her resilient despite tragedy after tragedy, beginning with the death of her father by suicide when she was ten. Perhaps it was her view of God. When she was asked if she knew what caused the fire that destroyed her coffee plantation in Kenya and caused her to lose her land to the bank, she replied, "I think God had a hand in it. He gave me my best crop ever and then He remembered." Or perhaps, it was the way she related to the men in her life.

"Jeff," I said, breaking out of my musings, "I wanted the story to end differently. All she had left at the end of her life were her memories of her 'fa-ar-rm in Afri-ri-ca,'" I said, mimicking the way her Danish accent lingered over each syllable. "She had a chance at love twice. The first man, a philanderer, was clearly wrong for her. The second man, the mysterious game hunter, handsome and full of passion and excitement, was aloof, unable to commit to her. He was obviously incapable of giving her what she needed, and yet she was bound to him."

"Nancy, do you hear yourself?" Jeff asked.

With a swift recognition of my similarity to this story, I suddenly sat straight up, leaned forward across the table, and grabbed Jeff's hand. "Jeff, that's me! That's why it disturbed me so much. I don't want to be at the end of my life, summing it up by saying, 'I was a law-yer in Wash-ing-ton.' I want more. I want to share my life with someone whom I can build a future with, not someone who tears me down.

"I guess that's why I was crying so hard. It was as if I was watching the end result of my choices. I was weeping for lost opportunities. Sure, Isak Dinesen was strong and resilient and people admired her for that, but she was lonely, left with only the memories of painful loves and broken dreams."

Jeff squeezed my hand and stared intently into my eyes.

"Nancy, that realization is important. You can start at any point to make different choices than you have in the past. Your future does not have to be determined by your past."

"We're talking about us, now, aren't we?" I asked.

"Yes."

"I have a lot to think about, Jeff." I replied. "Be patient with me."

"Nancy, I have been," he answered. "You know I have been!" We laughed and left the restaurant arm in arm.

The next day it was snowing, and we went to O'Hare Airport early to make sure I could catch my flight. We sat near a large window and watched the snow swirl in small drifts on the runways. As we waited, I tilted my head and studied Jeff. He was talking but I didn't focus much on what he was saying. My mind was engaged in a conversation of its own.

I have never known a kinder, more considerate person, I thought. *He appreciates people and their uniqueness and is able to affirm those things that are good in each person. He's never been anything but steadfast and caring in his actions toward me. His constancy in the midst of my brutal honesty has been amazing.*

Yes, all that is true, I countered to myself. *He is a remarkable man. And maybe you even love him—as a friend—but you are not in love with him. You can't marry someone without the feelings being there.*

But my feelings are damaged, I argued. *They aren't going to be speaking truth to me about Jeff. What is love anyway? Is it predominantly a warm, glowing feeling or a commitment? Could I commit myself to Jeff? I think so.*

Yes, but, what if someone better is down the road? Someone like Jeff for whom you would have these feelings?

That's possible, I admitted to myself. *But what if that someone is Jeff? What if my feelings are going to follow years into the marriage? That's possible too, isn't it?*

"Flight 1732 to Washington–Dulles now boarding."

"That's your flight, Nancy," Jeff said, interrupting my thoughts. As always, when we said good-bye, Jeff placed his hands on my shoulders and looked steadily into my eyes and said, "I love you, Nancy." I had never been able to return those words. Instead, I usually gave him a solid hug, letting him know that I did care. I hugged him again this time.

I gave my ticket to the agent and began to walk down the ramp. Halfway down, I turned and saw Jeff still standing at the top of the ramp, smiling. He gave me a quick wave and turned to leave. Suddenly, I dropped my carry-on bag, shouted, "Wait, Jeff," and half-ran back up the ramp. I threw my arms around him and whispered in his ear, "I love you, Jeff. I love you!" He drew back in surprise, and then looked in my eyes, half expecting to see me shut down once again. Instead, as he saw my clear commitment to him shining in moist eyes, he broke out in a big grin and said, "Oh, Nancy, I love you too!"

On April 19, one week after Jeff moved to Virginia, we were engaged. This had been no ordinary courtship and it would be no ordinary proposal. Jeff had asked me to join him on Saturday afternoon at Evergreen Farm. "Wear something medieval," he suggested. "We're going out to a special place I've found for a celebration dinner to thank the Lord for my new job and my move to Virginia."

I arrived at Evergreen Farm dutifully carrying an old bridesmaid's dress from the 1970s, forest green velvet and empire waist. It was as close to Maid Marian as I could get. Jeff, having planned all this in advance, told me to change and he would go get the car. After I changed into my dress, Sandy, Jeff's stepmother, said in her usually enthusiastic manner, "You look lovely. Why don't we go down to take some pictures while we wait for Jeff. It's such a beautiful afternoon and nothing is lovelier than Evergreen in the spring." We walked down the hill from the farmhouse. The Japanese maple by the white, wrought-iron bench, one of my favorite places on the whole farm, was a deep burgundy, set off against the crisp clean green of new spring grass. The rhododendron were in full bloom with large bouquets of purple flowers, and the dark green of the boxwood leaves seemed especially shiny in the afternoon sun.

I turned back to look at the farmhouse. It was just as lovely as the first day I had seen it. Three stories, with eighteen-inch walls built out of stone covered with white stucco, it was an imposing Quaker structure. The green tin roof had faded with the sun to a light green. Evergreen itself looked like a large bountiful blossom set against that crystal blue afternoon sky, where puffs of white clouds dotted the horizon. Such a peaceful place.

The front door suddenly swung open and striding out onto the porch of the farmhouse was Jeff, dressed as a knight in shining armor. His silver helmet with visor down was decorated with a purple plume. A purple velvet coat of arms accented his suit of mail. In his arm he carried a slender wrapped box, decorated with purple bows. His back ramrod straight, he began his descent down the hill to the dell where I was standing.

I laughed hysterically. *Jeff is always doing things like this,* I thought. *Only Jeff would make such a big deal out of a celebration dinner.* He approached me without a word. Jokingly, I said, "Good day, m'Lord," and curtsied.

Still silent, he pointed to the wrought iron bench. I sat down, trying not to laugh. Apparently, he was very intent on what he was doing. Still without a word, he offered me the present. I resisted the urge to make a joke and simply said, "Thank you." Sandy, with all her creativity, had decorated the package with her stylistic handwriting in a silver ink. Along the ribbon, she had written, "I have set before you life and death, the blessing and the curse. So choose life in order that you may live, you and your descendants. Deuteronomy 30:19" and "Blessed is she who believed there would be a fulfillment of what had been spoken to her by the Lord. Luke 1:45."

I opened the box to discover an antique black glove box with roses lacquered on the top and, again in Sandy's distinctive script in silver ink, the words, "Lady Nancy." I opened the black glove box and lifted the aged lace to discover a pair of long white gloves, now ivory with age, beautifully decorated with hand-painted flowers, again due to Sandy's remarkable artistic talents. On one glove I read this: "Delight yourself in the LORD; / And He will give you the desires of your heart. Psalm 37:4." I picked up the other glove, admiring Sandy's handiwork and read: "Arise, my darling, my beautiful one, and come with me. See! The winter is past; the rains are over and gone.... Arise, come, my darling; my beautiful one, come with me Song of Songs 2." Then I noticed a beautiful sapphire and diamond ring on the ring finger of the glove. I looked up at Jeff in surprise.

Jeff dropped to one knee, took the ring off the glove, and said, "Nancy, this ring is very special to me. It was Mom's. Dad gave it to her when they got engaged in 1959. Would you wear it? Nancy, I love you. Will you marry me?"

"Yes, oh yes," I exclaimed as he slipped the ring on my left hand.

When he got up, he took off his helmet, and sat beside me on the bench. I turned to him, still somewhat dazed, and asked, "Did you just ask me to marry you?"

"Yes," Jeff said tentatively.

"Did I just say yes?"

"You did." Jeff immediately thought of the time he asked me if I wanted to take back my proclamation of love to him and I had. *Oh, no,* he thought, *she still isn't ready.* Quietly, softly, he asked, "Do you want to take it back, Nancy?"

"Oh, no," I exclaimed and smiled broadly. "I want to marry you." Visibly relieved, Jeff hugged me and we kissed.

Later that evening at dinner, I looked down at the beautiful ring, an oval light-blue sapphire with two brilliant round diamonds on either side. I shifted my position in my chair, suddenly uncomfortable. "Jeff, do you think your mom would have approved?" I could not shake her concern she had expressed in the abstract about my family background being compatible with someone from a strong Christian home. Twelve years later, after Catherine Marshall had admitted that Christian parents would be right to be concerned about my background, I was not only marrying her son, I was wearing her ring. It seemed suddenly inappropriate. Jeff enthusiastically described all the reasons why he knew his mom would have approved of my marrying him, but I couldn't shake my unsettled feeling.

I couldn't sleep that night. I sat in the deep-set window frame of my second-story bedroom at Evergreen, with arms wrapped around my knees, looking down on the wrought-iron bench, now framed surrealistically by a full moon. It was 4:30 A.M. I lifted my left hand and watched as the moonbeams danced off the brilliant facets of the ring. "Oh, Lord," I prayed, "I am amazed that I am at this place, filled with so much love and commitment to You. I am amazed at Your goodness to provide me with such a wonderful man and such a loving family. Len and Sandy have accepted me as one of their own. They have prayed for us and stood with us as we struggled to come to this place of commitment. But in all of this, Lord, I feel a bit apologetic. It's like I want to say, 'Catherine, I know you felt strongly about the generational problems a person can bring to a marriage. I hope you don't mind that I am marrying your son and wearing your ring.' Lord, I know You did all of this. You gave Jeff an almost inhuman ability to stay committed to me, despite my attempts to drive him away. You worked with me over time to get me to the place I could choose to commit myself to Jeff. It's just that I can't shake this feeling that somehow I have snuck into the family. If Catherine had been here, she might have had some words of caution to tell Jeff. I know this is somewhat irrational, but it is how I feel."

Four days later, Jeff and I went to my church for the fourth in a series on God as Father, given by two counselors, Fletch and Betty Fletcher. After Fletch taught on God's ability to redeem families, Betty took the microphone and said, "I'd like to read a passage from one of my favorite authors, Catherine Marshall."

I looked quickly at Jeff and smiled. It seemed odd to be sitting with her son, wearing her ring, and now listening to her words.

Betty read from *Something More* from the chapter entitled, "The Law of the Generations":

It was about then that I was startled to find in the Old Testament a brief but applicable description of society's plight in our time:

Thou shalt beget sons and daughters, but thou shall not enjoy them; for they shall go into captivity.

...The author and compiler of Deuteronomy has Moses speaking to them as part of the prophetic warnings given him by God. The forty years of Israel's wilderness wanderings were over. The second generation stood poised, ready to enter the Promised Land...the venerable leader gave a farewell charge to Israel. This charge is the book of Deuteronomy.

Reading this book is like looking through a window into the amplitude of Moses' spirit. In his speech there is no note of an old man's sentimental nostalgia, rather the entire thrust is into the future. Warm with feeling and persuasively eloquent, Moses focused on this one significant point:

See, I have set before you life and death, the blessing and the curse...Therefore, choose life.

The rest of the Old Testament narrative tells us what happened: all too often the descendants of those to whom Moses had given his charge did not "choose life." History records that these descendants did go into captivity literally as well as spiritually. Each generation, then, as now, has a choice: life or death, the blessing or the curse.[3]

My eyes were riveted on Betty. Something in my spirit was acutely aware that something very special was taking place. The many other people in the church began to fade from view. I sat forward, eyes glued to Betty, hungry for the next words. Betty continued:

> ...In this Law of the Generations, as I call it, we are linked to previous generations behind us. Our ancestors are in our genes, in our bones, in our marrow, in our physiological and emotional makeup. We, in turn, will be written into the children who come after us.... We are accustomed to the idea that we pass on to our children a physical inheritance—in color of eyes, color of hair, even certain diseases.... I began to ask myself, is it possible that our spiritual inheritance is as real as the others?
>
> It soon became apparent that just as we can inherit either a fortune or debts, so in the spiritual realm we can inherit either spiritual blessings or those liabilities (unabashedly called "sins" in Scripture) that hinder our development into mature persons. These blessings or liabilities do not come to us solely by heredity. Obviously they are passed on by example and by teaching— conscious or unconscious.[4]

My mind raced back to that day in October some twelve years ago at Agnes Scott College. I remembered the devastation I had felt when Catherine Marshall told me there were generational problems I would bring to a marriage.

My pain at that response had been so great that I did not remember what else she said. I realized now that in some unspeakable way, God was allowing me to finish that conversation. I glanced down at the ring. Jeff looked at me knowingly. Tears began to pour down my face as I continued to listen with awe:

> In her delightful book about the "uncommon union of Jonathan and Sarah Edwards," Elisabeth D. Dodds gives us a composite portrait of the Jonathan Edwards family. . . . In this family where the hearts of the fathers and the children were so visibly turned one to another, it is possible to see how God blessed them down through the generations "unto thousands of them that love me, and keep my commandments." In 1900 A. E. Winship tracked 1400 of the Edwards's descendants and published a study detailing what astonishing riches this family had contributed to the American scene. By 1900 this single marriage had produced:
>
> 13 College presidents
> 65 Professors
> 100 Lawyers and a dean of an outstanding law school
> 56 Physicians and a dean of a medical school
> 80 Holders of public office:
> 3 United States Senators
> Mayors of three large cities
> Governors of three states
> A Vice-president of the United States
> A Comptroller of the United States Treasury

Members of the family had written 135 books. . . . They had edited 18 journals and periodicals. They had entered the ministry in platoons, with nearly 100 of them becoming missionaries overseas.

The Edwards family is a beautiful showcase of how God fulfills His promises when we do our part. For the greatest blessings that God has to give us are never offered just to the individual. Always, "the promise is unto you, and to your children . . ."

God is sending us a ringing call to understand that we cannot escape the blessing or the curse of the generations. If we will allow Him to, our Lord

> . . . shall turn the heart of the fathers to the children and the heart of the children to their fathers . . .

Here is God's singing, soaring promise of what this could ultimately mean to nations of splintered families.

"The generations" can start to assume their creative function **at any point** . . . Yes, even then can God turn this curse that goes down through the generations into a blessing. . . . For each of us—no matter what our situation or how we feel we have failed—there is hope.

> See, I have set before you this day life and death, the blessing and the curse. . . . Therefore, choose life.[5]

The hot tears continued to flow down my face and wash my soul with release. Suddenly, I understood. Catherine would have approved of my marrying her son. In fact, twelve years ago she was trying to share with me the secret I would ultimately uncover in counseling. Yet I was too emotionally wounded at that time to hear any words of hope. Instead, I had only heard the jarring pronouncement that confirmed my strongest fears.

That night I went through box after box of books in my basement until I uncovered the book I thought might be there. I pulled it out of the cardboard box: *Something More*. I opened the front cover and read the autograph: "To Nancy Oliver, fellow traveler in the Way and fellow Agnes Scotter—Catherine Marshall 10/25/74." I turned quickly to page 58 and read again the chapter on the Law of the Generations. The chapter ended with the challenge that had been the crux of my counseling, of my healing, and of my commitment to Jeff: "See I have set before you this day life and death, blessing and cursing.... Therefore, choose life."

I quietly spoke the remaining words of that verse from Deuteronomy, "Therefore choose life, that both you and your descendants may live" (30:19). I had chosen life—by facing my past and the self-destructive patterns it created and by making new choices—and now it would make all the difference, for me and for my children and for my children's children.

Epilogue

On Tuesday, November 21, 1990, at 9:30 A.M., I received a telephone call from the Agnes Scott Alumnae Association. My father wanted me to know that my grandmother, his mother, had died that morning. It was an odd way of communicating, but my father's preferred method. Rather than write or telephone me directly, he often used my college alumnae office as the mediator. I felt sorry for the woman at the other end of the phone, who undoubtedly was thinking that this was one of the weirdest calls she had ever had to make.

For the last ten years, except for a few letters and phone calls, I had not seen my father. Now he had left a telephone number for me to call between 11:00 and 2:00. And now I had a decision to make. Would I attend the funeral? I knew that my father would see my presence as a willingness to be involved with him again. That could open the door possibly to further abuse.

The next several hours I considered the reasons why it might be wise to attend. First, I am no longer Nancy Oliver. I am Nancy Oliver LeSourd, a wife and mother. My father needed to see that and to understand that dynamic. Second, I knew at some point, he would need to meet Jeff and our son, Luke. This provided a short encounter whose primary focus was to attend my grandmother's funeral. Jeff agreed that if I was going, he was coming with me. With Luke only three-and-a-half months old, he would be with us as well. Third, I knew I needed to face my father now after years of counseling. I was a different person. But somehow, until I could face him and not be victimized by that experience, I would never feel confident that I was whole. Finally, I also still had to trust that God could work in my father. I did not want to be a block to anything the Lord might be trying to do in him.

After the decision was made, I called my father at the number he had left at Agnes Scott. It was the Krystal, the very place my mother had taken us for breakfast several times a week in her escapes from my father. Now my father works there. Once a lawyer, he now mops floors. I talked with him for the first time in a long time. I remembered how he had always called attention to himself by his unusual dress or mannerisms, but I was not prepared for his affectations and dialect. When I told him I had a son, he said, "You does? Damn girl, I done good." This from a man who once had an outstanding vocabulary and facility with words. He didn't ask anything about my son, his grandson. He didn't ask his name, what he looked like, whether he is healthy, anything. "So I's a grampa then? Damn and double damn."

When the brief phone call ended, I was exhausted. We had exchanged basic information. He knew I was happily married. He now knew that Jeff and I had a child. He knew I practiced law, representing nonprofit corporations. I knew that he and my younger brother, Sam, were living together. It was unlikely Sam would attend the funeral, even though it was to be held at the cemetery only an hour south of Atlanta. As my father said, "He has his own life." I also found out that my father, like myself, had no idea where my youngest brother, Pete, lived or how to contact him.

I had enough interaction with him to know that the time

at the funeral on Friday would be intense. Not only would there be the natural emotion of father and daughter meeting after ten years, but there would be the tension of waiting for his inappropriate behavior. I had been away from it so long, I wondered how I would react. Would I feel sorry for him? Could I cooly say to myself, "That's the alcohol talking." Would I be embarrassed? Humiliated? Would all those old emotions of my childhood come surging back? And then I had natural concern for Jeff and especially, Luke.

Jeff and I spent a lot of time in prayer the next several days, asking for wisdom in conversation with my father and especially for protection. I had two desires for our time in Atlanta. First, I wanted my father to meet me as Mrs. LeSourd, the wife of Jeff and the mother of Luke. He needed to understand that I have my own family now. He also needed to meet Jeff and to understand that he is the head of our home, its physical and spiritual protector.

Second, I wanted to respond to him in truth and in reality. Not so much for his sake, but for mine. I needed to know that the little girl, the survivor, was healed. Never had I felt more strongly that I needed to stand boldly in the face of my past to know for certain that my future was free. It was here, meeting my father again after all these years, that I would understand fully the depth of the changes that I had made and the fulfillment of the hard work of counseling.

I had trouble sleeping the night before we left. At 3:30 A.M., I heard Jeff saying, "Nancy, wake up. You're dreaming." He told me I had been crying out in my sleep, "No, no stop it. Don't do it." In my dream, I was standing in our house near the French doors to our deck. I saw a little child, about nine years old, with her face pressed against the glass, peering into our home. She smiled engagingly and I let her in. But as soon as she was inside, she took a knife and plunged it into my heart over and over. I knew from my counseling experiences that the little girl was part of me. As I prayed through this dream and talked it out with Jeff, I realized how frightened I was deep inside that the little girl, terrified of the power of her father, would come back and destroy the person I had become.

We boarded the Delta plane bound for Atlanta at Dulles Airport at 8:45 A.M. on Friday, the day after Thanksgiving. The two-and-a-half-hour flight, the time spent renting a car and eating lunch, was filled with tension. Jeff and I took potshots at each other over each and every little insignificant thing: who should hold Luke and who should carry the diaper bag and who should sit next to Luke on the plane. Should we buy the ticket for the plane back now or after the funeral? Every small decision was a call to battle. For me, it was my way of acting out my fear. For Jeff, he was practicing. Not knowing what to expect from my father, he was gearing up for battle.

We arrived at the cemetery at 3:00, a half hour before the service. The first car to arrive, we drove down a dirt path between grave sites and parked behind the hearse. My father was nowhere to be seen. I picked up Luke and held him in my arms, and Jeff prayed for us one more time. We both breathed deeply and glanced at the time, 3:10 P.M. Other relatives and friends began to arrive. As we walked down the path towards the grave site to meet them, a light breeze caused the golden leaves to swirl around our ankles. It was a warm day with overcast skies. We clustered together in a small group, opposite the canopied grave site. I introduced Jeff and Luke to them and exchanged pleasantries, all the while feeling my stomach knot up more tightly. I turned to Jeff at 3:28 and whispered, "Do you suppose he's not going to come?"

As soon as I said that, I saw my dad about a hundred yards down the path, walking toward the group. He walked slowly in a stumbling, almost drunken manner. Everyone turned and watched him approach, their conversations stilled. No one moved. All eyes were on my father. And on me.

Still holding Luke, I stepped out of the protection of the circle of people and began to walk toward him. Jeff quickly fell into step beside me. My father and I both stopped short, about two feet from one another. He was dressed in a black nylon turtleneck and blue jeans. From three large loops of steel chain through his belt hung a pipe, a black leather pouch, and an identification tag, much like that you would put on a piece of luggage. A short tan flannel scarf was around his neck, and he wore a beige windbreaker, peppered with cigarette burn holes. He no longer wore a beard. Instead, his multiple chins hung down loosely and a closely cropped Hitler-style mustache framed his upper lip. A bright orange baseball cap protected his bald head. My father exclaimed, "——— Girl, it's good to see you. Yo sho is pretty."

"Thank you. It's good to see you too after all these years." Seeing that he was going to break down in tears, I quickly added, "This is Jeff, my husband, and this is Luke, our son." Fortunately, the other relatives closed ranks around us and began to greet my father. The funeral director ushered us to our seats under the canopy and the minister began the service. Jeff and I sat directly behind my father on the second row of chairs. I tried to listen to the brief remarks by the minister as I cuddled Luke on my lap and stared at the back of my father. At one point, my father broke out in uncontrollable sobs, seemingly expressing his grief at his mother's death. But I didn't think so. It seemed part of the show. Just like the slang dialect and the outrageous, inappropriate dress, his emotional outbursts were just another method of drawing attention to himself and further alienating others.

As soon as the minister finished his remarks, we all stood and walked away from the grave site. I handed Luke to Jeff, knowing that now was the time I would need to talk with my father. We walked away together and he said about his mother, "She was an ornery ol' cuss. I never liked her. I just managed her affairs." A sharp contrast to his being overcome with emotion just moments before and perhaps his way of dealing with his true emotions. "I tried to get ahold of your brudder, but I ain't got no idea where he is."

"When was the last time you saw Pete?" I asked.

"Well, lemme see. It was about five years ago. I sued him, ya know. He owed me some money and wouldn't pay it back, and I had to sue him to get his attention. The marshall came back after he served him with the papers and said Pete called me every name in the book."

I remembered this suit. Dad had tried to get money from Pete to pay him back for money he had spent for the costs of raising him. Totally irrational thinking. I recalled my goal for today. Try to respond rationally, no matter how twisted the conversation gets. "Of course, it is highly unusual for a parent to sue his child," I responded.

"But I's had to get his attention, you see. And I got it," he explained. "When he came over, then I told him I'd forget the debt he owed and let bygones be bygones. But he moved away to California, and I ain't never see'd him since.

"I don't know what happened with your mama," he continued. "I had the bestest family in the whole world. I had the bestest kids. I done did good, ain't I? Ya know, I knew that if I got myself straight that all you kids would come back. We're okay now, ain't we?"

"Do you remember the last letter I wrote you?" I asked.

"Oh yeah. I jes ignored dat letter."

"Well, what I said in that letter still goes. We can talk as long as we can work within those guidelines," I explained.

He quickly changed subjects and began to talk about why he had resigned from the State Bar of Georgia. "You don't mess around with Carl Oliver. Oh, no. Ever since that Supreme Court decision that let lawyers advertise, I knew I had to get 'em to clean up their act. That to me is when the legal profession lost its standards." I stared in amazement as he continued on about his antics in suing lawyers who had advertised. One sentence flowed into the other. He was not inviting any dialogue. He just wanted center stage.

"Did ya know I's a member of three denominations. Yep. I is. The Methodists, Church of God, and the Episcopalians. I sued them too. When they wouldn't do what I wanted, I sued the ———."

Maybe it is that I am a lawyer. Maybe he was reaching for some common ground. But as I stood there listening, I realized that what was happening here was the parting of two generations. He represented death to me. His way of life. His choices. All that he had done and continues to do spirals him further and further down a destructive path. I grew up with that. I saw over and over again his choices for death being played out in my choices. The generational legacy of self-destruction.

But as I stood there listening to him, I knew that my choices were radically transforming these generational curses into generational blessings. I knew that my self-image, my relationships, and my understanding of God had dramatically pivoted out of that spiral of death and destruction into life. I knew God had been faithful to me, meeting me at every point in this journey.

I was no longer the little wounded girl, Nancy Oliver. That girl would have pleaded with God to transform her father into a loving man who would act normally and responsibly. That girl would have believed that God loved her if only He would fulfill her deepest longing of a happy family. That girl would have hoped for a miraculous healing as we met in this leaf-strewn cemetery. The scene would have been played and replayed in her mind and prayers: a remorseful father and tearful daughter would walk, then run (all in slow motion of course, as the music would crescendo), falling into each other's arms. A changed, loving, and compassionate man, he would ask her forgiveness for all he had done to hurt her, promising to make up for the past.

Instead, as my father continued on, now quoting unrelated Scriptures and explaining some of his theology, I realized that living my life waiting for my father to change only kept me from knowing God's power in the present and His blessings for my future. The key that unlocked all of this for me was the understanding that I had choices. No matter how crazy my home life, no matter how damaged my generational legacy, my choices over the years could result in blessings. It was God's promise. It was my choice to believe it. And my life has never been the same. And the life of Luke and any other children the Lord may give us will be forever blessed. The generational legacy of Nancy Oliver LeSourd is for life.

Notes

Chapter 1

1. Sharon Wegscheider-Cruse, *The Miracle of Recovery* (Deerfield Beach, FL: Health Communications, 1989), 104.

2. Larry Crabb, *Inside Out* (Colorado Springs, CO: NavPress, 1988), 15.

Chapter 2

1. Jim Craddock, Pat Springle, and Robert S. McGee, *Your Parents and You: How Our Parents Shape Our Self-Concept, Our Perception of God and Our Relationships with Others* (Houston, TX: Rapha Publishing, 1990), 6.

2. Leo Tolstoy, *Anna Karenina* (New York: Signet, 1961), 17.

3. Sharon Wegscheider-Cruse, *Another Chance* (Palo Alto, CA: Science and Behavior Books, 1981), 86.

4. *Ibid.*, 95.

5. *Ibid.*, 107.

6. *Ibid.*, 105.

7. *Ibid.*, 139.

8. *Ibid.*, 140.

9. *Ibid.*, 144–45.

10. *Ibid.*, 85.

11. *Ibid.*, 128–30.

12. *Ibid.*, 133.

13. *Ibid.*, 136.

Chapter 3

1. "Castle on a Cloud," by Claude-Michel Schönberg, Alain Boublil, Jean Marc Natel, and Herbert Kretzmer. From the musical, *Les*

Misérables, by Alain Boublil and Claude-Michel Schönberg (New York: Alain Boublil Music Ltd, 1985).

2. Wilfrid Noyce, *They Survived: A Study of the Will to Live* (New York: E. P. Dutton, 1963), 189.

3. *Ibid.*

4. Andrew E. Slaby, M.D., Ph.D., M.P.H., *Aftershock: Surviving the Delayed Effects of Trauma, Crisis and Loss* (New York: Villard Books, 1989), 15.

5. *Ibid.*, 16–21.

6. *Ibid.*, 29.

7. Patience H. C. Mason, *Recovering from the War* (New York: Penguin Books, 1990), see chapter 8, "Post-Traumatic Stress Disorder," 221–67.

8. Timmen L. Cermak, M.D., *A Primer on Adult Children of Alcoholics* (Pompano Beach, FL: Health Communications, 1985), 25.

9. *Ibid.*

10. *Ibid.*, 27.

11. Timmen L. Cermak, M.D., *Diagnosing and Treating Codependence: A Guide for Professionals Who Work with Chemical Dependents, Their Spouses and Children* (Minneapolis, MN: Johnson Institute, 1986), quoted in Charles L. Whitfield, M.D., *Healing the Child Within* (Deerfield Beach, FL: Health Communications, 1987), 57.

Chapter 4

1. Mark Twain, *A Connecticut Yankee in King Arthur's Court* (New York: Signet Classics, 1963), 47.

2. Paul Tournier, *The Healing of Persons* (New York: Harper and Row, 1965), 96.

3. Marie Winn, *Children Without Childhood* (New York: Pantheon Press, 1981), 199.

4. Dr. David Elkind, *The Hurried Child* (Reading, MA: Addison-Wesley, 1988), 119.

5. *Ibid.*, 43.

6. *Ibid.*, 181–83.

Chapter 5

1. Sheldon Vanauken, *A Severe Mercy* (San Francisco, CA: Harper and Row, 1977), 213.

Chapter 6

1. Karl A. Olsson, *Meet Me on the Patio* (Minneapolis, MN: Augsburg Publishing, 1977), 16.

Chapter 7

1. Tournier, *The Healing of Persons*, 108.
2. Bryan E. Robinson, Ph.D., *Am I Addicted to Work?* (Deerfield Beach, FL: Health Communications, 1989), 1.
3. *Ibid.*, 2.
4. Interview with Douglas LaBier, "Healing the Wounds of Success," *Washington Post*, July 23, 1989, H1, H4.
5. "Waking Up to Workplace Depression," *USA Today*, January 7, 1991, 1–2.
6. LaBier, *Washington Post*, H4.
7. Dr. Herbert J. Freudenberger, *Burn-Out: The High Cost of High Achievement* (Garden City, NY: Anchor Press, Doubleday and Co., 1980), 16.
8. *Ibid.*, 19.
9. J. Patrick Gannon, *Soul Survivors: A New Beginning for Adults Abused as Children* (New York: Prentice Hall, 1989), 142–43.
10. Bronston T. Mayes and Daniel C. Ganster, "Exit and Voice: A Test of Hypotheses Based on Fight/Flight Responses to Job Stress," *Journal of Organizational Behavior*, 1988, vol. 9, 199–216.
11. Gannon, *Soul Survivors*, 137.
12. Freudenberger, *Burn-Out*, 49.
13. Eliza Collins, "Why Employees Act the Way They Do," *Working Woman*, December 1990, 60–61. Reprinted with permission from *Working Woman* magazine. Copyright © 1990 by WWT Partnership.
14. Janet Geringer Woititz, Ed.D., *Home Away from Home: The Art of Self-Sabotage* (Pompano Beach, FL: Health Communications, 1987), 47–49.
15. Dr. Michael Diamond and Dr. Seth Allcorn, "The Freudian Factor," *Personnel Journal*, March 1990, vol. 69, no. 3, 53.
16. *Ibid.*, 54–55.
17. Manfred F. R. Kets de Vries and Danny Miller, *The Neurotic Organization* (San Francisco, CA: Jossey-Bass Inc., 1984), 95.
18. *Ibid.*, 81.
19. *Ibid.*, 82.
20. Diamond and Allcorn, *Personnel Journal*, 54–55.

Chapter 8

1. George MacDonald, *Unspoken Sermons (Series Two)* (London: Longmans, Green, and Co., 1895), 142.
2. "It Must Be Him," ("Seul Sur Son Etoile "). Gilbert Becaud -

Maurice Vidalin. English adaptation by David Mack. Copyright © 1966 by Editions Le Rideau Rouge represented in the USA by BMG Songs.

3. Dag Hammarskjöld, *Markings* (New York: Knopf, 1966), 92.

Chapter 9

1. T. S. Eliot, "Little Gidding" from *The Four Quartets*, in *T. S. Eliot Collected Poems, 1909–1962* (New York: Harcourt, Brace, Jovanovich, 1971), 208.

2. Sandra Wilson, Ph.D., *Counseling Adult Children of Alcoholics* (Dallas, TX: Word, 1989), 105.

3. Gannon, *Soul Survivors*, 226.

4. David A. Seamands, *Putting Away Childish Things* (Wheaton, IL: Victor Books, 1982), preface.

Chapter 10

1. From a talk by Claudia Black, M.S.W., Ph.D., "Reclaiming Lost Childhood," a seminar sponsored by LifeCycle Learning held at the University of Maryland, April 4, 1990.

2. David Streitfeld, "The Addiction Habit: Breaking Step with the Self-Help Movement," *Washington Post*, August 28, 1990, C5.

3. Charles M. Sell, "Sins of the Fathers (and Mothers)," *Christianity Today*, September 10, 1990, 23.

4. A good discussion of relevant Scriptures can be found in *The Twelve Steps for Christians* (San Diego, CA: Recovery Publications, 1990), 113–20.

Chapter 11

1. Lit., "as he reckons in his soul."

Chapter 12

1. C. S. Lewis, *Mere Christianity* (Westwood, NJ: Barbour and Company, special edition published with Macmillan, 1952), 97.

2. Dr. Susan Forward, *Toxic Parents* (New York: Bantam Books, 1989), 191.

Chapter 13

1. A. W. Tozer, *The Knowledge of the Holy* (New York: Harper and Row Publishers, 1961), 10. This book is a classic on the attributes of God. For further study, InterVarsity Press publishes a Bible study guide entitled, "Recovery from Distorted Images of God," which examines from Scripture the reality of these distortions of His charac-

ter: the God of impossible expectations, the emotionally distant God, the disinterested God, the abusive God, the unreliable God, and the God who abandons.

2. Wilson, *Counseling Adult Children of Alcoholics*, 95–100.

3. *Ibid.*, 101.

4. J. I. Packer, *Knowing God* (Downers Grove, IL: InterVarsity Press, 1973), 184. This book is particularly helpful to anyone desiring a study of God's attributes. J. I. Packer has a fresh, intimate knowledge of God and supports his points with numerous Scripture references.

Chapter 14

1. Dr. Connell Cowan and Dr. Melvyn Kinder, *Smart Women, Foolish Choices* (New York: Clarkson N. Potter/Crown Publishers, 1985), 63.

Chapter 15

1. Cowan and Kinder, *Smart Women, Foolish Choices*, 72–73.

2. *Ibid.*, 155.

3. Catherine Marshall, *Something More* (New York: McGraw-Hill, 1974), 59–60.

4. *Ibid.*, 60, 63.

5. *Ibid.*, 73, 75–77.

ABOUT THE AUTHOR

Nancy LeSourd is a partner with Gammon & Grange in Washington, D.C., and provides legal counsel to tax-exempt organizations. She is a graduate of Agnes Scott College, has her M.A. in education and American history from Tufts University, and her J.D. from Georgetown University.

She and her husband, Jeff, live in the D.C. area with their son, Luke.